America at Random

Books by Herbert Mitgang

THE RETURN
LINCOLN AS THEY SAW HIM
THE MAN WHO RODE THE TIGER

Edited by Herbert Mitgang

THE LETTERS OF CARL SANDBURG
WASHINGTON, D.C., IN LINCOLN'S TIME
CIVILIANS UNDER ARMS
AMERICA AT RANDOM

America at Random

FROM *The New York Times'*
OLDEST EDITORIAL FEATURE,

"Topics of *The Times*,"

A CENTURY OF COMMENT
ON AMERICA AND AMERICANS

EDITED, WITH AN INTRODUCTION
ON THE JOURNALISTIC ESSAY,
by Herbert Mitgang

Coward-McCann, Inc.
New York

Library of Congress Catalog Card Number: 69-19027
PRINTED IN THE UNITED STATES OF AMERICA

Contents

6

Contents 9

IV. *ARTS, ESPECIALLY THE LITERARY*

Contents

V. *A BACKWARD GLANCE*

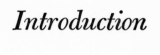

Introduction

HERBERT MITGANG

The Journalistic Essay

Of all the writing boxes to escape from, the essay is the most challenging. Like the novel, its subjects and methods are limitless; being without bounds, it naturally entraps the unwary. As with certain other literary forms—fine free verse, for example, which is more difficult to achieve than the fixed iambics of a Spenserian sonnet—the essay is deceptive creatively. Its normal hallmarks are brevity, informality and pungency. At best, an element of surprise in idea or phrase causes the writer's thought to linger long afterward.

But 400 years after Montaigne's *Essais,* the essay remains just that: an *essai,* only a try. It is always risky trying to write well for writing's sake, and the essay compounds the risk. Yet the essay survives while more immediate dissertations and descriptions of ephemeral events diminish with time. The antics of kings and cardinals, the ambitions of presidents and generals tend to belabor the familiar and become lost in the dying smoke of topicality. We forget the names of the monarchs and the details of their favorite battles; we remember what Swift said on the art of political lying and his meditations upon a broomstick. From century to century, the human risks and flavors and the mundane views of life on the cheap have continuity.

Inevitably, the philosophical and literary essays developed into journalistic broadsides, both serious and frivolous. The penny newspapers enabled Steele and Addison to instruct and amuse at the same moment. In the prospectus for *The Tatler,* Steele recognized that "this globe is not trodden upon by mere drudges of business only, but that men of spirit and genius are justly to be esteemed as considerable agents in it." Promising "all accounts of gallantry, pleasure and entertainment" in addition to poetry and learning, he forswore "musty foreign edicts or dull proclamations" when there was a dearth of news. Two and a half centuries later, there are editors who agree that human affairs and freedoms should be the first concern of public journals.

The distinguished American essayists in the nineteenth century were the heirs of the pioneering English journalists. It was while Emerson, Hawthorne and Lowell contributed their rich essays to the scholarly publications that the newspapers made tentative efforts to bridge the gap between literature and journalism. Tangents on the news took the form of elegant arabesques displaying knowledge of the classics, with many boring Greek and Latin references dropped in for seasoning. Few of these columns deserve resurrection; aging brings no guarantee of distinction, to writing or to wine. But the idea was planted, and the need soon seen, for occasional alarums and excursions between the solemn speeches and everyday disasters in the long news columns.

The editorial page of *The New York Times* was among those helping to blaze a trail for the newspaper essay over a century ago. At first these appeared as "casual notes"—shirttails of amusing items hanging down almost as afterthoughts. The fillers, still known around newspaper shops as "when-room" matter, were more pleasant to read than the pontificating editorials preceding them, for they did not worry the news a second time on the inside of the paper. The cold and distant events demanded more than factual repetition; there was need for the emotional response from what W. B. Yeats later called "the foul rag-and-bone shop of the heart."

Out of this long and sound heritage came the first "Topics" column in *The Times* on Saturday, March 16, 1867. More than a century later it is still running—still every Saturday—on the editorial page. The column was inspired by the first publisher, winked on and off thereafter, and revived by Adolph S. Ochs almost as soon as he became publisher in 1896. His heirs and editorial page editors have continued the column without interruption to this day.

"First invent a German and then let him invent something."

That, explained the first regular "Topics" columnist half-humorously, was the formula. William Livingston Alden's credentials were impeccable: He was the son of a minister and college president, a lineal descendant of John and Priscilla Alden, and a lawyer who turned to newspaper work. His short articles were familiarly called the "sixth column" because that is where they ran on the editorial page, under the heading "Minor Topics."

The column formally began as "Topics of *The Times*" on September 8, 1896, written by Frederick Craig Mortimer, a Maine scholar with a knowledge of science and the classics. For thirty years his brief essays touched on everything from French literature to Freudian medicine. But it was not all light comment. He campaigned vigorously in the column against the Ku Klux Klan when it was at its zenith. As he closed his desk each evening, his good-night to colleagues went, "I have rolled the stone to the top of the hill." Humorists and essayists understood the labors of Sisyphus.

The "Topics" column had various contributors on the editorial staff after Mortimer's retirement. Simeon Strunsky took it on in September, 1932, and remained the columnist for the next fifteen years. He had an avid interest in statistics and the ability to reduce complex subjects to simple terms. And he liked and often defended New York City in print. Strunsky was born in Vitebsk, Russia, and was brought at age seven to the Lower East Side. As a newspaperman, he wrote of America with an immigrant's devotion.

From Alden to Mortimer to Strunsky, all the "Topics" columns were unsigned. In a final section, called "A Backward Glance," examples of their essays appear as they did not in their own time—identified with by-lines.

After the last "Topics" by Simeon Strunsky ran in July of
1947, the column was written by a number of staff reporters
and editors, with occasional outside writers also contributing
to Charles Merz, editor of the editorial page. Among the dozens of people who wrote "Topics" there were *Times* regulars,
including L. V. Updegraff, H. I. Brock, Lewis Nichols and
Thomas Lask, whose pieces are represented here. The legendary knowledge of "Uppy" Updegraff, head of the Sunday Department copydesk, enabled him to quote what the Greeks and
Romans would say and do (better in most cases) about twentieth-century problems. He usually wrote the erudite Sunday
piece.

In recent years the column has undergone further changes
in looks and contents. To accommodate an increase in space for
editorials, letters and columnists, "Topics" went from daily to
twice weekly to Saturdays only. At the same time, it attained
greater prominence, changing from its old sixth-column verti-
cal spot after the last editorial to the horizontal upper right-
hand corner of the page. In the winter of 1965, the first columns
with a signature line began to appear, and in the spring of
1965 the author was raised to by-line status, a not insignif-
icant change after nearly a century of anonymity.

At the same time, John B. Oakes, editorial page editor since
1961, caused a change in emphasis from the ruminative essay
to more topical comments on the news. Distinguished diplo-
mats and college professors were invited to contribute to the
column in 1966. A more subtle change, reflecting current literary trends, occurred in 1967—the introduction of serious fiction
writers ("First invent a German," etc., as the 1867 "Topics"
columnist noted) in nonfiction raiment. Novelists, poets and
playwrights who had not been invited to write serious newspaper essays before, but who were aroused on such moral matters as the American involvement in Vietnam, were given their
say in the "Topics" column. Today there is a conscious balance
between the topical and literary piece. In our journalistic time
of strong opinion without special grace, it is fortunate that such

stylists as E. B. White and Brooks Atkinson still prove what humanists can do with the essay form.

When the sky is falling (as Chicken Little has correctly reported from Vietnam and other trouble corners in recent years), a need exists for the journalistic essayist with something to say of importance or nothing to say importantly. Certainly the Vietnam village burnings will remain a point of moral reference for years to come; but so will such timeless subjects as the length of a youth's hair and the mechanization of man. In this respect, the "Topics" column has recognized that—like Malraux, Camus and Silone among the Europeans—the American writer is moving in the direction of the engaged journalist.

We have tried (that word *essai* again) to strike something of a balance between pamphleteering and the pure essay. Impudent ideas and commonplace notions are often perishable; a few can be found here, too. The random for this generation has all too often emerged as panic-button America, which, when pushed, turns out to be cracked plastic. Unfortunately, most of the big answers will have to be sought elsewhere. And yet centuries before the first "Topics" column appeared in *The Times,* Montaigne and the litterateurs recognized that the essay might save the hour even if it could not save the day. That is the aim of these modern journalistic essays.

I
America and the Americans

E. B. WHITE

Dear Mr. ⑆0 2 ⑈⑈⑉ ⑈0 6 3 ⑆ ⑉⑈0 2⑈ ⑈0 7 3 0⑈ 8⑈

My bank, which I have forgotten the name of in the excitement of the moment, sent me a warning the other day. It was headed: "An important notice to all our checking account customers." The burden of this communication was that I would no longer be allowed to write checks that did not bear the special series of magnetic ink numbers along the base.

My bank said the Federal Reserve System had notified them that it will not accept for processing any checks that don't show these knobby little digits. For example, I would no longer be free to write a check on a blank form, because it would lack a certain magnetism that computers insist on.

I first encountered these spooky numbers a few years back and took a dislike to them. They looked like numbers that had been run over by a dump truck or that had developed rheumatoid arthritis and their joints had swollen. But I kept my mouth shut, as they seemed to be doing me no harm.

Now, however, it appears that we are all going to knuckle under to the machines that admire these numbers. We must all forgo the pleasure and convenience of writing a check on an ordinary, nonmagnetic piece of paper. My signature used to be enough to prod my bank into dispatching some of my money to some deserving individual or firm. Not any more.

This, I think, is a defeat for all—a surrender. In order to accommodate the Federal Reserve System, we are asked to put ourselves out.

The notice I received says that if I try to palm off a check that lacks the magnetic ink numbers, the check cannot be processed without "delay, extra handling charges, and possible embarrassment." I embarrass easily—it doesn't take much, really—and naturally I am eager to learn what form this embarrassment will take if I should decide to write a check using the old blank form that has proved so convenient, for I don't know how many decades, on those occasions when one is stuck without his checkbook or enough lettuce to carry the day.

"The tremendous increase in the use of checks," writes my bank, warming to its subject, "made it necessary for the Federal Reserve to establish a completely computerized operation for processing all checks from all banks. Their computer can function only when proper magnetic numbers are used."

Well, I can believe that last part, about the computer requiring a special diet of malformed numbers; but I am suspicious of that first statement, about how the Federal Reserve would have been unable to carry on unless it went completely over to machines. I suspect that the Federal Reserve simply found machines handy and adventurous. But suppose we had had, in this country, a tremendous increase in the use of checks before anybody had got round to inventing the computer—what would have happened then? Am I expected to believe that the Federal Reserve and all its members would have thrown in the sponge?

I know banks better than that. Banks love money and are not easily deflected from the delicious act of accumulating it. Love would have found a way. Checks would have cleared.

I'm not against machines, as are some people who feel that the computer is leading us back into the jungle. I rather like machines, particularly the eggbeater, which is the highest point the machine has yet reached. I'm against machines only when the convenience they afford to some people is regarded as more important than the inconvenience they cause to all.

In short, I don't think computers should wear the pants, or make the decisions. They are deficient in humor, they are not intuitive, and they are not aware of the imponderables. The men who feed them seem to believe that everything is made out of ponderables, which isn't the case. I read a poem once that a computer had written, but didn't care much for it. It seemed to me I could write a better one myself, if I were to put my mind to it.

And now I must look around for a blank check. It's time I found out what form my new embarrassment is going to take. First, though, I'll have to remember the name of my bank. It'll come to me, if I sit here long enough. Oddly enough, the warning notice I received contained no signature. Imagine a bank forgetting to sign its name! [9/23/67]

E. B. WHITE

An Act of Intellect to Turn the Year

Animals, as far as I know, do not create arbitrary lumps of time. They know and savor their day and their night, they accept the travel opportunities of spring and fall, but they have no week, no month, no year. Man, on the contrary, being a creature of caprice, has saddled himself with New Year's Eve, when he gives way to wistfulness, remorse, despair, fear, and resolve.

At this year's end I think everyone is asking: "What happened? What went sour? What did I do wrong? Who's to blame?" I don't pretend to know what happened, but something did; and to the last question there can be only one answer: "I am. I am to blame."

I feel personally responsible for 1967, and I hope a couple of hundred million other Americans feel the same way. There is always the chance, in the next lump of time, to correct our mistakes, mend our ways, and reshape our destiny.

This is a solemn year that is just coming to a close. The Republic slides downhill at an alarming rate—in many directions, and so fast it makes one wonder. The roar that will be heard in midtown—a blend of drunkenness, piety, and hope—will be louder and more savage than ever before. I feel involved in this mass despair, this hunger. I feel, too, that by a deliberate exercise of the intellect, an individual can purify his life, correct his compass, and that a nation can, too. All can be changed—in a single night. One has to believe this to stay afloat, in these times, in these seas.

I have always loved New Year's Eve, and still do, on this most awesome of evenings. In 1967 many things that had been commonly regarded as fixed and immutable turned out to be shaky and precarious. Much that we had taken for granted was challenged and upset. Our cities began falling apart, our families seemed to lose their grip, our races clashed, our youth drifted off to the simplicities of hallucination and the lethargy of flowers.

The uneasiness of a foreign war that was unpopular at home unsettled everyone and caused some to lose their balance entirely. The threat of disobedience by those who lacked the stature that is necessary for disobedience shocked and worried us. The faint, acrid smell of anarchy got into the air when those to whom law is intrinsically distasteful took charge.

In 1967 we heard the Vietnam War called "immoral": but I would like to submit that no war is immoral—all war is amoral, and will continue to be amoral until some decent substitute is established to settle the things that must be settled and defend what has to be maintained.

Americans feel sick and discouraged at the turn events have taken in the past twelve months. Our streams run brown, our dirty air sticks in our throats, our enlarged war sticks in our crops. The good earth, once golden, has begun to run out, as any neglected field, and we are discovering, a bit late, the consequences of fouling the only nest we have. To grow the perfect lawn we destroy the perfect bird. To kill the ultimate gnat we load the liver of the final fish. Even our national bird fights for survival and lays eggs that don't hatch.

Much that was hailed as progress has picked up the odor of

retrogression. Even the speed in which we delight may, in the long run, fail to save us a minute's time: There is evidence that jet flights, because of their throwing the body out of phase, do not save time at all—the time is subtracted from the traveler's life-span.

But, as I say, I feel guilty. I accept the whole sorry mess as my own fault. A man doesn't have to smoke pot to achieve lethargy, or admire flowers to fail as a citizen. So I plan to turn over a new leaf. In this resilient and greatly favored country, a new leaf should be no problem.

I am eager to begin. The country is always stronger than we know in our most worried moments. Its constitution is as flexible as it is compassionate. And there are always the surprises: We have a woman right now who wants to become a jockey. ("Kathy Kusner Breaks From Barrier Faultlessly.")

I believe our principles are sound and good. I believe our races can and will live peaceably and sensibly together. If I were to doubt these things, I couldn't last the night out. I believe that by an act of will, an act of intellect, the familiar dream will come true and the sky will again be bright, as it was many years ago on a memorable evening when the curtain rose on the first act of *Oklahoma!* and the sounds of the earth were like music.   [12/30/67]

ROBERT F. KENNEDY

"Things Fall Apart; the Center Cannot Hold . . ."

As 1967 came to an end, E. B. White observed in a "Topics" column that all Americans seemed to be asking the same questions: "What happened? What went sour? What did I do wrong? Who's to blame?"

President Johnson speaks of a mood of "restlessness." Cabi-

net officers and commentators, poets and protesters tell us that
America is deep in a malaise of the spirit, discouraging initiative, paralyzing will and action, dividing Americans from one
another by their age, their views and the color of their skin.

Demonstrators shout down government officials and the government drafts protesters. Anarchists threaten to burn the
country down, and some have begun to try—while tanks have
patrolled American streets and machine guns have fired at
American children. Our young people—the best educated and
comforted in our history—turn from the Peace Corps and public commitment of a few years ago to lives of disengagement
and despair, turned on with drugs and turned off America.

Indeed, we seem to fulfill the vision of Yeats: "Things fall
apart; the center cannot hold;/Mere anarchy is loosed upon
the world."

This is a year in which we elect a President. Yet it is a year
for us to examine not only the candidates but also the country;
to ask not only who will lead us but where we wish to be led;
to look not only to immediate crises but also to the nature and
direction of the civilization we wish to build.

For the many roots of despair all feed at a common source.
We have fought great wars, made unprecedented sacrifices at
home and abroad, made prodigious efforts to achieve personal
and national wealth. Yet we ourselves are uncertain of what
we have achieved and whether we like it.

Our gross national product now soars over $800 billion a
year. But that counts air pollution and cigarette advertising,
and ambulances to clear our highways of carnage. It counts
special locks for our doors, and jails for the people who break
them. It includes the destruction of the redwoods, and armored
cars for the police to fight riots in our cities. It counts Whit-
man's rifle and Speck's knife and television programs which
glorify violence the better to sell toys to our children.

Yet the gross national product does not allow for the health
of our youth, the quality of their education or the joy of their
play. It does not include the beauty of our poetry or the strength

of our marriages, the intelligence of our public debate or the integrity of our public officials. It measures neither our wit nor our courage, neither our wisdom nor our learning, neither our compassion nor our devotion to country.

It measures everything, in short, except that which makes life worthwhile; and it can tell us everything about America—except why we are proud to be Americans.

Children are starving in Mississippi, idling their lives away in the ghetto and committing suicide in the despair of Indian reservations. No television sets—not even 70,000,000 of them —can bring us pride in that kind of wealth.

Nor are we taking pride in our place in the world. Once we thought, with Jefferson, that we were the "best hope" of all mankind. But now we seem to rely only on our wealth and power.

So half a million of our finest young men struggle, and many die, in a war halfway around the world; while millions more of our best youth neither understand the war nor respect its purposes, and some repudiate the very institutions of a government they do not believe. There is something basically and terribly wrong in the spectacle of young Americans, however few, dodging the draft in Canada or deserting to Sweden.

Our power is enormous, the greatest the world has ever seen. Yet, as we see old allies pulling back to their shores, and old alliances dissolving in quarrels, we sense that even America cannot act as if no other nation existed, flaunting our power and wealth against the judgment and desires of neutrals and allies alike. We wonder if we still hold "a decent respect to the opinions of mankind"—or whether, like Athens of old, we will forfeit sympathy and support alike, and ultimately our own security, in the single-minded pursuit of our own goals and objectives.

Finally, we sense that as individuals we have far too little to say or do about these issues, which have swallowed the very substance of our lives. We have discovered that private accomplishment or affluence affords no escape from the perils and plagues that afflict the nation—and that these questions are far too important to be entrusted to remote leaders.

We search for answers to specific problems; but more than this, we seek to recapture our country. We have not yet discovered how to do it. That, perhaps, is what troubles these long nights of our national spirit. And that is what the 1968 elections must really be about.   [2/10/68]

ARTHUR MILLER

On the Shooting of Robert Kennedy

Is it not time to take a long look at ourselves, at the way we live and the way we think, and to face the fact that the violence in our streets is the violence in our hearts, that with all our accomplishments, our spires and mines and clean, glistening packages, our charities and gods, we are what we were—a people of violence?

Lincoln, Garfield, McKinley, John F. Kennedy, Martin Luther King, Medgar Evers—plus the line going into a sad infinity of lynched men, of men beaten to death in police cells, of Indians expropriated by knife and gun, of the Negro people held in slavery for a century by a thousand small armies dubbed chivalrous by themselves who long ago enchained black labor and kept black mankind from walking in freedom—Robert Kennedy's brain received only the latest fragment of a barrage as old as this country.

Here is a Congress literally face to face with an army of poor people pleading for some relief of their misery—a Congress whose reply is a sneer, a smirk and a warning to keep order.

Here is a people that would rather clutch hatred to its heart than stretch out a hand in brotherhood to the black man and the poor man. That is why there is violence. It is murderous to tell a man he cannot live where he wishes to live. It is murderous to tell a woman that because she has borne a child out of wedlock that she cannot eat, nor the child either.

There is violence because we have daily honored violence. Any half-educated man in a good suit can make his fortune by concocting a television show whose brutality is photographed in sufficiently monstrous detail. Who produces these shows, who pays to sponsor them, who is honored for acting in them? Are these people delinquent psychopaths slinking along tenement streets? No, they are the pillars of society, our honored men, our exemplars of success and social attainment.

We must begin to feel the shame and contrition we have earned before we can begin to sensibly construct a peaceful society, let alone a peaceful world. A country where people cannot walk safely in their own streets has not earned the right to tell any other people how to govern itself, let alone to bomb and burn that people.

What must be done? A decent humility, not cynicism. Our best cards are finally being called. Thomas Jefferson, a slaveholder, wrote the promise he could not keep himself and we must now keep it. "Life, Liberty and the Pursuit of Happiness." The pursuit of happiness is impossible for millions of Americans.

Let us take the $30 billion from the war, and let us devote the same energy and ingenuity we have given to war and apply it to wiping out the disgrace of poverty in this richest of all nations. Let us feel that disgrace, let us feel it for what it is, a personal affront to each of us that cannot be permitted to stand.

We are 200,000,000 now. Either we begin to construct a civilization, which means a common consciousness of social responsibility, or the predator within us will devour us all.

It must be faced now that we are afraid of the Negro because we have denied him social justice and we do not know how to stop denying him.

We are afraid of the poor because we know that there is enough to go around, that we have not made it our first order of business to literally create the jobs that can and must be created.

We are afraid of other countries because we fear that they know better how to satisfy the demands of poor people and colored people.

We are afraid of ourselves because we have advertised and promoted and sloganized ourselves into a state of contentment, when we know that desperate people surround us everywhere and we do not know how to break out of our contentment.

We are at war not only with Vietnamese but with Americans. Stop both. We are rich enough to wipe out every slum and to open a world of hope to the poor. What keeps us? Do we want peace in Vietnam? Then make peace. Do we want hope in our cities and towns? Then stop denying any man his birthright.

Because America has been bigger on promises than any other country, she must be bigger by far on deliveries. Maybe we have only one promise left in the bag, the promise of social justice for every man regardless of his color or condition.

Between the promise and its denial—there stands the man with the gun. Between the promise and its denial stands a man holding them apart—the American. Either he recognizes what he is doing, or he will take the final, fatal step to suppress the violence he has called up.

Only justice will overcome the nightmare. The American Dream is ours to evoke.   [6/8/68]

EUGENE J. McCARTHY

Thoughts on the Presidency

When I announced my candidacy, it was suggested that its main purpose might be to carry on an educational program in this country and to raise the issue of Vietnam before the American people. But now the response in the New Hampshire primary, and more recently in the Wisconsin primary campaign, has made it clear that my candidacy has become something more than that. It has become a challenge to win the Presidency of the United States.

Everywhere I have campaigned I have sensed a deep uneasiness about the war and about the equality of our leadership. It flows from a profound and growing conviction that something is wrong with the direction of American society; that since 1963 we have begun to lose much of the high purpose imparted to this nation by President John F. Kennedy. Yet people felt powerless to change our direction.

It is now clear to me that the discontent of the young is only the most dramatic sign of a feeling of paralysis that is shared by Americans of all ages. Although millions of citizens are deeply troubled over a situation in which the two major parties have been able to offer only candidates who promise to continue the present policies of proven failures, they feel that the political machinery in the country has become autonomous and beyond their influence.

Perhaps the most important result of my campaign so far has been to provide a reminder that, in a democracy, any political structure can be made to yield to the popular will.

People want to stop the war. They want to end the violence in our cities, not by suppression but by restoring basic rights to Negro citizens. They want good schools for their children. They want an end to rising prices. They want to see America return to a position of honor in the family of nations.

Americans are not by nature a people that wishes to oppress their fellow citizens or oppress the peoples of other nations, and they do not wish to be led by fear. Yet we see the growth of leadership by fear. We are finding among ourselves fear of remote enemies and fear of our fellow citizens.

I have found this unease among every kind of American, and my most urgent appeal is not to any ready-made political bloc or alliance of interests or constituencies in this country. It is to one constituency—a constituency of conscience, of hope and of trust in the future. Those who have come over to my cause have abandoned fear, disillusionment, defeatism and a kind of despair in America.

If I am elected I will never regard the office of the Presidency as a personal office. A President should not speak of "my country" but always of "our country," not of "my Cabinet" but of "the Cabinet." For once the Cabinet has been appointed it becomes something apart from the man who nominated its members and something apart even from the Senate which confirms them in office.

In this conception the office belongs not to the man who holds it but to the people of the nation. It is an office which must be exercised by the will of the majority but not in the sole interest of the majority.

The role of the President must be to unite the nation. But he must unite it by inspiring it, not unite it by just adding it up or by piecing it together like some kind of jigsaw puzzle. Rather than trying to organize the nation he must try to encourage the common purpose of creating an order of justice in America.

I believe that a man who is presented to the Presidency must know the limitations of power, and know the limitations that must be placed on the exercise of the office of the President, which has the greatest power of any office in the modern world. He should understand that this country cannot be governed by coercion, and that it needs a special kind of leadership, which itself recognizes that the potential for leadership exists in every man and woman.

America has great reserves of energy and high purpose, but at present our energy is being diverted and our idealism is being sapped by a war that seems to transgress our cherished tradition of prudence and decency. Much of our energy has been turned toward destruction, and the more generous and noble impulses of our people have been given little room to manifest themselves.

The next President must liberate these generous impulses

by reordering our national priorities. He must give direction
to the movement of the nation by setting people free.

[3/30/68]

HERMAN WOUK

One Vote for Conventions— Even with Hoopla

The hoopla and the boring procedures of the conventions
are in trouble. The cry against them swells. The Democrats actually banned demonstrations. I wait with interest to see if that
ban will stick in Chicago, 1968. Meantime, some perverse instinct prods me to suggest possible virtues in these supposed
weaknesses.

Let's take a general glance at this bizarre process we go
through every four years. It strikes me, first of all, that the electoral college concept, in a skewed way, has prevailed. The
Founding Fathers planned a shield against Presidents chosen by
mob surges of emotion in direct elections. We have that.

The constitutional college has been shaved to a legal fiction,
but the folk wisdom of America—for which I have no small
regard—has evolved a better idea. Two electoral colleges
pick two para-Presidents, who then go through a grinding
runoff, the election. The better man for the job usually wins.

In any case, the tortuous device of the double electoral
college slows down and chokes off demagogic sweeps. We have
been through some very unruly times, and we have had plenty
of demagogues. None has approached the Presidency.

The two electoral colleges are not wholly ill-chosen, though
that part remains vague and shaky. The Republican and Democratic parties are loose confederations of local political clubs
and machines that come to full life once every four years. The
delegates are workers in local politics, so at least they know
what the people think and want.

The two parties have real differences, but compared to their wide undramatized agreements these are minor. They do not offer the public clashes of ideology that strike to the root of our order. The right and left, even Communists and Nazis, are free to make all the noise they wish and try every legal device to take power and make policy, within the parties or without. By and large, they get nowhere.

In all this, the banal and corny hoopla of the conventions is antipomp, a fine American political invention. Hoopla is an old American folkway for breaking the ice and getting people friendly in large assemblages. At the conventions it has also become a mask for concern. The man chosen for President will wield unimaginably fearful power.

When the balloons cascade and the bands whoomp and the delegates cavort, their message is that familiar America can still produce the character and wisdom to handle vast new dreads; that we do not need some humorless, hooplaless, iron new way to do things.

The dragged-out procedures gain time, and allow shifts of strength to gather and sometimes explode. Of course, the game is to fix the unfolding of events long in advance. But the smartest manipulator can never be 100 percent sure that he has done it. It was during the protracted, much-abused Republican seconding speeches that the eruption against Governor Spiro Agnew caught the nation's eye, and exposed the sham of unity in Miami Beach, 1968. Richard Nixon got his man, but in that brief public show of his slip he may have lost the Presidency.

For under the eye of television, with the commentators mediating between the public and the pageant, the process has become more searching and revealing. Television usually serves only amusement, and it is disconcerting to watch the old slow-as-molasses political rites on the same glass screen. But these rites can flare suddenly and memorably into visible history, for the patient watcher; and they may decide whether and how, in the next four years, we will live or die. *Mission Impossible* only pretends to such importance.

The real mission impossible is to find men to bear the burdens of the age. Roosevelt, Truman, Eisenhower, Kennedy, Johnson—isn't the thing still working?

I honestly find in this rite of the double electoral college—for all the horse-and-buggy touches and sordid backstage hanky-panky—a serviceable instrument for the orderly transfer of terrible power with general consent. The clowning pageantry shows America's hatred of pompous might, its affection for old customs, its resistant health in international plague years.

Life is change, we all know that. But in politics I grew up under Franklin Roosevelt, and I remain one among many of his disciples. I believe he would tell us, with a shrewd and buoyant grin, that we had better go slow in dismantling the American political convention. [8/24/68]

MARGARET MEAD

The Road to Racial Irrelevance in America

Americans need not choose between integration and black power.

In fact, there are not two but at least three mutually supporting means for resolving racial inequality within the premises of American culture which are shared by whites and blacks: immediate integration for those with the education to use their gifts; political black power in the slums of the inner cities; a new economic and social base in the rural South.

The aim of integration is that race and color will become completely irrelevant and that each American will be judged on his merits and his skills. Such integration is most easily accomplished in the ranks of statesmen and scientists, lawyers and doctors, poets and musicians, where the requirements of gift or education are highest.

Simultaneously, in the ghettos of the inner city, black Americans are confronted by situations and political opportunities that faced other immigrants who came as strangers—uprooted, nonliterate and unskilled—to live in cities that had been built for and by earlier comers. That some of the ancestors of black Americans came to this country against their will long ago is not the issue in the North.

Their immigrant predecessors—Irish, Italians, Eastern European Jews and others—fled poverty, oppression and despair and crowded together in the enclaves of the slums. They came with hope and they found wretched housing, hostility and discrimination. They also found opportunity. Though they had to dig ditches and work under sweatshop conditions, when they organized politically and made demands on the society they moved up and out.

The waves of rural Negro immigrants arrived, and their educationally deprived adolescent children are leaving school at a time when automation and welfare have changed this familiar scene of exploitation. Nevertheless, because the Negro immigrants have settled in, because they live crowded into defined areas, the political roads to betterment that the earlier immigrants took are still open to them also.

It is a political gambit to call this racism when done by Negroes, in contrast to earlier ethnic solidarities. Political power belongs to the organized, foreign or native, white or black, on or off welfare. Black political power, based on urban concentration, can wring from politically susceptible leadership what the ghetto needs—housing, schools, policing, credit, financing, capitalization, and a chance together to develop stiff-necked self-respect, to cultivate a sense of identity, and to conserve their own traditions.

The development of political black power will inevitably involve separatism, but it must be at black, not white, initiative. If a black community wishes to bound itself, turn in on itself and gather strength to turn again and face the white community, that is its right.

In the old Southeast, especially in the rural areas, conditions are, of course, different. There black and white have lived together, locked within the different circumstances of their ancient immigration. Caste regulations governing close relationships, not the *de facto* segregation of the North, also have produced a state of deprivation, poverty and despair.

It may be that the South, with such a different history, can shift from the old pattern of kin and caste to a new pattern of kith and kin. Nevertheless, there must be many more new economic opportunities for the whole South, otherwise emigrants will continue to tax the resources of the cities all over the country.

New models are needed. Today, as the country with the greatest resources, we must recognize that our situation is unique. We cannot look to other nations for solutions to emulate or failures to avoid. We can no longer work with our own earlier proposed solutions. Holding our integration as the principal means—as well as the ultimate goal—has proved totally inadequate.

All movements toward change will need national planning and financing to expedite talent search and education, to meet the demands of the residents of the inner cities, and to reorganize economic opportunity in the rural South. Supported by the entire American community as a common goal, a combination of these three efforts can lead to the creation of a society in which ancestry no longer determines where a man stands and what he can do. [4/20/68]

JOHN A. MORSELL

Negro, Black or Afro-American?

The revival of controversy over the "correct" name for persons of black African descent includes, as it has in the past, an effort to repudiate the term "Negro." Opponents of "Ne-

gro" demand its replacement by "black," or by such hyphe-
nated variants as "Afro-American" or "African-American." In
other years, the term "colored" found much favor.

The contemporary reformers are not content to argue in a
context of personal preference or stylistic variety, modes
which have largely prevailed heretofore. They insist that the
psyche of the race is profoundly implicated, that "Negro" is
a white man's term of opprobrium, and that those who continue to use it are guilty of betrayal or, at the least, of failure
to identify with the masses of "black" people.

This was the burden of a young high school sophomore's letter to the late W. E. B. DuBois, answered by DuBois in *Crisis*
magazine for March, 1928. The DuBois who had published
Souls of Black Folk in 1903 and would publish *Black Reconstruction* in 1935 said:

> "Negro" is a fine word. Etymologically and phonetically it
> is much better and more logical than "African" or "colored"
> or any of the various hyphenated circumlocutions. Of course,
> it is not historically accurate. No name was ever historically ac-
> curate . . . [but] "Negro" is quite as accurate, quite as old and
> quite as definite as the name of any great group of people.

In point of fact, there is simply no other word we can use if
we wish to speak solely and exclusively of persons of black
African descent. Black Africans, New Guineans, aboriginal
Australians, East Indians (expecially the *harijans*) and a host
of diverse racial and ethnic strains are all properly called
"blacks," and "black" therefore fails the tests of exclusivity and
specificity.

"African-American" and "Afro-American" are equally deficient, since Ian Smith of Rhodesia is an African, as are President Nasser, the King of Morocco, and any of the thousands of
whites who hold citizenship in Nigeria, Ghana, Kenya, and
other black African states. Should any of these, or their descend-

ants, become United States citizens, they, too, would be "African-Americans."

Only "Negro" possesses, by reason of years of wide and continued usage, a clear, specific and exclusive denotation: a person of black African origin or descent. Proponents of other names may object that it is a white man's word; but so is "black" and so is "African-American." All these are "white man's words," by virtue of their being English. Moreover, it should be recalled that "blacks" was the white man's *first* designation for black Africans; historical circumstance brought into common English use the Spanish word for black, which is *negro*.

The intolerance with which the cause of this or that designation is pressed carries a special danger. We have already been told by some of the more extreme advocates of "black" that it is to be more than just an ethnic term: It is to be an elite designation, reserved for only those whom the extremists deem worthy, without regard to skin color or anything else.

Whether this absurdity gets very far or not, it is still a very likely prospect that, given *de rigueur* usage of "black," succeeding generations will indeed make darkness of skin an elite attribute which will irrevocably divide the Negro population. There could be no more ironic outcome of the generations of struggle against color prejudice than to find Negroes themselves split into rival camps on the basis of skin color.

This danger is great enough, it seems to me, to justify reasonable men in combating any effort to restrict our usage to a single term, whatever it may be. Whites in particular should not, in an excess of fear lest they offend, cater to a movement of intolerance and divisiveness.

As DuBois observed to young Roland Barton forty years ago:

> Suppose we arose tomorrow morning and lo! instead of being "Negroes," all the world called us "Cheiropolidi"—do you really think this would make a vast and momentous difference to you and me? . . . Would you be any less ashamed of being

descended from a black man, or would your schoolmates feel
any less superior to you? The feeling of inferiority is in you,
not in any name. The name merely evokes what is already
there. Exorcise the hateful complex and no name can ever make
you hang your head.

The truth has not been better stated since.   [7/20/68]

JOHN KENNETH GALBRAITH

Reckoning Day for the New Economics

As all know, a lively debate is now on over economic policy and whether in particular to increase taxes. If this debate is
to be fully understood, and the associated irony fully savored,
the reader should have information which, though part of the
public record, needs to be put in more organized form. Telling
the story requires that I repress the impulse to charity with
which one yearns to cover the embarrassments of his professional colleagues. I must even risk that most deplorable of all
public postures, namely the retrospective suggestion that one
was right. But this is the price of an understanding of the
present troubled situation of the New or Keynesian Economics.

In 1964, as everyone warmly remembers, the personal and
corporate income taxes were substantially cut in order to expand the demand for goods and thus to increase output and reduce unemployment. This was the most affirmative action to
date under the aegis of the New Economics. The ensuing increase in income and output and the associated decline in
unemployment seemed strong vindication of the policy. There
was considerable self-congratulation.

However, the decision to reduce taxes, as the ample histories
of the Kennedy era have told, was not unanimously supported

by the economists concerned. The division was not between the Keynesian and those who would balance budgets and advise fiscal orthodoxy. It was within the modern group between those who thought that tax reduction was the most expeditious way of expanding income and those who believed it a one-way street to a highly illiberal result.

In the latter view, taxes, once reduced, could not in the event of need be increased. Instead those whose income bracket makes them more sensitive to taxes paid than to public services forgone would argue for reduced spending. Were spending on education, urban environment, air and stream pollution, retrieval of the poor and like needs reduced (defense being sacrosanct), the contrast between private well-being and public squalor would be enhanced. Lower income groups, which depend most on public services, would suffer most.

Were spending not reduced there would be inflation. The wiser, safer, more liberal, although admittedly slower, course would be to expand demand by increasing outlays for necessary services. Then, in the event of reversal, the higher (progressive) tax rates would operate on the higher level of income. And any needed curtailment of services would be from a higher level of public performance.

As has also been amply told, I led the second argument. I doubt that my case suffered from reticence, desire to avoid repetition or an overly delicate concern for the patience of the opposition. Administration economists and advisers were overwhelmingly for cutting taxes. They discounted the above dangers. In time they persuaded President Kennedy and won. It was, I might add, a wholly amicable row.

Now with a kind of fatal clarity the day of reckoning for the winning team has arrived. There is always the happy possibility that liberty, democracy, the free world's test of will and the sanctity of the SEATO alliance will have an early triumph in Vietnam—I note that the nomenclature here is not mine but that of the Secretary of State. Apart from this and accident, taxes must now be increased. But an election, as always, is coming. And men of self-confessed soundness of judgment are, as predicted, arguing for a reduction in public services.

The president of the United States Chamber of Commerce, Robert P. Gerholz, observed that if the President and Congress could "effect a substantial reduction in expenditures," it would have an "electrifying effect." Others are echoing these thoughts, so-called, and the members of the chamber voted by a huge margin for expenditure reduction. So the reputation of those who said it would be possible to reverse course and increase taxes is now on the block. There is no hope that failure will be overlooked, as this very column shows.

Nor am I the formidable threat. For, waiting in the wings, one imagines, are those who will seize upon failure to act on taxes now, to discredit the whole effort to manage demand. This is the essence of the New Economics.

As noted, some accident, such as the triumph of Marshal Ky, or a terrible collapse of the stock market, could save the situation. But it is the pride of the New Economics that it relies on probabilities, not accident. So only a tax increase will safely return the reputation for miscalculation to those of us who— happily for our reputations for prescience but unhappily for price stability and our sense of modesty—now look so much like being right.   [5/14/66]

HARVEY SWADOS

The Inalienable Right of Selective Apathy

The forays of literary men against President Johnson on Vietnam have resulted neither in capitulation to good sense nor in the decline of hostilities, but simply in an increase in the number of requests for their services as writers of checks, signers of statements, and authors of new petitions, protests, and proclamations.

This is disconcerting not just because it is expensive and time-consuming, or even because it is mortifying to observe that one's *J'accuse* is not summarily followed by redress of the grievances that prompted the polemic. Although writers have at least the normal quota of self-esteem, they need not fall in with those whose rising hysteria would seem to stem not so much from dismay at the war's horror as from pique that their opinions do not win instant acceptance from the opponent whose policies they assail.

They ought to remain ready, if with no particular pleasure, to accept the necessity of continuing to speak out against what they find detestable, not from a forlorn hope that the politician will retreat or the war will end, but simply from a stubborn desire to retain their self-respect by keeping the record straight —and a suspicion that even in a democracy it takes a long time for the truth to prevail.

What disconcerts is rather the assumption on the part of readers that a writer's indignation about the course of an immoral war implies equal indignation about the course of projected neighborhood sewage lines. The more the literary man writes about war or political dishonesty, the more he is importuned to participate in school board elections and beautification projects. Like many another citizen he finds himself forced—if not because the range of his passions is limited, then simply from sheer self-defense—to indulge in selective apathy.

While this is a condition that ought to be an inalienable right, it is often violated, and not only by those eager to enlist writers in their particular variety of ax grinding. The modest housewife at the shopping center, asked by an inquiring television reporter for her opinion of Thomas Dodd or Adam Clayton Powell, is attempting to practice selective apathy when she says to the prodding microphone, "I don't keep up with politics," and it is to be inferred that other questions, such as the price of bacon, would elicit a less equivocal response.

Intellectuals tend to assume that the matters on which they choose to practice selective apathy are of lesser urgency than those ignored by the common man; and it is probably true that the voting procedures of the Miss Universe contest are not as consequential as those of the UN Security Council. But it is hardly self-evident that concern for local or "frivolous" issues combined with apathy about oceanic problems is in itself evidence of intellectual incapacity.

In this regard the classic response of the husband describing his household's decision making is worth recalling: "I handle the big problems, like whether we should recognize Red China; my wife handles the little ones, like whether we should have a baby."

We should not expect absolutely everyone—even a President or a poet—to be righteously indignant, or even to have an opinion, about absolutely everything. The assertion of selective apathy ought to be seen as a basic democratic right—like that of not being forced under penalty to choose between two abysmally unqualified candidates for the same public office. It was not a democrat but Benito Mussolini who proclaimed during his Ethiopian campaign: "Apathy will not be tolerated."

Contrariwise, the citizen who, having opted for apathy on local issues and dissidence on international ones, must be accorded not merely his formal constitutional right to dissent, but the same access to his fellows via the mass media as is now enjoyed by an establishment more powerful than any in world history, which sees as its most vital concern the maintenance of power through the enforced retention of the status quo.

On this matter, which may determine not only our national direction but our very existence, apathy might very well diminish as the issues clarify and become more urgent.   [8/19/67]

BROOKS ATKINSON

Thoreau's Message After 150 Years

By issuing a commemorative stamp for the one hundred and fiftieth anniversary of the birth of Henry David Thoreau, the government has performed a magnanimous deed. No one has ever spoken more contemptuously of government than Thoreau. It is impossible, he said, to be associated with "this American Government" without being disgraced.

His bitterness was provoked, one, by the Mexican War, to which in his opinion "the people would not have consented" at the outset; and, two, the institution of slavery. Denouncing the Mexican War, he declared that the time had come for honest men to rebel. Concerning slavery, he remarked, "This question is still to be settled—this Negro question, I mean: the end of that is not yet."

In 1967 the Vietnam War and the struggle for civil rights represent two ideas that alienated him from society in the nineteenth century.

When the Fugitive Slave Law of 1850 compelled Massachusetts to acquiesce in the institution of slavery Thoreau stepped up his opposition: "My thoughts are murder to the State and involuntarily go plotting against her." Although he spoke those words in special circumstances in 1854 they sound just as violent today. Perhaps the United States Post Office Department did not make a search of Thoreau's works before it commissioned Leonard Baskin to design the commemorative stamp.

In the 150 years since Thoreau's death his reputation has undergone a complete right-about-face. James Russell Lowell doubted that Thoreau had a healthy mind. Robert Louis Stevenson rejected him as a prig and a skulker. In those days Emerson was the accepted Yankee philosopher; his optimism and benevolence expressed the mood of the time. During most of his life Thoreau lived in the shadow of his illustrious neigh-

bor; and the sale of his works was overshadowed by the sale of
Emerson's works for many years after both of them had died.
But the situation changed between the two World Wars. It
appeared that Thoreau had been telling the truth all along. It
was true that most men lead lives of quiet desperation. It was
true that we live in a hurry with a waste of life. In his own time
most people regarded Thoreau as a misanthrope and curmud-
geon—ludicrous, harebrained, eccentric, clownish, to use adjectives that were flung at him.

But his *Civil Disobedience*, which he—a very provincial
Yankee—wrote at the age of thirty-one, became a handbook for
Gandhi and at one time for the British Labor Party in this century, and it has been a strong influence in the civil rights
movement of the last few years. "Unjust laws exist," he ex-
claimed. "Shall we be content to obey them . . . or shall we
transgress them at once?" That anarchic stance had already cost
Thoreau one rather folksy night in jail, but since then it has
sent a lot of other people to less neighborly jails all over the
world.

He was a militant solitary. When Emerson asked him to attend a Saturday Club meeting in the Parker House in Boston,
Thoreau replied that the only room in Boston he visited with
alacrity was in the Fitchburg Depot, where he could get a train
to take him out of town. Now many of his admirers and fol-
lowers attend meetings in his honor.

The Thoreau Society, which was founded in 1941, holds
its annual meeting in Concord, visits Walden Pond and dis-
cusses the rather prickly man who lived there from 1845 to 1847
in a small house he built with his own hands. The members of
the society are invited to visit with a second Thoreau organization—the Thoreau Lyceum at 48 Belknap Street, which would
like to raise enough money to buy the land next door where,
in the so-called "Texas" house, Thoreau lived with his mother,
father and sisters before the family pencil business succeeded.

And so there are two paradoxes about him. The government that Thoreau despised has issued a commemorative

stamp in his honor; and a society of cultivated Americans meets every year to do homage to a man who avoided meetings. The paradoxes can be accounted for very simply. Thoreau lived the life he preached with incomparable purity; and he wrote a classic that contains not only his philosophy of independence but great valor, great knowledge and wisdom, great beauty and cautious hope.

It took eight years to sell the 2,000 copies of the first edition of *Walden* that appeared in 1854. Probably 2,000 copies of "Walden" are now sold every week. An obscure citizen of Concord has become a powerful American. As he phrased it: "Any man more right than his neighbors constitutes a majority of one already"—a bold nineteenth-century maxim that has turned out to be prophecy. [7/15/67]

BROOKS ATKINSON

The Warfare in the Forest Is Not Wanton

After thirty-five years the forest in Spruce Notch is tall and sturdy. It began during the Depression when work gangs planted thousands of tiny seedlings in abandoned pastures on Richmond Peak in the northern Catskills. Nothing spectacular has happened there since; the forest has been left undisturbed.

But now we have a large spread of Norway spruces a foot thick at the butt and 40 or 50 feet high. Their crowns look like thousands of dark crosses reaching into the sky.

The forest is a good place in which to prowl in search of wildlife. But also in search of ideas. For the inescapable fact is that the world of civilized America does not have such a clean record. Since the seedlings were planted the nation has fought three catastrophic wars, in one of which the killing of combatants and the innocent continues. During the lifetime of the forest 350,000 Americans have died on foreign battlefields.

Inside America civilized life is no finer. A President, a Senator, a man of God have been assassinated. Citizens are murdered in the streets. Riots, armed assaults, looting, burning, outbursts of hatred have increased to the point where they have become commonplace.

Life in civilized America is out of control. Nothing is out of control in the forest. Everything complies with the instinct for survival—which is the law and order of the woods.

Although the forest looks peaceful it supports incessant warfare, most of which is hidden and silent. For thirty-five years the strong have been subduing the weak. The blueberries that once flourished on the mountain have been destroyed. All the trees are individuals, as all human beings are individuals; and every tree poses a threat to every other tree. The competition is so fierce that you can hardly penetrate some of the thickets where the lower branches of neighboring trees are interlocked in a blind competition for survival.

Nor is the wildlife benign. A red-tailed hawk lived there last summer—slowly circling in the sky and occasionally drawing attention to himself by screaming. He survived on mice, squirrels, chipmunks and small birds. A barred owl lives somewhere in the depth of the woods. He hoots in midmorning as well as at sunrise to register his authority. He also is a killer. Killing is a fundamental part of the process. The nuthatches kill insects in the bark. The woodpeckers dig insects out. The thrushes eat beetles and caterpillars.

But in the forest, killing is not wanton or malicious. It is for survival. Among birds of equal size most of the warfare consists of sham battles in which they go through the motions of warfare until one withdraws. Usually neither bird gets hurt.

Nor is the warfare between trees vindicative. Although the spruces predominate they do not practice segregation. On both sides of Lost Lane, which used to be a dirt road, maples, beeches, ashes, aspens and a few red oaks live, and green curtains of wild grapes cover the wild cherry trees. In the depths of the forest there are a few glades where the spruces stand aside and birches stretch and grow. The forest is a web of intangible tensions. But they are never out of control. Although they are wild they are not savage as they are in civilized life.

For the tensions are absorbed in the process of growth, and the clusters of large cones on the Norway spruces are certificates to a good future. The forest gives an external impression of discipline and pleasure. Occasionally the pleasure is rapturously stated. Soon after sunrise one morning last summer when the period of bird song was nearly over, a solitary rose-breasted grosbeak sat on the top of a tall spruce and sang with great resonance and beauty. He flew a few rods to another tree and continued singing: then to another tree where he poured out his matin again, and so on for a half hour.

After thirty-five uneventful years the spruces have created an environment in which a grosbeak is content, and this one said so gloriously. It was a better sound than the explosion of bombs, the scream of the wounded, the crash of broken glass, the crackle of burning buildings, the shriek of the police siren.

The forest conducts its affairs with less rancor and malevolence than civilized America.   [11/23/68]

GEORGE A. WOODS

What Did You Do in the War, Daddy?

There are some things a middle-aged man can't explain to his children—about his part in World War II, for instance.

Were you at Midway, Daddy, they ask, the Coral Sea, Omaha Beach, the Bulge, did you take any flak over Berlin, how many Zeros did you down, what island did you "take," what beaches did you "hit"? No, none of those.

Did you capture any of the enemy, Daddy, save a town perhaps? No. Daddy, did anyone shoot at you? And how come you don't have a German helmet, an Iron Cross, a Luger or a

Rising Sun flag with bullet holes in it like the other kids' dad-
dies? You were in the service, weren't you, Daddy? Yes. Well,
what did you do?

Try explaining to them about the business of supply, that
for every slogging infantryman it took many men to keep that
one supplied with ammunition, clothing and food. They don't
understand logistics. They have visions of their father cradling
a machine gun, storming or defending some shell-shattered re-
doubt while shouting imprecations at the foe.

If you're halfway lucky you can say you drove a truck. They
know about trucks, having seen them on TV going through hell-
fire to supply fuel for Patton's tanks or racing ammo to the front
lines. Maybe you can say you were in the Quartermaster Corps;
it's got a nice, official, intimidating ring, or even the Adjutant
General's Department. But try telling children, point-blank,
that you were a clerk.

There was a time—the children were little then—when you
could point to your appendectomy scar and say, "See that? A
Japanese soldier ran me through with a bayonet." Awed and
pained, they would ask, did it hurt? And you'd tell them jok-
ingly, of course, that the worst part was when the soldier put his
foot on your chest to pull the bayonet out.

Daddy was a hero, a brave and fearless man—for a while—
until they grew older and discovered that a good portion of
American males, and females, suffered bayonet thrusts in ap-
proximately the same abdominal region. But now you have to
stop the exaggerations and confess that you never saw an enemy
soldier except on a training film.

A clerk, a headquarters clerk at that, doesn't impress them.
The medals the children discovered in the bottom of an attic
trunk years ago—good conduct, Asiatic-Pacific, Victory Medal
—have tarnished. Stories of 14-mile hikes, hot nights and days
in the hold of a troopship, of munching C and K rations, of pro-
ficiency on the range with a Springfield rifle, of scrubbing

out your mess kit with sand, of leaky pup tents—these stories bore them now. They yawn. A clerk. Twenty-five years ago you counted yourself lucky; today you're an unlucky ex-clerk.

Maybe that's why so many middle-aged fathers snarl and growl like top sergeants of yesteryear in dealing with their children on weekends. Maybe they were clerks, too. "AAAaaright, you bunch of misfits, let's police the area. I wanna see nothing but backs and elbows."

Or in the morning when those ex-clerks get up early, ahead of their children, and pound on the doors: "Fall out, hit the deck, everybody up, drop your teddy bears and grab your underwear." And when a child is especially slow on an errand the bark becomes: "On the double." In the evening, too, it's "knock it off. Everybody into their sacks. Lights out in ten minutes." Maybe they even have their children stand inspection, reveille or sign the payroll for their allowances, deducting, probably, for rations and quarters.

These are things you still remember but the children will never understand: bulletin boards and duck boards, the endless buffing of shoes, the swabbing of rifles with oil and patches of cloth, the lines that never seemed to move, the shouts of "fall out," "fall in," "helmet liners, leggings and full field packs," "take ten."

Lectures, duty rosters, the way socks were rolled and stacked so they "smiled" at the inspecting officer, the loneliness of being a soldier in a soldier town, initials like USO, CQ, OD. You still remember your serial number—12240780, the omnipresent clink of dog tags, V-mail, the red, white and blue of the CBI Theater shoulder patch, the joy, when it was all over, of going home.

But long before that, somewhere along the line, they separated the men from the boys, the combat soldiers from the company clerks. It's just like the wise one used to shout at new trainees: "You'll be sorry." And now, twenty-five years later, how right they were.

"You were in the service, weren't you, Daddy?" "Yes." "Well, what did you do?" [11/12/66]

FREDERIC MORTON

The Nouveau Avant

Something funny has happened to the American Dream. For generations it was the Good Life: Maybe we didn't live in the Fifth Avenue mansion yet, but we had already placed one real Wedgwood vase on the imitation fireplace. Maybe our daughter could not dance in the Debutante Cotillion, but she already took ballet lessons across from the Plaza. Most of us would never make it, yet all of us had the feeling we might be getting there.

But now—whatever happened to "there"? Sheer affluence has gone sour; surrounded and choked by its facsimiles and artifacts, we've only grown more unhappy with ourselves, more aggressive to others. There's no longer much salvation in the opulence of objects. And because of that we are turning inward, listening for our soul, trying to "do our thing." Instead of dreaming rich, we've begun to dream hip.

The bearded hippie of the sixties, like the top-hatted swell of the thirties, is a caricature—a crucial one. He personifies radically what the rest of us feel dimly. The swell touched off a smile of recognition because a generation ago we were all a bunch of *nouveaux riches*. Today, every morning more and more of us wake up to discover that we've been bourgeois all our lives; now we want to liberate our wild, free, *avant-garde* persona from sodden prosperity. The generation of the *nouveau riche* has given birth to the generation of the *nouveau avant*.

Unfortunately, it's tougher for the *nouveau avant*. His pursuit of persona, like the pursuit of wealth, is just another

American dream—only more frustrating. Yes, it takes a lot to change a grocer into the president of the A & P. It takes much more to turn a podiatrist into a genuine flower child, the kind that can burp true poetry into his petaled beard. After all, there is only one Allen Ginsberg for every ten Horatio Algers.

Yet our American Dreamers tackle their new ideal with the same old bandwagon energy, the same bravura faith in self-improvement. The slogan of Dr. Leary's medicine show, "Tune in, turn on, drop out," is fundamentally the same make-it lyric as "There's a Ford in your future."

Yesterday, in the *nouveau-riche* age, Mr. and Mrs. Upward Mobile graced their split-level with *Vogue* and English hunting prints. Today, being *nouveaux avants,* they turn on their pad with the East Village *Other* and psychedelic posters.

Yesterday the young marrieds from Yonkers motored to the country club in their de luxe hardtop for a cocktail with prestigious friends. Today they split for the Electric Circus in their (American Motors) Rebel to freak out with fellow swingers.

Here you might object that I'm talking about the quixoticism of the *nouveau-avant* adult—adults being, by many hip standards, obsolete. But actually the demands of hip are even severer on the young. The regal young, poor things, have no excuse for copping out on their own reign. They must pick up on the proper underground books, display the right drug insouciance, wear buttons with the correct put-ons.

But each of them knows, better and more ruefully than his elders, that such status symbols don't guarantee that inner gnosis demanded by the devout young hippie. The *nouveau avant,* and there's one hiding in every switched-on beard, is not a materialistic but a spiritual aspirant—he yearns for the postlinear vision.

Yet despite the built-in grace of teen-age, despite his Indian beads, his painted face, he falls back on remedies familiar from an all too linear childhood: for stomach relief, Bufferin; for becoming St. Augustine, LSD. And in an all-American try at ridding himself of bourgeois taboos he is often as Calvinist about being properly unbuttoned as his progenitors were puritan about staying covered up.

Hell-bent on the polymorphous perverse, out to reject everything square and squarely upright, the *nouveau avant* will in the end amputate his own origins and do violence to his own reflexes. The *nouveau riche* never punished himself like that. He bragged of being a self-made man, proud of his rags 'way back, of his rough diction now—contrasts that made his yacht all the more mythic. For rich meant the fulfillment of poor, whereas hip means the exorcism of square.

Our *nouveau avant* must suppress the person he used to be before starting out in the East Village. The hip American Dream has the hippie by the neck, but bad. He's less likely to end up a guru than his father was to make that million. Maybe he could learn to avoid the old man's trap: not to get so uptight about it. [11/25/67]

JUSTIN KAPLAN

The American City Is in Trouble (*1890, etc.*)

"The government of cities is the one conspicuous failure of the United States," James Bryce wrote in *The American Commonwealth* in 1888. Even then the charge had a familiar ring. Bryce was only lending the scriptural weight of his authority to what any number of Americans (especially those who had been to Europe) had already decided for themselves.

Many American cities were crippled by machine politics and organized corruption, New York being the most widely publicized but not necessarily the worst example. Violence was familiar, municipal services were at the best meager and unreliable, and in some cities such paving as there was consisted of garbage and dead animals.

As a social agency, as an instrument of collective power and responsibility for the common good, the American city had scarcely even begun to exist.

The same year Bryce's book was published Jacob Riis published the first of those searing slum photographs which brought to the eye and the conscience the indisputable facts of how the other half lived. During the 1890's the infant science of American sociology, stirring chiefly at Johns Hopkins, began to address itself to the nation's urban problems.

"The city was the place where we had to begin," said one of these early urbanologists, Frederic C. Howe (who became a leader in the civic revival movement). An enormous sociological literature about the city sprang up, and as muckraking journalists moved in to swell it even Bryce, reading Lincoln Steffens's *The Shame of the Cities* in 1905, was sorry that such a story had to be told and wondered whether some of Steffens's sources might not have exaggerated the evils.

Still, many of those who believed that the city was a problem peculiar to democracy also believed that the solution to the problem was (as a favorite reform slogan went) "not less democracy but more." To mobilize the people to "smash corruption," "throw the rascals out," and build "the City Beautiful" became the holy purpose of reformers all over the country. Leading sporadic insurrections of virtue, they warred on the bosses and the interests, on the apathetic citizen, and also on the loyal citizen who was afraid that a reform movement would give his city a bad name.

In a few cities, such as New York in 1895, reform scored famous victories, but they rarely lasted. A kind of bitter comedy followed. A few months after the victory over Tammany and police graft, the moral temperature of the city dropped appreciably, as any politician could have foreseen. The amateurs began to squabble among themselves.

The machine professionals took over once again. The new

Mayor, William F. Strong, was so embittered by his one term that he vowed never again to offer himself for public service. All in all, the ups and downs of most morally fired reform campaigns bore out Mr. Dooley's claim that it was easier and more rational to train lobsters to fly than it was to turn men into angels by means of the ballot box.

For our time of urban violence and bafflement the moral reformers do not have much to offer. But there is something— not answers perhaps, but impetus—to be got from another school of reformers, those who rejected the standard good man-bad man morality, were both sociological and religious in spirit, had higher goals for the city than just cleaning it up.

Among these reformers were Mayor Samuel M. "Golden Rule" Jones of Toledo, a Tolstoyan anarchist with a taste for publicans and sinners; his successor, Brand Whitlock, who had been brought into politics by the fiery John Peter Altgeld; and in Cleveland, Mayor Tom L. Johnson, a former manipulator of traction franchises who was converted to the single-tax creed by a chance reading of Henry George's *Social Problems* (which Johnson at first thought was a book about prostitution and venereal disease). Under Johnson, Cleveland became "the best governed city in the United States," Steffens said.

These men accepted the realities of politics, but they also celebrated the possibilities of the city in the accents of the Psalmist. Their creed was summed up in the title of one of Howe's books, *The City: The Hope of Democracy*. They talked about "a city on a hill." They used the same metaphors of the abundant city that had moved men from Aristotle to Augustine and from John Bunyan to Oz. They believed that it was possible, and necessary, for the city to become not only a place of justice and honesty but also an agency of unprecedented social service for all the people. [12/9/67]

JONATHAN KOZOL

Teaching Life at an Early Age in the Slums

In future years many of us will be asked by our children and grandchildren what we were doing when the students in the schools of the Negro slums of America were dying in their classrooms. I hope that some of us—above all, some of our teachers—will be able to give better answers than the ones that we have been giving up to now.

So much of the behavior of our teachers is bound in and delimited by a terrible acquiescence to an outworn code of "professional" reservation, "professional" withdrawal, "professional" restraint. Many teachers, like the rest of the people who know what is happening in the slums, are torn with shame and overwhelmed with their perceptions of the daily desiccation of the hopes of a million Negro children.

The teachers know well what is going on within their classrooms, but time and the timeworn habit of automatic self-denial have silenced their recognitions and compelled them to suppress their knowledge in the effort to fulfill the specific and clearly delineated obligation of an obedient teacher.

There is a higher obligation, however, than getting across the reading lesson. There is also the obligation to be an honest human being. The bewildered teacher, terrified to the very fibers of her spirit and shaken to the very center of her soul, smiles out at her black pupils, turns with them to the soiled flag above the doorway, and parrots a daily recitation of required fealty to a government which still claims, despite all evidence, to be "one nation, indivisible, with liberty and justice for all."

At times the irony is overwhelming. The books are junk, the paint peels, the rooms are so overcrowded that pupils can scarcely hear each other talking. In the midst of it all stands the kindly well-intending white school-lady and she tells her Negro pupils to be thankful that they do not live in a nation like Russia or in a continent like Africa.

There is a great deal of talk right now about technological innovations in the public classroom—new kinds of science, new forms of social studies, new language laboratories, new gadgets and new gimmickry. But what is the use of all this clever and expensive hardware if the same old goals are still sought after and the same old sad deceits still sold to children?

There is also, as we know, a great cry now being voiced to involve the ghetto communities in more meaningful participation in their public schools. But, again, what is the use of involving a black parent in the life of a ghetto classroom if she arrives there only to hear a teacher lying to her child?

I do not like to speak in terms that are needlessly apocalyptic and I would not wish to be in the position of heightening the dangers that are ahead of us by making dire predictions. On the other hand, it is apparent to me daily—as I leave my apartment in a black Boston slum, as I talk to many of the kids and listen to their parents in the evenings—that "rebellion" and "revolution" are no longer inappropriate terms with which to describe the kind of mood that is developing.

What I am trying to say, without rancor but in the most serious and absolutely urgent tone that I can muster, is that the American teacher, no matter at what level, is somehow going to have to figure out a way to *join* this revolution and to become a part of living history. If she can, she may not only command—she may also for the first time be able to deserve— her pupils' loyalty.

There are thousands of young, bright, brave and revolutionary pupils in the liberal colleges of this country. It is up to our government to find a way to get the best of these young people directly into urban classrooms, to make it worth their while, to spare them from repressive educators and to enable them to achieve a strong and swift liaison with the black communities:

a liaison based upon their mutual recognition of the need for immediate and overwhelming social change.

If we can do it for the poor and wretched of several dozen other nations, surely we can do it for the city-bound black people of our own society. [6/15/68]

HERBERT J. MULLER

The Uses and Abuses of a University

The end of the school year indicated clearly that the American campus is as confused as the state of America. The radical activists who make the headlines represent a very small minority. Most students remain complacent, as American students have always tended to be. Although they complain about this or that, chiefly the restrictions on their social or sexual life, they seem basically content with their education and their prospects.

But somewhere in the middle lie many earnest, thoughtful students who question the violent tactics of the demonstrators, yet sympathize with their indignation and their ardor. It is these students I am most concerned about, if only because they are still willing to listen to those of us past the unspeakable age of thirty.

In a way their dissatisfaction with the universities is surprising. So far from being oppressed, American students are in general the most pampered students in the world. Today they can look forward to more and better opportunities than ever before because of the change in the universities.

With the many billions going into "research and development," the knowledge industry has become the biggest business in America, growing at about twice the rate of the economy. One hears that the university bids fair to be the primary institution of our technological society, more important than the big corporation.

But here is the trouble. Educators might rejoice in their new eminence, as in fact most research men and administrators appear to. There are those, however, who describe the booming universities as superservice stations for government and industry, and deplore their willingness to play along with the powers that be.

Now, American universities must of course meet the demands of their society. The question is whether they are meeting them on their own terms. Traditionally these terms have included some independent idea of what society needed, not merely what it wanted.

Thus universities were supposed to uphold ideals of freedom of inquiry, criticism and dissent—ideals never really popular with most businessmen and many legislators. They were also supposed to provide intellectual and moral leadership, radiate a devotion to civilized values and the good life, dedicate themselves to the lofty aims annually paraded in our commencement oratory.

Students might feel edified by this oratory, but most of them remained content with the economic and social value of their degree. Today, in spoiled, affluent America, the surprising thing is that so many students really want the universities to be true to their proclaimed ideals.

They too seem pretty confused. The thoughtful ones complain that their education is not "relevant," but when asked relevant to what—to immediate burning issues or to broader interests than the subject they are specializing in—they are usually vague.

Except for freedom in their social life, they are as vague when they talk of "student power," seldom making clear how much power they think they ought to have in determining academic policy, and always tending to forget that this power might be exercised by the complacent, conservative majority. While demanding more attention to their needs as students, they are no clearer on just what these needs are, just what kind of education they want.

They want to be "committed" to some positive cause beyond private, selfish interests. They are looking for an idealism they too seldom find in the authorities in their universities. Their dissatisfaction is, finally, not so much with their curriculum as with the state of America, whose military and business interests the universities have been serving too faithfully and uncritically.

As a professor (known to the young radicals as an old liberal —the dirtiest word in their lexicon) I agree that the whole establishment has been letting down the thoughtful students.

Only I am not satisfied with my own efforts. I don't have a clear idea, either, of just what the universities should do for students today—just how to give them the professional training they need in a technological society, but also give them an adequate understanding of such a society, make them good citizens with a proper concern for human, civilized values, develop them as independent individuals, and prepare them for responsible leadership in a future that the experts in forecasting tell us will be still fuller of problems.

All I am sure of is that I'm glad so many students are as dissatisfied as I am.   [6/22/68]

MITCHELL WILSON

The Fountain of Eternal Adolescence

With the invention of the atom bomb, the demand was made more urgent than ever that scientists and inventors examine the social effects of their innovations before loosing them on the world. Actually scientists and inventors always had very clear ideas of what their creations were intended to achieve. The history of science shows that almost no one, though, is able to predict all the unexpected ways a discovery will be used by one's own generation and those that follow.

Dr. Richard Gatling, a Civil War surgeon, invented the machine gun, hoping that the tenfold increase in individual firepower would mean fewer men required for military service. Instead, armies grew even larger. The Wright brothers were sure their invention would put an end to war. Instead, the airplane became the deadliest weapons carrier in history.

The biggest miscalculation by scientists in our era seems to have been in the field of medicine. Medical researchers defeated puerperal fever, malaria, cholera, pneumonia and dozens of other diseases; and generally added decades to the average span of human life which, it was assumed, mature adults would use to deepen their experience and knowledge. Wisdom would become more profound, more widely shared.

Instead, most of the extra years have been preempted by the young. For many, childhood now lasts ten years longer, maturity begins ten years later. It is no surprising thing any more to run across a fully developed hulking male of twenty-five who refers to the "adult generation" as something to which he does not—he thanks God—yet belong. Even though physical maturity comes three to five years earlier than in 1900, many people of twenty-five today have more in common with those ten years younger than with those ten years older in terms of clothes, manners, values and esthetics.

The very word "adult" is synonymous now only with advancing age and deadening responsibility. Previously young people were anxious to escape adolescence for adulthood because only adults had freedom of movement, freedom to earn the money to satisfy one's appetites, freedom to assert oneself as a member of the community. To be adult paid off in privilege.

Today in rich, permissive America many young people have all the privileges once reserved to adults. They travel, find jobs almost for the asking and get educational grants—it sometimes seems—by merely filling out the required forms. In terms of self-interest they are right. What's in it for them to join the adult world?

Instead of the hoped-for increase of maturity, there is an increasing childishness. Twiggy's huge, empty eyes spoke to more hearts than Einstein's tragic gaze. Self-gratification is the order of the day. Let's get married; our fathers will go on supporting us. On the other hand, who wants that marriage bag —with its responsibilities: husbands, kids and a house?

In certain areas, art no longer need be consciously meaningful, liberating artists and audience alike from the responsibility of thinking or feeling. Or else the game of symbolism is played, in which the point is no longer the profundity of the artist's perception, but the cleverness with which one can read concealed statements into obscurities. The word today may be diffusely critical, but invariably platitudinous enough to be printed in Chinese fortune cookies, such as: Life Is Cruel, Men Are Mad, Hypocrisy Reigns.

The music that accompanies all this is deafeningly loud, the lights are blindingly bright, the colors stupefyingly vivid—in the greatest, most prolonged children's party since the invention of peppermint candy.

None of this was the aim of the army of dedicated researchers who worked to make man's life less of a torment in time of disease. Only one major lesson seems clear from the history of science—whatever the invention or innovation, regardless of the intention that gave it birth, man is apparently so constituted that he will take each new benefit science gives him and find some way to use it either for pleasure—or to kill.   [7/6/68]

MARYA MANNES

The Young in Hair

Two youths walked down the street. Each wore luxuriant hair not only down to their brows but below their turtlenecks. A middle-aged woman with a tight mouth and pixie glasses turned to look at them in scorn and distaste, and said, to no one or anyone: "I think it's disgusting. If they were mine, I'd shave every hair off their heads!"

This appears to be the reaction of all good citizens (the "clean ones" who don't march) to an increasingly familiar sight. They feel affronted and threatened by these masculine locks, they find them somehow evil, they don't understand them. They are quite unable to view them dispassionately.

To do so might, however, be a useful exercise. There is something to understand about all this hair on the youthful male, because it is more than a simple fad, more than a rebellion against the staling of age and custom.

For one thing, the conventional short crop may display the shape of the skull but it does not convey the texture of the hair. It imposes a conformity only partly mitigated by color and density. What you begin to see for the first time in this long hair, and which comes as a surprise, is the degree to which a man's hair, left to itself, can curl, wave, shine and spring.

Hair becomes much more than a cover crop, it becomes an individual adornment that sets a man apart from his fellow and can be admired for itself. Riffle through any history of costume and coif and this will become self-evident in any number of eras and peoples from Visigoth to Knight of the Round Table, from French troubadour to Arab sheik. Abundant hair has been just as much a sign of masculinity as the long robe or tights.

Ironically, these same young people who may seem so far

from romantic in their speech and their dances are true romanticists in the business of hair as well as clothes. A year ago this writer saw the reevocation of a medieval marriage celebration in a small Bavarian town. The youths and maidens in this thirteenth-century pageant were dead ringers for our own. There were the girls in their long, shining hair, there were the boys in their boots and leather jackets, their tights— and their waving locks. And they looked very good indeed.

So what is all this fuss about? Some of it is certainly aggravated by those of our young males who do not bring to their new adornment the carriage and grace it demands. The slouching lout with straggling hair falling over an unclean collar is an unlovely sight, and some of the combo singers and pluckers who elicit the loudest teen-age female squeals belong in a zoo or a psycho ward. Very few male faces are improved by hair that comes down to granny glasses in front and covers the ears and jawline.

But abundant hair, provided it is controlled at nape and sides, is a blessing to many boys who would otherwise look bleak and ordinary. Our sharp emotional reaction to it may be more a sign of our own rigidity than of their folly; one more example of a society grown set in its ways, resistant to change, hostile to difference. We seem to want everything neatly packaged and labeled.

That this society usually prevails is nothing to celebrate. All too soon the youths with the shining long hair become the shorn gray men with the black attaché cases or the close-shaven digits in boot camp or battlefront. The swagger goes, the color dulls, the clothes confine, the pressures erase the precious differences.

So let youth have its short span of freedom. If adults admired their long hair more, the young would probably cut it off themselves. The only thing apparently intolerable to them is our approval, for then what are they revolting against?

They are, in any case, preferable to the good ladies who hiss at them and the good men who sneer at them. And anyway, it's *their* hair, isn't it? [10/8/66]

MARIANNE C. MOORE

In Fashion Yesterday, Today and Tomorrow

Some phase of altitude manifests itself in every age. Dante says Beatrice walked like a crane—*come una crana*. And in Jacopo Amigoni's painting entitled "The Embarkation of Helen of Troy," Helen is wearing a long dress, holding by the hand a child in a miniature long dress. They were not depicted in mini-skirts or tennis-net square-mesh stockings. In fact, the mere tip of Helen's foot shows.

In keeping with a tradition of noble behavior, for the defense of children Venice by ordinance forbids the citizen to wear dress too strangely shaped or scant. A narrow sheath or pant (if I may use the word) does not set a "hippomoid" figure off to advantage.

The sound hole in a cello, an upper-case Caslon Old Style S, an approaching swan, a swiftly twirling sea lion reversing direction, fifty elephants with heads touching the ground as honoring majesty in Thailand—these symbolize fashion rightness as unfreakishly right as Siam is distant from Manhattan. In an exhibition of historic designs in the Brooklyn Museum not long ago, dresses or a wrap by the House of Worth were as pleasant to wear or try on as any dashing innovation in an uptown shop on Madison Avenue.

I have a tintype, taken about 1880, of eminently dressed Philadelphians. The men wore boating straws with university bicolored ribbons; the ladies' basques have sleeves that *fit*, which make our current blouses look like dressing gowns. One synonym of aplomb among the ladies in the tintype wears a silk basque, tightly fastened by about twenty-nine bullet buttons almost touching, and a close-fitting small hat, covered by stiff ribbons ended diagonally. Nor did they slouch.

The greatest change in fashion from Victorian times is in boys' clothes—long trousers instead of knickers. The yachtsman's double-breasted Navy jacket, and cap with white flannels or ducks, are the man's most effective garb, I think. (These modifying words are appropriate to any dogmatism expressed here by your fashion reporter.) Ballplayers' uniforms seem to me not so trim as formerly. They should not look like babies' sleepers or snowsuits.

Not only potential buyers applauded S. Klein's Mink Maids when exhibited there. A nineteen-year-old electric utility clerk said, "It sure breaks the monotony of lunch hour," as the Mink Maids paraded mink stoles, jackets, and a mink trench coat. An elderly Manhattan widow kept murmuring afterward, "Beautiful, beautiful. I wonder if they have any seconds that they're giving away."

The most expensive coat in the show ($3,987) was a floor-length white mink with a detachable flounce. This coat I view with partisan interest, since I am an incurable sufferer of thrift. If I were not the recipient of a donated French brocade emerald jacket and purple velvet skirt of papal quality I could be mistaken for a mere citizen of Times Square at the rush hour.

May I digress to shoes? Fontana of Rome makes a pale elephant's-breath suede blucher with cotton tie that might well be standard. At least, *did* make.

The cuffless trouser ought not to draw attention to itself —should be worn by a connoisseur of legs. Vests, slowly coming back, omitted to save cloth during the war, add four pockets to the suit and an inside one to carry a billfold.

Men's hats are still to be seen abroad. The New Haven between Stamford, Greenwich and New York is said to carry 40,000 commuters and the New York Central the same; and not a hat to be seen, except with a uniform. A Stetson or wide-brimmed Panama should not be merely an ornament, cost what it may! Sir Winston Churchill had nine hats.

The New Guinea Tari tribesman's bunch of leaves at the back, steadied by a vine string, is perhaps the least hampering concession to fashion.

Today? We are menaced by inexplicable epidemics of violence. Mr. Ortega y Gasset, quoted on television by Professor Floyd Zulli, sees violence, such as the stoning of cars and the defacing of churches by between-age girls and boys, as caused by empty minds—vacuity is interpreted as nobility that is action. But how can probity or fashion be instilled by parents who find sacrifices too inconvenient in providing children a home?

Tomorrow? The Italians have a saying: "It's a queer bee that makes honey only for itself." To what life and fashion principle may one adhere? Confucius, translated by Ezra Pound, said, "Sympathy." [11/4/67]

ELIOT ASINOF

The World Series Is No Autumn Classic

If you were born before the last great war, you know that the phrase "autumn madness" refers to the annual October classic called the World Series. America had a national pastime in those ancient days called baseball. Every village in the then forty-eight states, no matter how small, had a ball team, and there was hardly a kid who didn't take his baseball glove to bed with him, just to be sure it was broken in properly. The older you are, it would seem, the more the game means to you.

Once there was something marvelously special about the World Series. It was a national event, as celebrated as the Fourth of July, and its reverberations were felt even in hamlets whose citizens never came closer than a thousand miles to a big league game. Before the days of radio, people in the hinterland would gather at the local railroad depot and wait for the telegraph ticker to send reports.

Not so long ago thousands of the hopefuls would line up at the ball park gates twenty-four hours before game time and sit out the frigid night on the chance of getting in. During that first stirring week of October, much else in America would come to a standstill.

It is not so any longer, except in the two contending cities. On the days the Series draws to its climax, more people tune their television sets to college and professional football. Over 12,000,000 Americans now play golf, and there are not going to be fewer golfers on the links. Even the weekend afternoon movies will do good business, especially since the biggest percentage of movie fans are young.

Baseball, sad to report, has gone out of universal fashion.

In the exciting four-team American League race, real pennant fever seems to have hit only Boston. Chicago, with a history of being one of the great baseball towns, is too intimidated by racial turmoil to pour into Comiskey Park. Minnesota and Detroit have been playing crucial home games to less than 10,000 fans. True, there are still a great many baseball fans (according to official figures, more people attended big league games than ever before). But this must be considered comparatively; the trend is moving steadily away.

The New York football Giants draw more to a single summer exhibition than the New York baseball Yankees in a week of regular season games.

Baseball no longer grabs the young and it has alienated many of the old. It moves too slowly for a speed-conscious, action-hungry society. With the rising emphasis on home runs, there are too few base runners and even fewer who know how to run the bases.

"Only long-ball hitters drive Cadillacs," they say, but the end result seems to be that the average wing in hockey is driving a better car than the clean-up hitter who seldom averages over

.250. The tradition of great ball clubs in historic relationships with their communities—like Connie Mack with the Philadelphia A's—has all but dissolved with the maddening city jumping of money-hungry club owners.

The great American sport (remember, the Supreme Court says it's not a business) has become the desperate American hustle: A team that wins a flag in New York one year, say, may be shooting for another in San Francisco the next. This is not the kind of system that commands the loyalty of kids, and "the kids," as Babe Ruth once said, "are what the game is for."

It is inevitable that our affluence has changed our styles. The teen-agers who used to gather at the sandlots now prefer guitars and sports cars. The sandlots themselves no longer exist, having been swallowed up by the realty needs of expanding suburbs. As in boxing, baseball is becoming dominated by minority groups (despite the Baseball Establishment's desperate past try to forestall it), for this is a way out of poverty and into the limelight. Meanwhile, indispensable minor league farm teams have dropped in number from 500 to 120, and only a few are self-sustaining.

For all its dwindling popularity, however, the World Series remains at the heart of the American sporting scene. There will be more than enough drama in the competition for anyone who wants it.

Anything is likely to happen in the best four out of seven games. Great athletes will put out with the best that is in them to give, spurred by the happy combination of pride and prize money. [9/30/67]

LEWIS NICHOLS

A Den's No Den for Long

Not long ago the head of the house sat daydreaming. Having declined an invitation to help with the dinner dishes, he found a comfortable chair for himself and a comfortable coffee table for his feet, and drifted into a set of adventures all having the same likable hero. The radio played softly, old show tunes, each dripping with memory.

Presently there came an interruption for a commercial. A finance company was offering free money. Among several uses for this money, the unctuous voice suggested "build Dad a den."

The head of the house emerged with a yelp from his revery, the coffee table spinning across the room as his feet hit the floor. In the silence of the quickly stilled radio, a conspiratorial giggle and whisper in the kitchen suggested that local jokes were being exchanged out there. It was to be hoped they had not heard the evening's most grisly suggestion, for having heard, they immediately would have acted, rushing downtown even before the start of the next business day. For building Dad a den is the thing they like best to do. They do it all the time.

Down the years Dad has had dens in the far end of the living room, behind a screen at the near end of the dining room, in the spare bedroom, in two separate parts of the attic and behind the furnace in the cellar. Each of these came about in the same fashion. Their eyes greedily devouring advertisements for new sofas and rugs, they said that every man should have a room of his own, and just by chance there were the old sofas and rugs with which to furnish it. Each of these dens has ended in the same way. With Dad barely settled, they took over.

This is not to charge dishonesty in their intentions, for to do so would invite thunders sounding like the crack of doom. It is simply to set down a singular train of pretty odd coincidences. For a new television set now occupies that end of the living room which once was a den. A sewing machine is in the spare bedroom. A washing machine churns away in what was Dad's den behind the furnace in the cellar. What happened is that Dad's den, once established, became the most desirable spot in the house. And allowed in as visitors, they stayed.

The head of the house would like to read in this a compliment, for he would much enjoy having others share the pleasant pictures he has of himself. Alas, he knows better. The initial step of their getting into the den at the near end of the dining room was an evening's request for assistance with knotty problems in algebra. These solved, it seemed practical just to remain near the source of information. The initial step of their getting into the den in the cellar was one of finances. They did not wish to discuss the budget before the children, and what gave more privacy than a quiet den behind the furnace? The budget never has been settled upon although they settled in, bringing the washing machine with them. And so it has gone.

Not wishing to belabor the point, but as he considered his dens, the head of the house felt that the one in the living room most completely typified what had become of dens. The downfall of this one was in several stages, none of them easy. That one in the living room was potentially the ideal. It was on the same floor level as the kitchen and thus gave easy access to three meals a day. It was created on a Saturday, when it was raining outdoors and so everyone was available to help with the heavy work. It had a comfortable chair, a reading light, bookcases into which the head of the house placed his meager possessions.

But almost before he could put his feet up for the first Sunday siesta, the decline began. Some phonograph records were placed in the bookcase—only temporarily, of course—and these were followed by a portable phonograph with which to play them. Again this was temporary, and indeed it so turned out. For not long after Dad had left the living room, the new TV replaced the phonograph—but not those who had brought both of them in.

On the evening of the daydream, the head of the house reviewed Dad's dens, and then, struck with a morbid thought, wandered into the kitchen. The dishes all were done, no one was there, but the kitchen radio was tuned to the same station as his. And that conspiratorial whisper had indeed been heard just after the commercial. [11/13/65]

HERBERT MITGANG
Sunglasses Without Sun

As anyone can plainly see, sunglasses occasionally have something to do with the sun. There are some people who actually wear them to block out the rays and prevent squinting. Obviously, those who wear sunglasses only when the sun is out are unaware of their versatility and psychological advantages. Anybody can wear sunglasses when the sun is out, but that's so obvious. It takes somebody to wear sunglasses only when the sun is *in*.

The natural superiority of the sunglass wearer in the office, the subway, the nightclub and other areas of our subterranean life is established the instant he or she confronts a bare-eyed person. The advantage lies with the sunglass wearer, who can see but cannot be seen. The sunglasses may be a Berlin Wall hiding insecurities on the far side; behind the green smoke screen may lurk a Dorian Gray. Or reddened marital eyes. Or the rivulets of a hangover. Or, indeed, nothing at all but the vacant look of somebody who is nobody without his sunglasses.

Important People wear sunglasses. The Kennedys often wore them when the sun was out. His plain; hers Continental. Audrey Hepburn wears sunglasses that are shaped like big saucers. So Henrietta Plainface, a wide-eyed young lady with an out-of-town accent who is researching her way through the ranks

of the unmarriageable senior editors on a news weekly, went
out and bought expensive goggle sunglasses, too, but—she
still doesn't look like Audrey Hepburn. Her sister, Prudence
Plainface, wears the bulging wraparound sunglasses that
Brigitte Bardot helped to popularize, but on her they (the
sunglasses) seem to stick out in the wrong places. Actually, they
looked a little bug-eyed on Brigitte, too, but nobody noticed.

What do wearers of sunglass monocles do about the other
eye? Nothing, for the sad fact is that monocle wearers are the
only ones for whom special sunglasses have not yet been mass-
produced. (You read it here first.) There are curved-side no-
glare sunglasses for skiers, two-toned sunglasses for those who
want to match the glasses to their clothing, sunglasses with short
earpieces that cling to the temple without joggling the pin
curlers, mood-matched colored sunglasses designed to match
almost every mood—from sick green to blue funk.

The sunglass dreamers are the old Army Air Corps types who
wear their old flying goggles in the office while memos fly by
dangerously . . . .

Executing a chandelle, an ex-AAF man entered the elevator, waved "contact!" to the operator, and shot upward to his
floor. Pulling back on the joystick, he flew directly into the office
of his superior, Manfred von Richthofen, whose circus was lurk-
ing behind a cloud cover of secretaries. He immediately went
into a dive but he couldn't shake him off his tail. Then he remembered the lesson of yesterday's dawn patrol! He twisted the
rudders into a half-Immelmann, but the Hispano-Suiza engine
was no match for the Albatross D.3. Slowly the Spandau tracers
began to spell the Red Knight's initials across the nacelle of his
French Spad S.7.

There was only one thing that stood between him and the
Blue Lady of the Sky. He hated to do it but he did it: He ripped
off the old Air Corps sunglasses from his despised enemy.
It worked! Exposed for all to see, his nemesis went down in
flames. [10/29/63]

HERBERT MITGANG

Short Atlantic Snorters

The airlift of an American armored division from Texas to Germany was achieved with such ease and swoop recently that it caused an old transatlantic military traveler to search— of all places—deep in the recesses of his wallet for evidence of earlier flights. Sure enough, right between a card entitling him to Red Cross doughnuts on the Boulevard Baudin in Algiers and a second card giving him permission to take a public bath on the Via Roma in Palermo was another souvenir of (let's see, which war was it now, World War I or II?) that suspended life in uniform. It was a $1 bill. A short snorter.

All the long days of the Furious Forties, flying the Atlantic was so privileged an experience that it entitled one to boast. Boasting occasionally required proof when backed into the corner of the bar. At this point, the alleged passenger would have to produce the evidence—a bill with his name, date and flight signed by the captain of the airplane. If he did not have this vital document in his wallet, he would have to pay a buck to the short snorter who challenged him—or buy the drinks for the evening. Otherwise, each signed the other's short snorter.

What about those who flew the wider Pacific in those days? Why, they were still more exclusive. Long snorters.

The magic letters for military travel by aircraft in those days were three, all in caps, no periods in between: TDN. Travel Directed is Necessary. Beautiful words! They sang, they were poetry, they winged you home by air instead of troopship. Home could be either way: to the States or back to the old outfit overseas. (The very word "overseas" rather than "abroad" had an Atlantic snorter ring to it.) Occasionally TDN had to be stretched a bit by fast talking because military language managed to touch all bases. Written orders (correction: orders

weren't written, they were "cut," due homage to the mimeo-
graph stencil) might read, "Water, rail, government motor vehicle, and/or military aircraft, as necessary and available."

Since taking a train or truck across the Atlantic was as difficult
then as now, that left the and/or of ship or plane. The option
often rested with the man carrying his own travel orders—who
could always miss a boat.

And how did one finally get on a Flying Fortress or Liberator
or other converted air transport to earn a snorter? Often simply
by going out to the aerodrome (correction: aerodrome was another war; better change it to read airfield) and hitching a ride.
You walked up to a captain, asked if he had room for one
more, he'd glance casually at the cut orders, and tell you to hop
on.

Nowadays, on some transatlantic flights, you are almost there
before the air hostess has had a chance to say coffee, tea or me.

Not so in that was the war that was.

One earned one's snorter the hard way. So that's why some
Army types referred to the citizens as "bodies"! A transatlantic
crossing was a bone-breaking affair. Aluminum bucket seats, designed for inhuman shapes, resisted all efforts at stretching out.
And, 10,000 feet up they were colder than a witch's heart (or
however the original of that pungent Army line went). Instead
of pressurized cabins, one went on individual oxygen almost automatically high up. Those little masks were not conducive to
today's jet catnapping.

At the end of his transatlantic journey, recalled the half-nos-
talgic man with the short snorter, he remembered one thing in
particular. Stepping off the plane, after a few years in a war
theater where mines were placed by the enemy along every
route, he discovered that he couldn't bring his feet down on the
grass. There were no safety tapes running along the edges of the
airfield in New York; how could he be sure that there were no
mines buried below? It took a long time to walk on the unswept
grass, even without ACHTUNG MINEN signs.

The grass, he hoped, was greener for the new flying armorers in the strange new wars of peacetime.   [10/27/63]

HERBERT MITGANG

The Winter Bank

The first cold snap caused a man to examine the sums in his winter bank. This is where he saves up his dreams and imaginings; these seem to last longer than his limited tangible resources. When wintry winds blast, and city shepherds blow their nails, he has his own peculiar account to tide him over the sharp black nights. His adult piggy bank has memories on deposit of the bright moments and the wash-and-wear scenes of summertime. They return with compound interest now.

At the far right of the shirt drawer, for example, one of the vacation shirts has in due course worked its way up to the top of the pile. Neatly stitched through one of the tails is a piece of red thread knotted carefully: a laundry mark in the secret code of a Parisian laundress. Although unseen, the seamstress or laundress is no doubt a hidden beauty, a granddaughter descended from a character in Zola's *Rougon-Macquart* novels, living obscurely but happily, without the poverty and slow demoralization of her literary ancestors. No wonder the tiny red thread brings the thrill of recall every time the shirt comes up.

The bank also includes a Roman vocabulary lesson. The jangling cleaning woman in the little hotel, heavily weighted down with keys, knew not a foreign word except what might be called hotel English. The phrase book was searched in vain for the precise word. How could the American on the move ask her if his special raincoat could be cleaned and returned in one day without getting it mixed up with all other raincoats? He struggled, pointed and grimaced—until the wise woman came to the rescue. "Ah, si," she nodded. "Il trench." Perfect! How else would you say trench coat in hotelese? Through all the long, slushy days from November to March, his "trench" would speak to him of Mediterranean sunshine.

Indeed, a number of international words in the lingua franca of America abroad had been safely deposited in the memory book. A Sorbonne professor calls the new words "franglais." His favorite was a bistro which featured Le Quick-Snack. It was handy for those who were in the city only for (as a Parisian newspaper ad put it) Le Week-End. Under the circumstances, it was not strange to find a pinball parlor (Salle de Jeux) featuring machines named Gaucho, Paris Swing and Slick Chick. These latter names, unfortunately, became debits in the book. But discussions of Britain's great train robbery one summer were referred to in a heist phrase worthy of Hercule Poirot: Le Hold-Up.

A caravanserai in London caused our depositor to come up with his own secret method of classifying hotels. Everybody knew, of course, about superior two- and three-star restaurants in the guide and road books. And that hotels were classified from bathless third class up to de luxe or luxury. Yet even the unfamiliar traveler always discovered places of his own to stay or dine.

A concierge who had played both sides of the English Channel conveyed a tip himself: "Always look for three buttons next to the bed lamp. If there are three separate buttons to summon concierge, valet or waiter, it can't be all bad."

The rule of thumb added up and made sense wherever tried. It was information expensively gathered and therefore all the more carefully deposited—surely one of the sums that could be drawn against when the dreariest days ahead stormed the invincible winter bank.   [11/3/63]

WILLIAM G. WING

Christmas Comes First on the Banks

The Christmas sun rises first, in America, on trawlermen fishing the undersea meadows of Georges Bank.

At the moment before sunrise a hundred miles east of Cape Cod, the scene aboard a trawler is so unchanging it can be imagined. The net has been hauled and streamed again. The skipper is alone in the pilot house, surrounded by the radiotelephone's racket and the green and amber eyes of electronic instruments, instruments that are supposed to tell him not only where he is but where the fish are, too.

But this is only hope, not science. Despite the instruments, despite the boat's resemblance to a plow horse, methodically crisscrossing the meadow, her men are not engineers or farmers, but hunters who seek their prey in the wilderness of the sea. The trawlermen are, in fact, the last tribe of nomadic huntsmen left in the East.

The skipper is alone, then, with a huntsman's anxieties: the whereabouts of the prey, the uncertainties of the weather, the chances of hitting a good market.

On deck before him the men are processing the catch just brought aboard. They sit in a circle of brilliance, the deck lights reflecting from their yellow and Daybrite-orange oilskins and from the brown curve of the riding sail above.

They sit on the edges of the pens, holding the big white and silver fish between their knees, ripping with knives and tearing with hands, heaving the disemboweled bodies into a central basket. Nothing is visible beyond the cone of light but the occasional flash of a whitecap or comber.

There is much noise, though—wind and water and seabirds that have gathered in mobs for the feast of haulback.

There is an appropriateness to Christmas in this scene, east of the sleeping mainland, so marked that it seems quaint. The names of the trawlers themselves—*Holy Family, Immaculate Conception, St. Mary, St. Joseph*—give the flavor. On the engine room bulkhead of the trawler *Holy Cross,* beyond the ugga-chugging Atlas diesel, is a painting of Christ at Gethsemane.

There is an appropriateness, too, among the men. They share alike—equal shares of profit, equal shares of danger. To work together in such small quarters and stern conditions requires a graciousness of spirit that is the essence of Christmas.

The sun is up and the pens are empty. As the deck is hosed down and the trash fish pitchforked overboard, the noise from the birds rises hysterically—barnyard sounds, shrieks, whistles, klaxon horns.

Now the birds can be seen flying in a circle around the boat. Each can hold position for only a few moments beside the point where the remains of fish are washing over. Then it falls astern and has to come up to windward on the other side of the boat, cross ahead and fall backward to the critical point. The birds pumping up the windward side look like six-day bicycle riders, earnest and slightly ridiculous, but when they reach the critical point there is a miraculous moment of aerobatics as the birds brake, wheel and drop in the broken air.

Gulls snatch, gannets plunge, but the little kittiwakes balance delicately, their tails spread like carved ivory fans. There is a column of descending, shrieking birds, a scintillating feathered mass. The birds revolving about the boat have made themselves not only guests at the feast but have formed the wreath as well.

Christmas Day has begun, but for the men it is time to sleep. They hose each other off and then disappear through the whaleback for a mug-up below.

Boots and oilskins off, they will have a minute or two for a James Bond novel or a crossword puzzle in the bunks, braced against the elevator motions of the hull, not hearing the sounds of Niagara outside. Then the instant unconsciousness that seamen and children know. The skipper alone remains awake, watching Christmas come.

Christmas came first to men on lonely meadows. It will come first again to the men on the lonely meadows offshore, fishing the Bank in boats wreathed by seabirds.   [12/24/66]

JAMES T. FARRELL

Woodrow Wilson Remembered

Woodrow Wilson died at his house in Washington. He had always liked Thomas Gray's "Elegy Written in a Country Churchyard." When "the paths of glory" led him to his "inevitable hour," Wilson is supposed to have said to his wife:

"Edith, I'm a broken machine, but I'm ready."

As I look back, I can summon from my imagination and memory and from my reading several different images of this man who became President when I was nine years old, and a War President when I was thirteen, and who, when I was fourteen, was the Hero of the World, as though he were a savior of mankind, and then lost and crumbled. Repudiated politically, paralyzed physically, he left office at the end of his second term, and the exponent of "normalcy" succeeded him.

When I was passing through adolescence and young manhood in the 1920's, Wilson then seemed to me to focus the tragedy of the world into which my contemporaries and I were growing up. With the years, he becomes one of the many characters of that tragedy, not the sole protagonist. I cannot think of him but with sadness.

Even in my first hot moments of postwar disillusionment, with the anger of a young man's feeling of betrayal, and the expectation that my generation and I, myself, would pay the price of Wilson's historic failure as a peacemaker at Versailles, I did not lose my underlying sense of sadness. For it was not the fail-

ure of a man, but of human hope for a better and much
different kind of world, which imbues the story of Wilson with
the somber tones of tragedy.

But those were not my first impressions of Wilson. As an
Irish boy in Chicago I grew up thinking that he was a great man,
the greatest President since Abraham Lincoln. My father had
voted for him. He was brainy, a scholar; he had a big vocabulary.
I was a trusting boy. My trust extended to the President, and I
wanted him to do right and to be right.

With the succession of days from 1914 to 1917, the First
World War slowly penetrated my consciousness, as it did
that of most Americans. The war meant death and suffering,
the death of countless thousands; it meant soldiers going over
the top on bayonet charges and being mowed down by machine
guns. But President Wilson knew what to do. I didn't even have
to tell myself such a thought; I knew it and believed it as I believed that the sun would shine in the morning that must follow
the night. President Wilson was a hero of mine.

Wilson at one point early in the war proclaimed that the
United States was "too proud to fight." I later perceived that
this famous statement reflected one of Wilson's outstanding
traits. He was a phrasemaker who, too frequently, substituted
words for the deeds of decision. Such a statement was a phrasemaker's remark. Americans have never to my knowledge been
"too proud to fight," but they were reluctant to fight at that
time because they didn't quite know what the fighting was all
about.

Wilson understood intellectually that the Presidency is, first
of all, a place where power has to be exercised and action taken.
As he said shortly after his election in 1912: "This is an office
in which a man must put on his war paint. Fortunately, I am
not of such a visage as to mind marring it."

But Wilson, a minister's son, a scholar and a man of words
who came to the practice of politics late in his career, was not
by nature at ease with himself when he had his "war paint" on.
H. L. Mencken described him as "the perfect model of the

Christian cad." That was once a fashionable judgment which I largely shared, though I never wholly lost my compassion for him. At times, Wilson may have acted in a way that justified Mencken's description.

At the climax of his life, however, Wilson died bravely for his conduct, his actions, his signature. Beaten, with the people turning against him, he went out to face them to try to persuade them. Self-deluded as he was at Versailles and as J. M. Keynes so graphically described for us in *The Economic Consequences of the Peace*, Wilson faced the people in defense of his conduct. Vanity, in part, appears to have been a source of his courage; but how many of the vain have courage?

His conduct suggests that if his health had not failed he would have convinced the people or would have walked in loneliness to his grave. "For nothing less depends upon this decision [whether or not to ratify his signing of the Versailles Treaty], nothing less than the liberation of the world . . . ," he declared.

But when Wilson became no more, the hopes which he had lifted out of the mud and blood and agony into a dreamlike euphoria of faith—those hopes had died. He had outlived his oratorical idealism.

Our world, our tragic century, had truly begun. [2/5/66]

JOHN W. GARDNER

America in the Twenty-third Century

To gain perspective on our own time, I decided not long ago that I would look three centuries into the future. I am able to do this thanks to a Cornell scientist who recently discovered how man may step off the time dimension and visit the past or future at will. You may be surprised you haven't heard about this, but he's finding his capacity to know the future profitable.

He doesn't want to publicize his findings until he has won a few more horse races.

The first thing I learned is that in the last third of the twentieth century, the urge to demolish long-established social institutions succeeded beyond the fondest dreams of the dismantlers. They brought everything tumbling down. Since the hostility to institutions was a product of modern minds, the demolition was most thorough in the most advanced nations.

Unlike the fall of Rome, this decline was not followed by hundreds of years of darkness. In fact, there followed less than a century of chaos and disorder.

In the latter part of the twenty-first century the rebuilding began. Since chaos is always followed by authoritarianism, this was a period of iron rule, worldwide—a world society rigidly organized and controlled. I don't think I shall tell you what language was spoken.

But tyrannies tend to grow lax, even under futuristic methods of thought control. By the end of the twenty-second century, the sternly disciplined institutions of the world society had grown relatively tolerant.

In the new, more permissive atmosphere, men were again allowed to study history—which had been under a ban for two centuries. The effect was electric. Twenty-third-century scholars were entranced by the variety of human experience, shocked by the violence and barbarism, saddened by the stupidities and exalted by the achievements of their forebears.

As they studied the history of the twentieth century, they discovered that human expectations had risen sharply in the middle years of the century.

Men came to demand more and more of their institutions—and with greater intransigence. But while aspirations leapt ahead, human institutions remained sluggish—less sluggish to be sure than at any previous time in history, but still inadequately responsive to human need.

Considering the disastrous outcome, twenty-third-century scholars concluded that if society is going to release aspirations for institutional change—which is precisely what many twentieth-century societies deliberately did—then it had better be sure its institutions are capable of such change. In this respect they found the twentieth century sadly deficient.

Because of failure to design institutions capable of continuous renewal, twentieth-century societies showed astonishing sclerotic streaks. Even in the United States, which was then the most adaptable of all societies, the departments of the federal government were in grave need of renewal; state government was in most places an old attic full of outworn relics; in most cities, municipal government was a waxwork of stiffly preserved anachronisms; the system of taxation was a tangle of dysfunctional measures; the courts were crippled by archaic organizational arrangements; the unions, the professions, the universities, the corporations, each had spun its own impenetrable web of vested interests.

Such a society could not respond to challenge. And it did not.

But as one twenty-third-century scholar put it, "The reformers couldn't have been less interested in the basic adaptability of the society. That posed tough and complex tasks of institutional redesign that bored them to death. They preferred the joys of combat, of villain hunting. As for the rest of society, it was dozing off in front of the television set."

Twentieth-century institutions were caught in a savage cross fire between uncritical lovers and unloving critics. On the one side, those who loved their institutions tended to smother them in the embrace of death, loving their rigidities more than their promise, shielding them from life-giving criticism. On the other side, there arose a breed of critics without love, skilled in demolition but untutored in the arts by which human institutions are nurtured and strengthened and made to flourish.

As twenty-third-century leaders proceeded to redesign their own society for continuous renewal, one of them commented on the debt they owed to the twentieth century: "It is not just that we have learned from twentieth-century mistakes. We have learned from twentieth-century insights. For in that troubled time there were men who were saying just what we are saying now. And had they been heeded, the solutions we have reached would have come 300 years earlier. But no one was listening."

[7/27/68]

II
World Watching, Including Vietnam

ARCHIBALD MacLEISH

The Seat Behind the Pillar

History, like a badly constructed concert hall, has occasional dead spots where the music can't be heard. Everything in the United States today—the boredom of the young, the numbness of the arts and the ineptitude of the politicians— indicates that we are caught in one of them. No matter how we crane our necks and cock our ears we seem unable to catch the tune.

The reason, I think, is fairly clear. We can't make out the tune of the time because we are still back behind it in the 1950's with the dilapidated bulk of "anti-Communism" against our faces. If we could bring ourselves to look around, it might occur to us that we are not, whatever the ushers may have told us, in the best seat in the house.

Some, of course, have already noticed. Even fifteen years ago when the place was first proposed to us a few protested. "Anti-Communism," meaning Joe McCarthy at home and containment abroad, looked like a queer location for the United States, a nation not previously given to squatting in the lee of anything.

But fifteen years ago the whole state of the Union was so preposterous it seemed easier to laugh. McCarthy, for all the noise he made and harm he did and pain he inflicted, was a comic figure whose monstrous revelations of treason in the Department of State and disloyalty by the noblest American soldier of the century kept blowing up in his face like a clown's balloons.

And as for the containment, which meant the redefinition

of the American purpose in the world as the negation and denial of the Russian purpose, it was so palpably inappropriate to a country which had just planned and engineered and supplied and fought the greatest victory in military annals, that no one but the professional Holy Warriors could take it seriously.

The Truman Doctrine was justified by the Marshall Plan, which had a creative and characteristically American purpose of its own, but nothing could justify the worldwide wall of Foster Dulles—nothing in American history at least. And so we merely smiled at SEATO and the rest and let the protest go.

That, however, was back before the sixties. Now that the better half of a new decade has pushed its predecessor into the past, the perspective alters. McCarthy has disappeared—but only to be replaced by the apparently ineradicable reek of McCarthyism. And containment has turned into the disaster implicit in it from the start—the disaster of Vietnam.

With the result that what was preposterous in the fifties has become tragic in the sixties. Where the question fifteen years ago was why in the name of sanity and common sense the American revolution of independence and self-government which was redrafting the map of Africa and shaping a new society in India and Japan should be betrayed at home—turned into a mere counterrevolution to the Russian, a static and defensive state of negation and neurosis and downright fear—the question today is a soberer question.

It is the question whether an unachievable victory in Vietnam is preferable to an unthinkable defeat or an unthinkable defeat to an unachievable victory.

Which is not precisely intellectual progress, but does throw light upon the cause of our predicament. It was not when we began to escalate the war in Vietnam or even when we first decided to fight in it ourselves that the sad mistake was made. It was made when we allowed ourselves to be frightened into "anti-Communism" as a national policy and posture.

Our involvement in Vietnam is our inheritance from containment and McCarthy. And it is for that reason more than any other that we get so little sympathy from Europe. For it has long been obvious to European intelligence, even including the intelligence of the Vatican, that "anti-Communism" is dead as a policy and worse than dead as an intellectual position.

The past cannot, of course, be revised, but there is something to be said for recognizing what it was and where it has left us and what our actual situation is. When, in a hypothetically sane universe, a problem proves insoluble by the exercise of sanity, it is usually because it has been stated in mistaken terms.

Vietnam is insoluble as a military conundrum: An unachievable victory is neither better nor worse than an unthinkable defeat—it is merely equally unthinkable, though for different reasons. Conceivably, therefore, the problem of Vietnam should not be posed in military terms but in different terms: terms which would recognize the error of the fifties and move us out from behind the obstructing column. Once we recognize as a nation that "anti-Communism," like all the rest of the anti-isms, is not an effective policy or, indeed, a policy at all—once we recognize as a nation that the only defense against the purposes of others is a better purpose of our own—we may very possibly regain the freedom of action we have been progressively losing ever since Vietnam began if not since Foster Dulles.

After all, we *have* a better purpose of our own. It is now evident to anyone who cares to see that it is the Revolution of 1776, not the Revolution of 1917, which is providing the dynamism of the waking world from the west coast of Africa to the islands of Japan. [1/21/67]

J. WILLIAM FULBRIGHT

The United States and "Responsibilities of Power"

In the vocabulary of power politics large nations are referred to as "powers," the assumption being that the truly important function of a nation is not the maintenance of law and order, nor the advancement of human welfare within its borders, but the exercise and expansion of power beyond its frontiers—to which function all others are necessarily subordinate.

To that school of political thinkers who call themselves "realists" it is irrelevant sentimentalism to question the primacy of power politics in terms of its costs, purposes and human rewards. There is—so they tell us—no choice involved. A great nation, it is said, devotes its major energies to the exercise of power because its own inner nature requires it to do so; to ask why is as useful as asking why donkeys bray or why cats eat mice instead of cabbage.

Power politics is practiced under different names. The British called it the "white man's burden"; the French called it their "civilizing mission"; nineteenth-century Americans called it "manifest destiny." It is now being called the "responsibilities of power." What all these terms have in common is the assumption of involuntariness. "Realists" might call it a "law of politics"; romantics might call it their "mission." Both regard it as something outside of rational choice.

History appears to support them. Powerful nations have always devoted the major part of their resources to building empires; only a few small nations, such as the Scandinavian countries, have devoted their main energies to human satisfactions, presumably for lack of any other choice.

Just as the great empires expanded, inevitably they began to contract, culminating, as in the case of ancient Rome or the Austria of the Hapsburgs, in total disintegration, or, as in the case of Spain, in a long, gradual decline. No empire stood stronger and prouder than the British Empire a hundred years ago; today we are witnessing its sad, final sunset.

Can America escape the same fate? Accepting the gloomy determinism of the "responsibilities of power," in effect our present policymakers tell us that it cannot. They do not, of course, predict our decline and fall, only the extension of power, the drain of material and human resources, and the neglect of domestic requirements that precede and precipitate the fall of empires.

Our very success condemns us to spend the lives of our sons in distant jungles, and to waste our substance on the costly horrors of modern weapons and the glittering vanity of trips to the moon and supersonic airplanes.

I do not think we are condemned to this. History and psychiatry and religion tell us that, for all our human susceptibilities, we do have some choices. Experience suggests that we are well advised to join in *collective* measures—through the United Nations and our alliances—to prevent the arbitrary and unwarranted interference by one nation in the affairs of another.

Beyond that we are free to use our vast resources for the enrichment of life, for the improvement and enjoyment of things, for the setting, if we will, of a civilized example to the world.

Nations, like individuals, have some freedom of choice, and America of all nations is equipped to exercise it. Our nation was created as an act of choice; our Constitution was designed to protect and perpetuate the right of our citizens to freedom of choice. Most of us are descended from people who came to America as an act of choice. Unlike any other great nation in history, we are a rich composite of cultures, united not by race or religion but by the choice made in becoming Americans.

If ever a nation was free to break the cycle of empires, America is that nation. If we do not, it will not be because history assigned to us an imperial role. It will be because we *chose*

to believe such pompous nonsense, because power went to our
heads like a superdose of LSD, leading us to betray our history
and the purposes for which this nation was founded.

That, I suspect, is what the hue and cry is about. That is
what the dissent and protests are about. Our leaders speak of
our stars, of the travail to which we are condemned by the
"responsibilities of power."

But our youth are wiser than their elders; they know that
our future will not be shaped by some nonexistent "law" of
politics but by human choice or susceptibility. They see their
country succumbing, sliding toward an imperial destiny, and
they are crying out against it. They are crying out for America to
return to its history and its promise, and in their crying out lies
the hope that it will.   [1/27/68]

ARTHUR SCHLESINGER, Jr.

Dissent and the Vietnam War

General William Westmoreland's lecture tour has
brought to the surface a proposition muttered *sotto voce* around
Washington for some time by administration supporters: that
dissent in the United States prolongs the war and costs lives in
Vietnam. This thought carries with it the agreeable implication that, if only everybody would rally behind the President,
then Hanoi would stop doing what it is doing and the war
would be over.

Two points are worth considering here: (1) If the proposition is true, should it be controlling? And, even more interesting, (2) Is the proposition, after all, true?

The suggestion that we can persuade the world that we are
united on our Vietnam policy does not seem on examination
very practical. The sad reality is that, if Ho Chi Minh *thinks*
the American people are divided, one reason surely may be,

as Clayton Fritchey has crisply put it, that "they *are* divided."
Such division is not easy to conceal, like a spot in the carpet.

Suppose that we succeed in abolishing protest marches and
those other things which General Westmoreland considers unpatriotic? Must we next abolish public opinion polls in the interest of demonstrating national unity behind the escalation
policy? And why should we suppose that, even if we abolished
all evidence of division in the United States, the North Vietnamese Marxists would not, as true believers, still continue to
think that the oppressed workers were about to rise against the
imperialists' war?

Suppressing a national debate is not only pretty impractical;
it also would seem at odds with the values for which we are presumably fighting. Secretary of Defense Robert McNamara put
this well in language his circuit-riding generals might usefully
ponder: "Whatever comfort some of the extremist protest may
be giving our enemies—and it is clear from Hanoi's own statements that it is—let us be perfectly clear about our own principles and priorities. This is a nation in which the freedom of
dissent is absolutely fundamental."

So, even if the administration proposition were true, it
would be hard to act upon it without trampling on older, and
conceivably more important, national commitments. But is the
proposition really all that true? Secretary McNamara has said
that the extremist protest gives Hanoi comfort, and unques-
tionably this is so. But cheering the enemy is one thing; affect-
ing his military decisions, prolonging the war and costing American lives is something different.

Are we really expected to take seriously the notion that
marches down Fifth Avenue are keeping alive the will to resist in Hanoi? Serious leaders base their military decisions on
the actual battlefield balance of force, will and opportunity,
not on speculations about antiwar protests on the other side of
the world. The evidence suggests that our adversaries are fighting not because they expect us to collapse but because they believe fanatically in their own cause.

If history tells us anything, it is that our bombing has hardened the resolve of North Vietnam a good deal more than anything said by Martin Luther King. Moreover, no serious American—including Dr. King—has proposed unilateral withdrawal;
and this, after all, would be the only action which could hand
the game to our enemies. The call for a holding action in the
South instead of escalation in the North is no formula for a
Hanoi victory.

Not only is the administration's argument poor on its merits,
but it recoils on its own proponents. For surely it is precisely
those who insist on widening the conflict beyond political or
strategic necessity who are prolonging the war and costing
American lives. The most effective way to save lives would
plainly be to slow down the war, not to escalate it.

If the administration's proposition is, on reasonable examination, so manifestly unpersuasive, why then the official excitement about it? This phenomenon would not greatly surprise
historians. For, when a policy fails, those responsible, instead
of entertaining the horrid thought that the policy may have
been wrong, often tend to argue that the failure is someone
else's fault.

They devote themselves, as Senator George McGovern has
suggested, to the exercise of "trying to blame the failure of their
policy on their critics." This is, after all, a well-known reflex of
military disaster. Consider only the *Dolchstosslegende*—the
stab-in-the-back myth concocted by the German military to explain their defeat in 1918.

The proposition that dissent in America is losing the war in
Vietnam is, on the existing evidence, much less a fact than an
alibi. When this is understood, then we can forget so feeble a
digression and return to the serious issues of this complex and
tragic war.   [5/6/67]

ARTHUR MILLER

The Age of Abdication

Man's capacity for deluding himself has always been cited as one of the chief causes of war, but the reporting from Vietnam is making even a little honest self-delusion hard to come by. On television the other night they showed how another 15,000 Vietnamese peasants were forced out of their villages by Americans who then proceeded to burn down their thatched houses to deny shelter to the Vietcong.

Watching this short piece of film, I thought once again how ineptly this era has been characterized. Nearly every play and novel is about the lack of human communication, the unreality of contemporary life, but here was the kind of incident visible to the whole world which in former wars would have been a state secret for fifty years after the war was over. Watching it, I thought that it was not a lack of communication we suffer from but some sort of sincerity so breathtaking that it has knocked us morally silly.

The peasants involved here, the reporting disclosed, had not wanted to have their homes burned; our people had no land to give them to replace what they were being forced to vacate; and some of them had had to leave so quickly that they left their working tools behind.

Horrible as the whole spectacle was, I could not help feeling for a few moments afterward that despite its clarity and completeness, something remained unspoken in it. And soon the question formed itself which, I think, now goes to the heart of the matter. How is it that we never see Vietnamese peasants burning down their own houses?

This is not as ridiculous as it sounds when we recall the Yugoslavs, the Russians, and if a dim memory is not mistaken, the Americans during the Revolution who destroyed buildings to deny them to the enemy. Even the Nazis scorched the German earth before the advancing Russian armies. I am certain that where I live more than one citizen would feel no pain as he fired his house to keep it from an invader, if we ever faced a war here.

Frankly, I am amazed that our Psywar people haven't thought of this. Here we are, pumping blood and money into a fight to help these people retain their freedom, and we can't even find a native pyromaniac, let alone a patriot, to fire his own roof. Instead there is always the same old Zippo torch, the GI's standing around looking rather uneasy, and the villagers looking on with Oriental resignation.

Imagine the effect if for once we could see villagers lighting the flames and maybe even a few shaking their fists toward the jungle where the wily Vietcong must be biting their nails in futile anger at shelter lost. It would be enough to get Senator J. William Fulbright to stop trying to drag Secretary Dean Rusk before a Senate Foreign Affairs Committee hearing, for in one stroke we would have understood why we're in Vietnam.

What we have come to, it seems to me, is the level of belief we accord most advertising. We know perfectly well our teeth will never be white again but we go on buying teeth-whitening dentifrices; we really don't believe that any good will come out of this war, but most of us go right on paying for it and will as likely as not vote back into power the men who escalated it to its present size.

But there is no secret about any of this, and no lack of communication either. Since it is we and not the Vietnamese who are burning down their houses, it can mean only that they don't share our urgency and would much rather live where they always lived and work the land they have always worked, Vietcong or no Vietcong. In short, it is our war against Hanoi and not the war of the people of Vietnam against the Vietcong.

So what's the moral? For one thing we might think seriously about changing the name of the age. It is not the Age of Anxiety, not any more; nor the Age of the Credibility Gap, not with the mountain of facts available about this war. We see, we hear, and from Bishop Fulton Sheen to U Thant to General

Matthew Ridgway we are given an understanding of the futility and the moral insanity of what we are doing.

But we do not affirm or deny what is given us, we simply abdicate. Ours is the Age of Abdication. I'm speaking of the great majority, of course. The protesters, in and out of the Senate, merely prove the rule, and there is nothing at present in their favor but history. [12/23/67]

MARGARET HALSEY

Selective Morality and Citizen Loyalty

Once when I was picketing in an antiwar demonstration a policeman said to me, "What does a nice lady like you want with peace?" What indeed?

The advocates of peace in Vietnam do not want just "peace and quiet." There are two reasons why they persevere in their efforts despite domino theories and official deafness to entreaty. The first is that the policy in Southeast Asia exemplifies the most antisocial of sins—namely, selective morality. The second has to do with the quest for identity.

An obvious instance of selective morality occurs when a policeman beats up a Negro in the back room of the station house but does not lay hands on a white man for the same alleged offense. Morality—and this is not theology but plain common sense—must be a seamless garment like the shroud of Christ if it is to be a force in human affairs.

Selective morality on a small scale often characterizes personal conduct. Perhaps a father rewards or punishes one of his children but does not behave in the same way toward another. But selective morality became institutionalized as a national American *modus operandi* during the McCarthy period.

The silent but effective lesson the American public learned from the late Senator was that it was all right to lie if you were uncovering "Communists" in the State Department. With the passage of time, however, the conditional clause got lost in the shuffle. We ended up with the principle that it was all right to avoid the truth.

Actually, the domino theory applies much more demonstrably to Western morality than it does to the politics of Southeast Asia. If the rampart of morality, justice and fair play is breached for any reason at all, the whole moral structure is weakened. College students today who have barely heard of Joseph McCarthy are unashamedly cheating on exams because of the social climate created in the period that bears his name.

What do nice people want with peace?

They want a a cessation of the American adventure in Vietnam because they cannot live comfortably with selective morality—with a government which proclaims democracy at home and supports puppet dictators abroad; which talks law and order when ghetto populations rebel at home but winks at torture in the Mekong delta; which supposedly believes in self-determination of peoples but is trying to impose on the Vietnamese a government that lacks popularity.

We hear a great deal about young people in high school and college going through a crisis of identity. But the Vietnamese conflict is creating a crisis of identity for many older people, too.

Human beings identify in many different directions. They identify with their parents even after the parents have been long dead. They identify with a profession. Some people identify with a particular church. People identify with their children when the children are hurt. They often identify with the part of the country where they grew up.

Not the least important of identifications—though often taken for granted—is our overall identification as Americans. We are not Swiss or Chinese or Patagonian or Italian. We are Americans. Being American is one of the important ways by which we know ourselves.

But here we are living safe, normal, comfortable lives while carnage is committed in our names in a conflict which, in my opinion, has no moral or legal justification and is at variance with our professed beliefs. Commenting on the war, the *Arbeiter Zeitung* of Vienna speaks of "the strange mixture of political slyness, unlimited naïveté and cold cynicism which marks the Johnson era."

We do not believe that such a description fits us personally, but every time we identify ourselves as American we must take on part of the burden of it.

Even President Johnson remarked in his State of the Union message on the strange restlessness which characterizes prosperous America. Part of this feeling is due to the loss of an important source of self-identification.

"Ask not what your country can do for you," said John F. Kennedy.

But a lot of blood has been spilled since then. If the administration represents us, then it is time to ask what our country can do for us. Loyalty is a two-way street.   [4/27/68]

ARTHUR L. GOODHART

Draft Resistance and the "Nuremberg Defense"

As World War II ended, the United States, Great Britain, France and the USSR signed an agreement establishing the International Military Tribunal. Attached to it was a charter setting forth the procedure to be followed at the trial, and stating the principles of international law which were binding on the court.

The most important of these principles can be found in Article 6, which provided that there shall be individual responsibility for (a) *Crimes against peace* (waging a war of aggression); (b) *War crimes* (violations of the laws of war); and (c) *Crimes against humanity* (murder and other inhumane acts against the civilian population). It was only (a) that was novel, as (b) and (c) had long been recognized to be international crimes.

These principles were followed in the other war crimes trials, and have been accepted by most of the authorities on international law, although there has been some doubt concerning crimes against peace. (In motions at the conspiracy trial of Dr. Benjamin Spock and others for counseling draft resistance, the principles of Nuremberg were raised as one defense.)

The relationship between international law and state law can be understood only if it is realized that they are two entirely separate systems with two different sources. The rules of the former are based on general international recognition, on international legal precedents, and on international conventions, such as the Kellogg-Briand Pact, 1928, to make aggressive war illegal.

On the other hand, state law is found in the constitutional system of the state, which prescribes what body or bodies have the power to create rules that are binding on the courts.

The distinction between the two systems is illustrated by Article 8 of the Nuremberg charter, which provided that "the fact that the defendant acted pursuant to the orders of his Government or of a superior shall not free him from responsibility."

This gave rise to heated dispute, as it was argued that a defendant ought not to be punished because he had obeyed the law of his own country; on the other hand, if this was a defense, then a defendant whose country had a particularly brutal system of law could never be found guilty. How can this conflict be solved?

The answer under English law is a simple one. The British Constitution, which can be stated in a single sentence, provides that any statute enacted by Parliament, with the consent of the Queen, which is purely formal, is absolutely binding on the courts and all officers.

The American Constitution is a far more complicated one,

so that it is difficult to give a categorical answer to any question. It gives exclusive control over foreign affairs and the conduct of war to the President and to Congress (it does not matter here how these powers are divided), but it does not necessarily follow from this that the Supreme Court may not be able to place a limitation on the exercise of these powers.

It has also been argued that the "due process" clause of the Fifth Amendment can be used to limit the war powers of the United States on the ground that it is not due process to force a person to serve in a war which violates the three Nuremberg principles.

If this were accepted, then the Supreme Court would have to determine whether the American action in Vietnam was an aggressive one, whether the conduct of the war was in violation of the laws of war and whether any crimes against humanity had been committed. Such a general inquest may be desirable, but it is difficult to believe it part of due process.

The consequences would be remarkable if such a power were attributed to the courts, because it would always be possible in any future conflict to delay all action while the character of the conflict was being debated. This is a question of state law; if the state law says that a person shall be conscripted it is a most doubtful answer to say that the war is in violation of international law, even if this were true.

Whether a person is morally entitled to resist what he considers to be an immoral law is not a legal question at all. It is an ethical question which a lawyer has no greater claim to answer than anyone else.

We Americans can point to one occasion when such resistance was clearly justified: In 1776 the American colonists refused to obey a law which at that time was legally binding on them. On the other hand, in the Civil War the moral conviction of the Southern states that they were entitled to secede was met by the moral conviction of the North that secession was wrongful.

Which step a man should take when such a conflict arises

depends on his conscience, remembering always that a breach of the law in a particular instance may in time lead to a breakdown of the law in general. That, however, is a consideration which may carry more weight with a lawyer than with a layman.

[5/25/68]

DAVID VIENNA

Let's Put It on the Train to Hanoi

It is apparent that President Johnson is having a hard time convincing the North Vietnamese that he would rather quit than fight. Maybe what is needed is an advertising agency to help the State and Defense Departments sell the idea of peace to the Communists.

Since he took office the President has been fighting the advertising agencies and he's lost every battle.

He asks Americans to travel in their own country rather than abroad so that the outflow of gold can be slowed. An agency places pictures of little cars with the caption "Beetle" in magazines and newspapers across the country, and Americans begin seeing the U.S.A.—in cars made overseas.

One of the President's advisers suggests that cigarette smoking may not be the healthiest practice. An advertising agency promptly sticks a cigarette in a cowboy's mouth and makes him wear a hat just like the one the President wears. Before you know it more people are smoking now—and maybe enjoying it less—than they were before they were warned about smoking.

An agency may be the means to a solution in Vietnam. The campaigns it could provide are undoubtedly the most peaceful way to end the war. The weapons are harmless but effective: washing machines that are 10 feet tall; white tornadoes, armored knights on horseback—the list is a long one.

Now if Mr. Johnson were to seek the help that only Madison Avenue specialists can provide, the first thing nine out of ten advertising men would do is make him more appealing to the Orientals. A new image—even a new name.

Nationwide, worldwide, you can depend on men to be more friendly to other men with names they trust. Lyndon Baines Johnson is the enemy, but "Lindin" could be a friend.

Then there would be a campaign to send a dove flying into Ho Chi Minh's kitchen. Everybody knows that a dove is a sign of peace. And the Madison Avenue dove is a special kind of bird; it'll get Ho out of his kitchen fast. He'll move even faster when he hears the Jolly Green Giant in the dining room calling "Ho! Ho! Ho!"

In this carefully planned advertising campaign, Ho would, of course, be surprised to see Lin at his dining-room table. The President would stand to greet the leader and as a sign of friendship he might say: "Ho, mah friend, how 'bout lettin' me send your sinuses tah Arizona?"

Impressed with the gesture, the Vietnamese leader would sit down at the conference table with the President. They might sip an American soft drink that would help them think younger or livelier. And while they're both there thinking lively, they just might call a truce.

But in case Ho continued to believe that coups do more for him, there must be an alternative campaign.

The President would suggest that Vietcong brush their teeth for one year with a leading Communist brand and the Americans would do the same with a United States toothpaste. The group with 21 percent fewer cavities at the end of the year wins the war.

Or they could try something different for a change—something with more spirit to it. A race in cars from Hanoi to Saigon.

"Let me put you in the driver's seat of this fine new convertible," the President might offer. No doubt Ho would refuse, choosing a weapon with which he is more familiar: a Soviet model. Mistakenly believing that the tiger in LBJ's tank is a paper one, Ho would feel like a Giant Killer. But the President, driving an American car that combined the best features of a Barracuda, a Fury, a Marlin and a Mustang, would win the economy run to Hanoi with miles to spare.

Or an advertising campaign could get the Vietcong asking themselves, "Do capitalists have more fun?" Even though they can never be certain because only their accountants know for sure, they can be convinced that they will be in good hands with the United States.

It is too early for President Johnson to despair about Vietnam. A man who has gone as far as he has with the slogan "All the way with LBJ" should realize that he has not mobilized America's full resources as long as the advertising agencies remain unused.   [5/7/66]

HAROLD LAVINE

1898 and All That

About seventy years ago, the United States stumbled into a war against a ragged army of Asians. It was a war that at first seemed merely a distraction, and it dragged on and on. The American generals and admirals were steadfastly optimistic, for they commanded overwhelming power. Yet victory eluded them.

Even as they assured the administration they were winning the war, they asked for more men, more guns. For political reasons, the administration hesitated to send them what they wanted, but eventually it did, it always did, because, as the President of the United States proclaimed, they were fighting for "the world's best civilization."

In the mountains and the jungles, as they cleaned their weapons and washed their socks, the missionaries sang:

Underneath the starry flag,
We'll civilize them with a Krag.

This was the War of the Philippine Insurrection, a war long since forgotten. We had just destroyed the Spanish empire in two of the most dazzling battles in naval history; and though, in a fit of absentmindedness, we had renounced all claim to Cuba, we considered the Philippine Islands ours, by right of conquest and by right of moral superiority.

Unfortunately for us, there was a ragtag of Filipinos who did not agree, men characterized as "misguided" by President William McKinley. Organized into a military force of sorts by Emilio Aguinaldo, they sought to establish a republic.

The very first dispatch to Washington announcing the conflict foreshadowed the rest. It read in part: THE AMERICAN ARMY AND NAVY IS GENERALLY SUCCESSFUL . . . REQUEST AMMUNITION REQUISITION DOUBLED. It was signed by the hero of the Battle of Manila Bay, Admiral Dewey.

At the outset, General Eldwell S. Otis had 20,000 troops under his command. He assured the President he could quickly suppress the insurrectionists with 30,000. His men fought well. To Washington's bewilderment and dismay, General Otis then said that what he needed was 30,000 "effectives."

In the United States, critics of the administration clamored for withdrawal from the islands. President McKinley denounced them collectively as "the prophets of evil."

General Otis asked for 40,000 men.

The trouble was that no matter how many Filipinos we killed, Aguinaldo found men to replace them. We drove them from the villages, but the moment we left, they returned. We chased them into the jungles. They disappeared, only to reappear elsewhere.

General Otis asked for 50,000 men.

General Otis's strategy was based on the assumption that all but the handful of Filipinos in Aguinaldo's army believed we were "liberators." He granted that many Filipinos had for a while been "intoxicated by the cry for independence and self government." However, he said, the cruelty of Aguinaldo's troops had disillusioned them.

He asked for 60,000 men.

He was convinced that, once he destroyed Aguinaldo's main force, the rest would be easy. He would have nothing to cope with except scattered bands of guerrillas. He did, finally, shatter the main force; and then he discovered the guerrillas were even a worse problem. They were villagers one day, savage soldiers the next.

This was the beginning of the bloodiest phase of the War of the Philippine Insurrection. One of Otis's commanders, General Henry W. Lawton, called for 100,000 men.

In a way, the story did have a dismal kind of happy ending. General Arthur MacArthur (the father of Douglas MacArthur) took command of the United States forces. He adopted a new military strategy based on the assumption that our enemy was the people. He issued a proclamation renouncing "precise observance of the laws of war." Among other things he permitted his men to torture prisoners, even civilians.

He instituted the *reconcentrado* policy that General Valeriano Weyler had followed in Cuba. Under this policy he forcibly removed people from unfriendly villages, burned the villages down and put the people in concentration camps. Only a few years before, when Weyler was doing the same thing, Americans had called him "Butcher Weyler." No matter. MacArthur did succeed in suppressing the insurrection.

[1/12/68]

BROOKS ATKINSON

Home Front Thoughts of Vietnam

In every war the inequities between the home front and the fighting front are distressing. No contribution a civilian makes can compare with one casualty on the battlefield.

But the inequities in the Vietnam War are monstrous. In a distant, backward, muddled part of the world about a half million Americans are obediently slugging through the mud and jungles on an elusive mission their government has assigned to them. Every week 150 to 250 of them are killed. More than 13,000 of them will never enjoy the beauty and bountifulness of America again: They are dead. Their parents, their wives, their children, their friends have made a sacrificial contribution by having relinquished someone they love.

For the rest of us the war is an ugly mirage that worries but does not hurt us. Life at home goes on much as usual—heedless and gay, angry and acquisitive. During the summer the roads were choked with passenger cars full of adults, children and bizarre impedimenta on the way to vacation. Life in the White House goes on cheerfully. Like thousands of other Americans, the President's daughters take vacations in the West Indies or Europe; and the White House lawn is the scene of a charming carnival for children.

Riots demonstrate the frustrations of some of the citizens; strikes reveal the aspirations of others. With a few exceptions, no one at home is required to share the awful burden of a war that has settled down to futile routine somewhere beyond our horizon.

In Vietnam millions of people are suffering—not only the Americans but Australians, New Zealanders, Filipinos, South Koreans and, of course, the unfortunate Vietnamese on both sides of the Demilitarized Zone. The poor excepted, most Americans at home eat well, sleep well and conduct their lives with a minimum of inconvenience. The men in Vietnam have a right to resent this cruel disparity between their jungle warfare and our continuum of self-interest at home.

If the Vietnam War hardly disturbs the life at home the logical conclusion is that it is not an essential American responsibility. Everyone at home would be part of it if it were a part of the national welfare. But it is not. It is a distant skirmish that no one foresaw, no one wanted, no one controls and no one can finish. Most of us have forgotten how it started.

For many years the United States government has been pouring money and military supplies into Vietnam to keep Communists from conquering the whole of Asia, although Communism has been failing everywhere with dull regularity—in Greece, Korea, the Congo, Indonesia, the Middle East. In 1962 there were 16,000 American soldiers in Vietnam to keep Communism at bay. Now the American forces have become massive. By easy steps we have advanced to the barbarism of bombing civilian areas in the traditional manner of ruthless imperialism.

After serving for ten months in the Central Highlands a New York soldier, who has the Purple Heart, remarked to a *New York Times* correspondent: "Does anyone back home care about this place? Guys are dying here. Does anyone really care? Why don't we just chuck it?"

We can't chuck it as if nothing had happened. If and when the time comes, the withdrawal will have to be responsible and orderly. Nor is it true that people at home don't care. Whether they believe in the war or not they care about their countrymen assigned to this Asiatic limbo; and also about the millions of people throughout Vietnam who are trapped in this cruel struggle.

But Americans have not made this war their first order of priority because it is alien to the traditions of a peace-loving nation, founded on the principle of liberty and committed to the ideal of self-determination among nations. It is in the nature of imperialism that power should become progressively more inhuman the farther it stretches away from home.

"Let us raise a standard to which the wise and the honest can repair," said Washington when the Constitutional convention opened. It is still a wonderful idea. [10/7/67]

BROOKS ATKINSON

Russians as People and Politicians

Since the United Nations headquarters is located in New York, Premier Aleksei N. Kosygin has had to come here to present the Soviet Union's policy case. No doubt he would be much happier if the UN were located in Moscow, where no prudent citizen is likely to carry a placard lettered KOSYGIN GO HOME.

Mr. Kosygin is not a showman, like his ebullient predecessor with the loose footwear; and the political decision to fly to a huge city where he is not universally welcome must have involved a few misgivings. It would be more fun to be a tourist in New York than the head of a powerful state.

For politics distorts human relations. Russians and Americans can get on very pleasantly together as individuals—both being emotional, energetic, good-humored and sociable, and the Russians being especially hospitable to foreigners. If it were not for Israel, the Arab nations, Vietnam, Cuba and a few thousand other intractable issues how happy we could all be! Heads of state have to deal with the issues that divide nations. People can relax over the simpler matters that all human beings have in common.

Standing on their dignity as representatives of a sovereign nation, Russian officials can look so forbidding. After all these years of international diplomacy Andrei Gromyko still exudes massive disapproval when he debarks or embarks at our airports. Mr. Kosygin looks neutral; he does not visibly approve or disapprove. But he has brought his daughter with him, which is a happy circumstance for us as well as for him.

She not only has a bright personality, but she also speaks English, which shows more interest in our civilization than most Americans can show in hers. Like other Russian women of similar backgrounds, Mrs. Lyudmila Gvishiani has grace and charm. When Nikita Khrushchev was swaggering across America, taking a good look at us before burying us, Mrs. Nina Khrushchev conquered America by behaving like a woman of sense and manners and by speaking English. No one could resist her comfortable personality.

Mr. Kosygin cannot be expected to have a sentimental interest in the fortunes of Mrs. Svetlana Alliluyeva, whose defection to America must have been a painful experience to all patriotic Russians. But her womanliness, her candor and also her fluent English made many friends for the Russian people. If the Russians would send us more of their women the relations between the two countries would sweeten. Women are less pedantic than plenipotentiaries.

Many of the differences between our two countries cannot be solved rationally; at best they can be endured in the hope that nothing catastrophic happens. But the things our two peoples have in common are numerous, wholesome and enjoyable. They have borrowed our Mark Twain and Hemingway. We have borrowed their Gogol and Pasternak. They have borrowed our O'Neill and Arthur Miller. We have borrowed their Chekhov and Gorky. They have borrowed our Gershwin. We have borrowed their Prokofiev. Both of us have Shakespeare.

In America we have borrowed a great many others that are more difficult to compare: Ilf and Petrov, the comic writers; Mikail Zoshchenko, the satirist; Yevgeny Yevtushenko, the poet; Mikail Sholokhov, novelist of the quiet Don, who hates us and nearly everything. We would also like to borrow Andrei Voznesensky, the poet, but the old fogies of the Soviet Writers Union prevented his coming to the Lincoln Center's Summer Festival. He does not distrust America enough.

On the top levels our countries disagree sharply. The fact that our two peoples agree on many things does not cancel disagreement at the top. For power becomes inhuman the higher it rises. But Russians and Americans can still enjoy each other as members of the human race who have worked hard, accomplished much and at least spoken kindly of the human spirit. Probably Mr. Kosygin knows this as well as Americans do. But heads of state do not have the latitude of private citizens. Among their duties is making the best case they can for bad causes.

[6/24/67]

ANTHONY EDEN, Earl of Avon

The Diplomatic Way Out of Vietnam

There are many in non-American lands who years ago would have advised against United States intervention in Vietnam. These same observers would not, however, now wish to see an American withdrawal without an arrangement which could not give fair confidence of an enduring and peaceful life for the countries of Indochina.

Repeated attempts have been made to revive the activities of the two Geneva conference cochairmen, Soviet Russia and Britain, but without success. It is, however, worth considering whether another grouping of powers might not be activated to play a part in reducing the area of differences.

Canada, India and Poland have been members of the Supervisory Commission since 1954. Theirs has often been a frustrating task, but in the course of it the governments of all three countries have gained familiarity with the detailed problems of the area. It should be worthwhile to make an attempt to bring those three powers together with the two cochairmen in a meeting, however informal.

The purpose would be to prepare the ground for a reconvening of the Geneva conference. If that initiative is not successful, variants of it should be persisted in without respite.

Much, of course, must depend upon the intentions of Soviet Russia. The Geneva Agreements of 1954 would never have been reached without Soviet cooperation. Admittedly the relations of Moscow with Peking were very different in those days, which no doubt made it possible for the Soviet representative to counsel restraint upon the Vietminh, as he certainly did.

Today the general opinion seems to be that Soviet Russia would like to bring the conflict to an end, but that Hanoi is the intransigent capital. If this is so, it should not be above the wit of resourceful Soviet diplomacy to work to bring the parties to the council table, yet it does not seem to do so with any of the earnestness displayed in 1954.

However this may be, and Moscow probably has its hawks and doves like every other capital, there can be no question of the influential part which Soviet diplomacy could play in encouraging new diplomatic moves to promote a settlement in Indochina.

Time is not necessarily on the side of the Communist powers. They would be wrong to ignore the increasing authority of the United States in much of the area of Southeast Asia, in Malaysia, Indonesia and Singapore as well as in Thailand. Admittedly, the American presence brings local criticism, yet broadly speaking, these nations welcome American support because of their deep suspicion of China's intentions. Soviet Russia must share these suspicions, for she ranks high today in the catalogue of China's enemies.

All this is argument for the general advantage which is to be found in a negotiated settlement whereby the territory of South Vietnam and its neighbors would be internationally guaranteed by agreement among the powers concerned. Admittedly, such a negotiation presents formidable difficulties, as do the military arrangements which must be dovetailed into it, but not more so than some other problems which have been resolved before now.

Those who contemplate that the fighting can peter out without a negotiated settlement are only prolonging the span of the war, even if they do not realize it. Nor is there anything in the record of escalation to establish that it can do other than intensify suffering and multiply the risks of a wider conflict.

Time is an essential ingredient in any settlement which is to be of service to South Vietnam. After the terrible ravages which that country has endured, a full period of years, perhaps as much as ten or fifteen, is necessary before it should be asked to express its will about its relationship with its neighbors.

Probably North Vietnam could continue to infiltrate forces into the South on the present scale for many years to come. On the other hand, the United States cannot be defeated militarily, and it is unwise for any country to count upon political events in a foreign land to reverse its policies.

Any nation that is determined upon a 100 percent victory in a war of this character, where so much is indeterminate, may live to regret that it has not opted for half that figure.

This at least is certain: It would be an immense relief to the world if peace could be brought to Indochina. Yet that can happen only if all the powers on the sidelines will make their contribution to get negotiations opened. It could take weeks or months, but if it eventually led to the guaranteed neutrality of the North and of their neighbors to the South, it would be to the best interest of all concerned. If only they could be brought to believe it.

In negotiation as in so much else: "Perseverance, dear my lord, keeps honour bright."   [1/6/68]

ANTHONY EDEN, Earl of Avon

The Message of Czechoslovakia

Thirty years ago the Munich agreement left a weakened Czechoslovakia little chance of survival. Russian spokesmen have often denounced that agreement and its consequences. Now

Czechoslovakia is occupied by military force once again, this time by its ally and big brother in Communism and in the Warsaw Pact, Soviet Russia. The unprovoked harshness of this deed has aroused indignation in the free world and in the Communist world also.

The judgment of the Yugoslav newspaper *Politika* merits quotation:

> Never, in the postwar period, has the tragedy of a country so deeply and so painfully shaken the world of our planet as has the tragedy sustained by Czechoslovakia. Never before was the world so united in the condemnation of the aggression as it is these days.

Czechoslovakia is the first casualty. This land which looked for freedom is now a land of fear. Though still a Communist state and loyal member of the Warsaw Pact, it is helpless before Russian armor and the still more dreaded secret police.

We must cherish no illusions. Repression has come again and with it the terror of the knock on the door in the dead of the night. All this for no crime, except that the Czechoslovak Communist leaders sought, with the full support of their people, to practice a little more freedom than the rulers of Russia were prepared to permit, so sharp was the fear of contagion.

There are other casualties. International Communism is split wide open, the greater part of it siding with Czechoslovakia at the first shock, even though the temptation to palliate the deed may grow with the passage of time.

No less significant is the impact upon hopes of negotiation in Europe. At intervals since the summit conference in Geneva, in the summer of 1955, efforts have been made to get discussions going with the purpose of agreeing to some mutual reduction in the number of troops, perhaps determining their location and even considering the possibility of a neutral zone.

At times during the Bulganin-Khrushchev era some progress on these lines seemed possible. Now not only these but other attempts at negotiation between Moscow and the West must be ruled out, unless one condition is first fulfilled. The Soviet armies must be withdrawn from Czechoslovak soil and that country's government allowed to function free from the imposition of foreign nominees or dictated censorship.

This is the indispensable minimum, for all negotiation must rest on confidence, and there can be none in the conditions which Russia has imposed upon Czechoslovakia. To condone what has happened would be base; it would also be foolish. The history of the thirties has taught us mercilessly that to attempt new agreements, while ignoring flagrant breaches of the old, earns contempt, not progress.

The record of attempted negotiation with Hitler and Mussolini cannot be ignored. There have also been more recent examples of appeasement with its predictable consequences.

When Sukarno claimed Western New Guinea, to which he had no right either ethically or ethnically, and threatened attack upon its territory, pressure was applied upon the responsible power to yield. It was no doubt expected that, satisfied with this notable concession, the Indonesian dictator would rest content. As usual, the reverse proved the truth and Sukarno was soon claiming Malaysia.

"Confrontation" followed, which Malaysia, with the help of her ally, successfully repelled at a heavy cost, not least to Indonesia, which to this day is burdened by the aggressive adventures of her previous ruler.

There is a course for the free nations to follow. NATO should review its needs in the light of the changed conditions in Europe. That organization is essentially defensive and to improve its effectiveness can threaten no one. Admittedly the European nations would have to contribute to this effort, but it has to be made, for it would be irresponsible to ignore that the optimistic assumption of steadily improving relations across the Iron Curtain is now belied.

But this local action, though important, is not enough. The influence of Czechoslovakia's ordeal is already worldwide. Relations between the Communist powers have deteriorated sharply. The uncommitted nations are alarmed and acutely conscious of their uncertain future, while the smaller free nations are understandably anxious.

In conditions where Communism's repute is much damaged, the leading free nations have both a duty and an opportunity. Together they should examine the existing situation in each continent, politically, militarily and economically. The purpose of this exercise would be to determine the wisest policies to be pursued in each of these spheres.

To make this effective, closer consultation would be necessary between the leading nations across the world. Something of the spirit of the earlier years of NATO would have to be rekindled for this more comprehensive work, but that is not impossible and the outcome could offer the leadership and inspiration which the world so sadly lacks.

No less important, a joint endeavor such as this could counter the world's greatest danger, the widening spread of anarchy.

[9/14/68]

L. V. UPDEGRAFF

Mirabile Dictu, Indeed

Two Russian savants, Professors N. Deratin and I. Nakhov, protest in the *Literary Gazette,* according to a Reuters dispatch, against the neglect of Latin and Greek in the Russian schools. These scholars go so far as to say openly that there is a prejudice against classical education in the Soviet Union. "In their concern for the great tasks of the present," they say, "people have apparently forgotten about antiquity. The study of ancient literature, art, philosophy, aesthetics and languages is lagging behind the general level of Soviet science." Strange language to have passed the Russian censor. Soviet education has been concentrating on turning out scientists by the thousands—specialists in all fields from nuclear physics to the management of farm tractors—and no word has reached the outside world of any attention paid to the classics. If there is any lingering interest, it is further proof of the resistance of these so-called dead languages to time and change and the most varied political fortunes.

The evidence of any Russian interest at all in Latin and Greek would be the more remarkable considering the revulsion against classical education in Russia that began back in the last century—at about the time that American secondary schools and colleges were also turning away from the old classical curricula. Michael T. Florinsky in his history of Russia, published in 1953, says that what was called the "Graeco-Roman bondage" was brought to an end in the late 1890's in a strong reaction to "the Tolstoy brand of classicism." After 1902 Latin and Greek were taught in only a small number of gymnasiums.

Russians came late to an interest in Greek and Latin literature, long after these studies had been made the basis of Western education. After Russia's "Time of Troubles," about the time that Harvard College was being founded in Massachusetts Colony, Russians seemed to have lost faith in their old culture and turned to the West for something better. Learning was in a deplorable state. But three monks were found in a Kiev monastery who could translate the Greek Testament into Slavonic. For the study of the Latin authors the Russians took as teachers their neighbors, the Poles, who had been schooled in the Roman Catholic universal tongue. Some few Russian youths were sent to Poland to study and were applauded when they were able to make a speech in the Polish-Latin jargon of the scholars. With Peter the Great, Russian education became almost entirely utilitarian, but the Czar chose for himself the Latin honorary titles of Imperator and Pater Patriae.

When the Russian scholars say that the Russian people have forgotten about antiquity they obviously mean more than Russian antiquity. Here the Bolsheviks have shown some interest if only to prove that the Eastern Slavs are quite as ancient and honorable as the Western Slavs. The scholars would also apparently look beyond Russia's Byzantine heritage to the Graeco-Roman civilization which is the common heritage of all Europe. That Russia received less than her full share of this latter heritage is probably the fault of the Byzantine Empire, which was such a long time dying. It is one of Arnold J. Toynbee's interesting theories that the world would now be better off if the Eastern Roman Empire had collapsed completely, like the Western Empire, after the age of Justinian, last of the Emperors in the Western or Latin line. Then Eastern Europe might have developed more like Western Europe and the sharp division represented by language and religion might not have been drawn to plague later generations.

If by any chance the Russians should become interested in classical antiquity, there would be something to bridge the wide gap which now separates Eastern from Western peoples. Russian students might be less than enthusiastic in the pursuit of Greek and Latin grammar and the works of classical authors. Yet they might welcome these as an escape from the boredom of large doses of Marx, Lenin and Stalin. The Commissar of Education might even adapt the classics to the Communist line. Plato's *Republic,* for example, might be read as an early Communist tract—a plan for a Communist state that could exist only in heaven and not on this earth. Messrs. Khrushchev and Bulganin might be presented in the role of Plato's guardians of the state, although their training for the job is not the kind that Plato outlined.   [1/22/56]

ALAN PATON

The Yoke of Racial Inequality

It is a hard thing for many white people to believe that their own racial attitudes could be the fundamental cause of the hatred, fear, dislike, or indifference, of so many black people toward them.

It is much easier and much more pleasant to believe that the fundamental cause is the laziness and fecklessness and irresponsibility and innate savagery of the black man.

It doesn't do much good to argue with people who believe this. Their psychological need to hold such beliefs is so great and deep that one cannot reason with them. There is only one therapy that can do them any possible good, and that is to bring them into contact and communication, and collaboration if that is possible, with the people they fear and despise. Most of them will not submit to the therapy, for why should one wish to know more of such irresponsible and savage people? But there is hope in applying the therapy to their children.

It was the sudden leap forward in man's understanding of and control over his physical environment that led to our present racial situation, because this leap forward took place in the West. Why was this? Some of us believe that it was due to the innate superiority of the white races, others that it was due to an accident of history and luck and climate.

I don't think the answer to this question is yet established. All I can say is that I believe that it was an accident. I believe this because it is my experience, and a very common one, that the Africans of my own country, when they have enjoyed the same benefits of education that I have enjoyed, speak to me in my own idiom, and understand my thoughts, and cherish the same ideals for man and his society.

This almost miraculous flowering of the human intellect did not occur in every part of Europe at once. It took place here,

and then there, but in the end it was characteristic of the West
as a whole. In like manner I believe it will spread throughout
the world, at least to those countries which are reasonably well
endowed.

Or are we to suppose that the Japanese, for example, are superior to all other Eastern peoples, and that what happened
in Japan will not happen elsewhere in the East? I myself shall
not believe this until some other proof not now available is
brought forward.

Whatever may be the solution of this fascinating riddle, some
of the consequences of this Western flowering were catastrophic
for the rest of the world; they were exploration, colonization,
exploitation, and slavery. It is the white man's boast that he
brought law and order to many a community torn by tribal
wars, and this was often no doubt true.

But we Westerners are only now beginning to understand
the cost of it, and the depth of the traumatic wound that we inflicted on the non-Western world. Indeed many of us not only
cannot understand it, but believe that there is no wound at all,
except that which exists in the imaginations of sentimental
visionaries.

In my own country the ruling white group is hostile to any
persons who say that there is a wound, and can silence them
and severely restrict their movements and their actions, not by
any process of law, but merely because the Minister of Justice
considers such persons to be "advancing the aims of Communism." When antichange people hold the power, they can act
as ruthlessly toward those who advocate change as the revolu-
tionaries can act toward those who resist it.

While colonization had catastrophic effects on the non-Western peoples, the undoing of colonization is also having catastrophic effects, and will, in my opinion, continue to have them
for generations to come. Antichange extremists derive pleasure,
and seem to be justified, by the catastrophic nature of these
events, just as the segregationists of America derive pleasure
and seem justified by the unrest of the cities.

Yet it is clear—to persons like myself, of course—that the United States cannot return one step along the road she has taken, and that no matter what the consequences, it was the right and only road to take.

Does the world now face an inevitable and implacable conflict between the white and the other races? Is there no measure that can be taken to prevent or lessen it?

There is one, I believe, and we all know what it is, but we take it half-heartedly. It is for those nations who are so far ahead to devote more of their skill and energy to the intellectual and technological development of the others, for modern racism is not only a heritage of the colonial era, with its wounds and hurts, it is also a direct product of the various inequalities that the era has bequeathed to us.

And this is true within the nation itself; not until these gross inequalities have been removed will we have any hope at all of building the great society. [11/30/68]

LEONARDO SCIASCIA

The Human Earthquake Goes On in Sicily

The earthquake that completely destroyed five villages in western Sicily, more or less seriously damaged at least twenty more, and made hundreds of houses in the oldest district of Palermo uninhabitable, suddenly and tragically revealed to the Italian nation and to the world a human condition that Sicilian writers and artists for more than a century have been representing and denouncing, but which neither the Italian leading class nor public opinion has ever seriously worried about.

The newspapermen and students who came from northern Italy found themselves facing a reality quite different from that of Florence hit by the floods. What had to be saved from the rubble was not paintings and statues (which aren't lacking in the churches of Sicily) but, instead, the mule, the ass, the goat.

They were facing, in a word, the peasant world. It was the one that the Arabs, a thousand years earlier, had formed and left—landed property divided and structured as it was then, the soil tilled with the same criteria and implements, the people sticking to the same way of life and of seeing life.

This condition was, and is, not only that of the Belice Valley, which was hit by the earthquake, but of all of Sicily's interior: The earthquake violently revealed what the sense of shame and the dignity of the people concealed elsewhere, in all the other peasant villages.

And it is this truth, this fact, that one must bear in mind when one speaks of Sicily and the earthquake. Otherwise, one runs the risk that the compassion and the help that today flow into the villages struck by the earthquake serve as alibis, as relief for the conscience, as a screen behind which the Italian leading class once again hides its old guilt with regard to Sicily.

Actually, Sicily has been an earthquake victim for centuries, devastated not only by the seismic events, which have been frequent and terrible, but also by the human events, by history. Had any other zone of Sicily now been hit by the earthquake, it would have revealed the same poverty as Montevago, as Gibellina. The problems are ancient, so ancient that people have become resigned to them, and the state has forgotten them.

The government autonomy granted to Sicily twenty years ago by the Italian state (apart from the fact that it is a very limited and controversial autonomy) has, one may say, deepened the problems instead of solving them.

A regional Parliament that wants to imitate the national Parliament in outward dignity, and brings forth government without political stability and with little administrative competence; a bureaucracy that was created out of nothing, enormous, and almost useless; a constellation of agencies that have not served, and do not serve, any other purpose than that of giving power and funds to political parties—that is the balance that one may strike today after twenty years of autonomy.

By hitting a vast agricultural zone and destroying land reclamation installations along the Belice River, the earthquake thus has worsened and exasperated Sicily's problems. Among other things, it has caused a new wave of emigration toward Switzerland, Germany, Venezuela and Australia; the villages of the interior have lost almost all their young population. Sicily, by now, is for the young people a cursed land, full of misfortunes, immobile for centuries, without opportunities and without hope. The youth flee as soon as they can, toward any place in the world where they can find work.

The law for the villages struck by the earthquake that was adopted by the national government, and which calls for 300 billion lire expenditures for reconstruction, will solve (if it does solve) only the immediate problems of a limited area; but the problems of all of Sicily can be tackled neither with 300 billion lire nor with a political class such as that which at present rules Italy.

And, in fact, months after the earthquake, thousands of persons still live under miserable conditions. In how many months will they have permanent huts? And when they have them, will they not end up remaining in them for half a century, like the people of Messina after the earthquake of 1908?

[5/11/68]

MORRIS GILBERT

America and Le Mans

The city of Le Mans in France, where the annual twenty-four-hour motor race ended in unprecedented victories for first, second and third places by cars of the Ford Motor Company, has several other associations for Americans. Modern aviation, for instance, had its first real takeoff in Le Mans and the American Wilbur Wright, at the controls of his biplane, achieved it.

That was in 1908. Wilbur and Orville Wright had first demonstrated the possibilities of powered heavier-than-air flight in 1903 at Kitty Hawk, North Carolina. In the next five years nobody could have cared less about this stupendous feat than their own government, particularly the military.

France played it differently. After sending a mission of inquiry, the French government offered the Wrights a flattering and financially liberal invitation to bring their flying machine over and try it out for them.

Le Mans is the pleasant, unimportant, provincial capital of the Department of the Sarthe, and lies about 130 miles west of Paris. It is in flat country, and even in Wilbur Wright's day was a center of automotive industry. Wright picked the grounds of a local automobile factory, that of a certain Léon Bollée, for his tests. He presumably needed access to shops familiar with internal-combustion engines. So here, with the secretiveness characteristic of him, on August 8, 1908, he made his first test in France.

On that day it happened that one of those present was Eric Hawkins—later, for many years, the esteemed managing editor of the Paris *Herald*. The plane, he reported, was catapulted "to a height of eight or ten meters [a little more than forty feet], circled twice, took turns with ease at almost terrifying angles and alighted like a bird. The flying time was 1 minute 45 seconds."

Mr. Hawkins was back at Le Mans on December 18 that year to see Wright set three records—in distance, altitude and time. Wright flew in circuits over the field for 113 minutes and covered 99 kilometers (more than 60 miles) at a height of 80 feet.

For Americans, the next occasion when Le Mans engaged their attention was about 1920. This was a great ceremony. For a number of years air-minded Frenchmen had sought to raise a monument there, honoring the Wrights and other aeronauts.

But fund raising had gone badly. Then an American of considerable means entered the picture and subscribed the sum needed to set it up.

So on the given day a special train pulled out of Paris, bearing a distinguished company including the American donor, the eminent French statesman and Americophile André Tardieu, and the cream of the Paris-American colony, a prestigious group, indeed, in those days. Also modestly among them was the present writer, then a young reporter for the Paris *Herald,* on his first out-of-town assignment.

The monument was by the celebrated sculptor Landowsky. It stood on a splendid site, on a promontory above the Sarthe plain, beyond the sanctuary of the Cathedral of St. Julien. The statue itself was a symbolic affair, with Icarus, who first sought to violate the skies in the Greek myth, climbing and raising an arm heavenward, and it was dedicated to "The Precursors of Aviation."

After the unveiling, at a sumptuous luncheon, the American benefactor, to nobody's astonishment, was awarded the Legion of Honor. The distinguished company returned to Paris, and the report of the event was in the first edition of the Paris *Herald.*

As far as Americans were concerned, Le Mans remained dormant (except for the internal-combustion set) for decades. Then, in early August 1944, General Patton's Third U.S. Army surged through it. And there, attached rather anomalously to General Wade Haislip's Fifteenth Corps ("that psychological fella," General Haislip called him) was the reporter who, twenty-four years earlier, had attended the unveiling of the Wright memorial.

He duly noted, in moments apart from his duties, that the monument still stood on its prowlike eminence above the Sarthe prairies.

And now, the great annual race again over, Americans will surely leave Le Mans in repose until next year, when the unbridled and insolent racket of all those engines will once more disturb its natural tranquillity. [6/25/66]

DENIS W. BROGAN

Britain's Oxbridge Problem

In the national stocktaking that is going on in no very amiable way in Britain today, two issues are coming to the surface: the position of "the public schools," *i.e.,* private prep schools; and the related problem of "Oxbridge."

The problems are linked, for the disillusioned public is coming to think that it is suffering from the products of an exclusive educational "establishment" which takes all the good jobs, runs all the country and is both overpaid and incompetent. The public schools question can, however, be put on one side. How far it is a really burning problem is doubtful. But Oxbridge is another matter.

The term was coined by a disgruntled and distinguished academic at the University of Liverpool to describe the odd, privileged and, as he thought, indefensible position of "the ancient universities," Oxford and Cambridge, or, as the alumni of these two celebrated institutions still simply say, "The Universities," for it is this assumption that there are only two real universities in Great Britain that is the problem and the cause of irritation rising to anger.

Oxford is for the English upper classes and upper middle classes "The University." If they use the horrid modern locution "at university," they mean at Oxbridge. If they can't get a son into Oxbridge, they will descend to Harvard. Trinity College, Dublin, will just do and Saint Andrews will do for girls. The ancient and famous universities of Glasgow and Edinburgh won't, even for girls.

This is the aspect that egalitarians fasten on. For them, Oxbridge is a citadel of privilege where rich young men waste their time and where poor boys, admitted on scholarships, are educated away from their families and class. For this increasing group England will not be a democracy till Eton is a coeducational comprehensive high school of the American type and Oxford and Cambridge are, at best, left to serve as graduate schools. But the social exclusiveness is a minor nuisance.

A more serious problem has arisen. A great program for university expansion was pushed forward in the first two "Labor years." That expansion has been nearly stopped.

What does it matter if the government tap is turned off, if the great American and British foundations still pour their bounty on Oxbridge? Why should anyone doubt the wisdom of the Ford Foundation (of New York) and of Sir Isaac Wolfson (of Glasgow) in founding a lavishly endowed new college at Oxford under the rule of Sir Isaiah Berlin? Isn't the money going where it should go, to the places where it will be best spent? And that means, in the sciences, Cambridge, Oxford, London. There are the clusters of Nobel Prize men outshining the constellations on the Charles and San Francisco Bay.

There the cream of youthful academic talent is separated from the milk that is good enough for London, Manchester, Glasgow, Edinburgh.

There money will be best spent. Such is the theory which justifies a policy which I think is one symptom of our national troubles, the concentration of wealth, prestige, recognized talent in the triangle: London-Oxford-Cambridge.

If universities are really research institutes, does it matter much where they are? Why shouldn't Rockefeller University be in New York, Churchill College and Wolfson College be in Cambridge and Oxford? No reason if so many other things were not concentrated there. London is now much more the capital of Britain than Paris is of France. Our rulers are either born inside this triangle or enticed to live in it. Political and economic decisions are made by people who don't know how the other half lives. And that ignorant group includes the faculty (in the American sense) of Oxbridge. Eighty percent of Oxford and Cambridge teachers are graduates of Oxbridge. Till recently, more than half of the teachers in "Redbrick," *i.e.*, in the new civic universities, were alumni of Oxbridge.

There is a slight improvement, but slight and slow. This is bad educationally, socially, politically. It is fortunate that Cambridge (Massachusetts) and Berkeley (California) are at a distance from Washington and New York. Of the Prime Ministers of Britain since Sir Winston, all have been Oxford graduates.

The result has not been so edifying as to make us think that there is a monopoly of political talent at Oxford and, while Cambridge might have done better, the fundamental alienation of our rulers from so many of the problems that have to be lived with would remain. The power of Oxbridge has increased, is increasing and ought to be diminished. [2/25/67]

KENNETH CAMPBELL

Wagons-Lits People

A throng of men and women sometimes called the Wagons-Lits people moves restlessly about the world, especially now when tourists are taking off. They are so called because they are as rootless as the people who seemed to have their being on those crack frontier-traversing sleeping car trains made up of cars from the Compagnie Internationale des Wagons-Lits. This could be translated as the International Bed Wagon Company, but this would convey nothing of the glamour that once surrounded these trains, now sadly reduced in prestige.

Let us sit with this charming and handsome middle-aged Wagons-Lits type on the terrace of a fashionable hotel at Cannes. His accent is mostly excellent English public school, but there is just a hint of something like a top-drawer Irish brogue. There is an extraelegant handling of the umlaut *u*. He has an accent in all languages.

"You see, my father and mother and my oldest sister were

forced to get out of Ruritania in a hurry back in the 1920's when Black Michael became dictator. Actually, my mother was Irish. I was born in Copenhagen while my parents were waiting for visas for us to go to Bolivia. They'd put my sister in school in Switzerland. When my father died my mother left La Paz to live with a sister in South Africa and I was sent to school in England. But I went back to Bolivia to do my military service. I lived in Turkey but I kept my South African citizenship. I like it here in Cannes, don't you? Yes, I can speak Polish. It isn't hard when you know Russian."

There he is in all his gentle glitter—the typical Wagons-Lits.

In a way, this is the golden age of the Wagons-Lits type. He is useful as never before. Diplomacy, commerce, international law and banking and journalism can't find enough Wagons-Lits characters. Frontiers are softer now if they have not exactly melted and he can waft himself across them like smoke. He may be your humble but capable travel agency courier who relieves you of worry about your luggage and often prevents you from being relieved of the luggage itself. Or he may be the trusted adviser at the embassy or consulate.

Of course, just after World War II, many a Wagons-Lits clinked with black market watches as he went through the Bellegarde customs checkpoint near Geneva like an ectoplasm. But on the whole your Wagons-Lits is just as likely to be honest as the next man, although there are temptations when you know all languages. The Wagons-Lits world isn't a Sunday School.

The great frontier upheavals after World War I; the trek of whole peoples across frontiers, wasn't calculated to make for iron virtue. Your Wagons-Lits may have searing memories not known to the chap who was born and raised in, and who stayed all his life in, Van Wert, Ohio. Your Wagons-Lits may remember coming into some place like Salonika from Smyrna with a big tag pinned to him and of being roughly handled when he was deloused. If he kept decent during his travels, and he often did, he learned the word honor in many languages. Or maybe he simply drifted into the world of currency fraud and smuggling. His story is the story of man.

Your Wagons-Lits character is eating well at present, and probably will until that dim, distant day when nothing is heard but Esperanto and there is an end to the snobbery of people who don't know what to do in a de luxe hotel and who don't want it known that they don't know. This pays off for the Wagons-Lits and it is only fair. You will never in your life have as much get-around know-how as a good Wagons-Lits. [6/8/64]

KENNETH CAMPBELL

March Now, Study Later

The world's universities are bulging at the seams with students who always seem willing to go into the street to demonstrate. When do they study? Perhaps they grab a minute at the university library between picketing a United States embassy building and throwing decayed vegetables at their own unpopular Foreign Minister.

Weariness may come over them sometimes. One says: "This is all very well, but I've got a term paper due tomorrow and I haven't even started it. We were up half the night hooting that guy—what's his name—from Moscow."

His friend says: "Well, you aren't any more bushed than I am. I've almost lost my voice screaming insults about John Kennedy. If I can only get that back seat in the Humanities lecture hall —the one behind the pillar—and get some sleep. I've used up my last class cut mixing that stuff we're supposed to smear on the walls of the Ministry of Culture and Enlightenment tonight."

Education can only come the hard way at the University of Graustark, where student interest varies from generation to generation. Since the kingdom of Graustark was invented by the novelist George Barr McCutcheon around 1901, we may assume that students' penchant for doing anything except study has something in it of middle Europe, where Graustark enjoyed its nonexistence. Intervals of uninterrupted instruction have been rare here. In the past, students of dear old U. of G. specialized in Sigmund Romberg close harmony. They wore student dueling corps pillboxes and big gauntlets and waved beer steins as they sang of sweetheart and country.

It's different at the University of Graustark today. The students roam the streets looking for foreign newsmen to assault. They are handy at turning over embassy cars and count themselves lucky if the Ambassador is in it. Maybe the students at another fictional seat of higher learning—Joel Sayre's Canarsie College in his novel *Rackety-Rax*—were better employed. No one shouted at anyone that he was a Fascist beast or a dirty Red. They just played football for a college that no one could ever find because nobody ever went to Canarsie.

Demonstrations were already old by the 1840's, when students battled in the Munich streets for beautiful Lola Montez, mistress of King Louis I of Bavaria. They were only doing fieldwork in practical politics. You didn't have to bother with lectures and classes after a night of hauling Lola around the streets in her carriage and bellowing insults at her enemies. In nineteenth-century Russia, the university students were cutting classes as they brought the idea of revolution to the peasants and plotted the assassination of the Czar and the Grand Dukes.

In Belgrade fifty years ago this winter a few pale faces began to disappear from the lecture halls of the university. Certain students were moving on to graduate work under officers of the Serbian general staff. They studied the uses of the bomb and the pistol and their work ended with the assassination of the Archduke Franz Ferdinand and his consort at Sarajevo.

One doesn't readily associate the late John Foster Dulles with student riots, but he was in several brisk ones. He was a young man at the Sorbonne when Joan of Arc was a fighting name, and he was in favor of her. He wore a bowler hat stuffed with news-papers to dull the thump of police truncheons.

Students seldom mind if a seminar has to be postponed for a session of street brawling. Anyway, it's better than passing up lectures in order to engage in burglary as a certain famous Paris M. A. named François Villon is supposed to have done.

If Harvard and many other former male domains take to the streets for revolution, resolute young ladies' voices will be heard for the first time. Can coeducation on the university level be a master plot to do away with student demonstrations?

[11/17/63]

CHESTER BOWLES

Who Owns the Land?

Many years of observation in the developing nations of Asia, Africa and Latin America have convinced me that in these vital areas the most important economic and political question is: Who owns the land?

Where the land is owned by the few, millions of landless la-borers are inevitably left with a deep sense of insecurity which makes them an easy target for determined Communist agita-tors. But peasants who own their own land have a major stake in political stability and in economic progress.

On this score the record of achievement in some parts of Asia is dramatic. In 1946 in Japan, at the recommendation of Gen-eral MacArthur, a sweeping land reform program was launched which placed a limit of seven acres on each family holding. As a result, 94 percent of all rural families acquired land which they could call their own.

With the application of fertilizer, improved seeds and pesti-cides, with adequate water and with hard work by the cultivator and his family, these small plots of land were soon producing the highest yields of wheat and rice in the world.

This same pattern was applied by the Nationalist Chinese government on Taiwan, where the limit on the size of land holdings was set at ten acres per family. Later in South Korea, where the size of farms was held to seven acres, the same dramatic gains in agricultural production and political stability were made.

The team of American specialists who sparked the reforms in Japan, Taiwan and South Korea made a similar effort in South Vietnam in the mid-1950's. However, reactionary forces in the Diem government and lack of strong support from the United States blocked the necessary changes.

If this effort had succeeded, it is unlikely that American troops would now be involved in this tragic country, fighting against peasant guerrillas.

Agrarian reform, particularly in countries without large tracts of uncultivated land, is no easy matter. In a democracy, where the rights of private property are respected, it is particularly difficult, for land reform is almost inevitably—if mistakenly—associated with coercion and expropriation.

Whatever the obstacles may be, it is difficult to see how any developing country can achieve political stability or rapid economic growth unless it puts the land into the hands of the men and women who till it.

In most developing countries the peasants constitute 60 to 80 percent of the population. If that large a percentage of a nation's population is without significant purchasing power or a clear stake in the future, it is impossible to build a vigorous national market. But when rural income rises, so does the demand for sewing machines, flashlights, transistor radios, cloth, shoes and a hundred and one other items which make life more comfortable for the farmer who buys them, for the industrial worker who makes them, and for the businessman who sells them.

In the countries where Communists have come to power they

have inevitably used the promise of land reform to whip up revolutionary sentiment, only to go back on their promises once the peasants had served their purpose. The newly emancipated peasants of the Soviet Union soon found themselves forced into collective farms. In China, the farmers who were given land by the new regime saw it repossessed and their families herded into communes.

The record of the United States in this area has by and large been solid and constructive. Our recommendations to the Japanese, South Korean and Taiwanese governments have resulted in enduring agricultural revolutions.

Still, tens of millions of Asian, African and Latin-American peasants are still held in semifeudal bondage by traditional patterns of land ownership and tenure. The liberation and integration of these peasants into the mainstream of twentieth-century life is essential to democratic development and, in the final analysis, to international stability.

It is an issue on which the United States must take a firm and positive stand.   [7/22/67]

III
The New York Scene

FREDERIC MORTON

I Love West 83d Street

People used to inhabit neighborhoods. Now they're more
and more stranded in the world. Street corners are no longer
much lived in, candy stores fray away, and still I can't help feeling neighborly rather than worldly. The fact is that I have two
neighborhoods, one in the past tense, one in the present.

The first is a tiny baroque street called Thelemanngasse,
which houses my childhood. It was a miniature Vienna. On one
corner (right below my very own window) a plaque announced that Edmund Eysler had composed many of his lilt-
ing operettas and songs here. In the middle of the block Frau
Gimsch's store displayed *Powidltatschkerln* and other legendary Viennese pastry. At the far corner stood a wine house where
Eysler's songs were sung, and opposite it hung a street sign saying THELEMANNGASSE in nineteenth-century gingerbread let-
tering—almost in the accents of the good Emperor Franz Josef.

The length of my streetlet was tailored to a boy's deepest
need: You could kick a soccer ball easily from the first cobble
to the last, even while achieving casual transubstantiation
through a *Powidltatschkerl*.

Indeed the Thelemanngasse was an idyll so *echt* that it developed a serpent. In 1938 the Anschluss arrived, more or less in
three-quarter time. The wine house became more colorful still
with the gay brown and black of storm-trooper uniforms. Frau
Gimsch's butter pastries were munched, just as idyllically,
under steel helmets. Only the Edmund Eysler plaque vanished,
since he turned out to be Jewish.

Being Jewish ourselves, we tried to vanish too, and managed just in time. Others have the leisure to outgrow their childhood paradise. I ran from mine the instant before it could destroy me.

But I'm addicted to neighborhoods, and today the Thelemanngasse sign hangs with all its Franz Josef curlicues in the foyer of my apartment. Somebody municipal by the shores of the Danube sent it to me as a touching gesture and, intentionally or not, as a paradigm. The writing on my wall points to my origins, to the underbelly of nostalgia, and, somehow, deep into the crevices of morality.

Good and evil are enormous abstractions that dizzy through the front page each day. They become more human in scale, more digestible to the individual conscience when they materialize in your particular little alley.

For the same reason I keep in my study a balloon saying "I Love West 83d Street." It celebrates my adult neighborhood. Of course, West 83d Street is much longer than the Thelemanngasse. No soccer genius could kick a ball through its entire length. Yet I've watched a police car traverse it wholly within a single siren cycle, and that's about as small and cozy as New York streets come in 1968.

I share the same roof with Mrs. Babe Ruth, a Broadway star, and an occasional cockroach, presences that certify the folk character of a New York house. So does the Hudson outside my window, a typically indigenous sweep of grandeur festooned with pollution. That's to the west. To the east, 83d Street fords West End Avenue and Broadway, two middle-class streams, though the latter is a bit swampy.

And from Broadway to Central Park, the street is one all-American slum, with sullen stoops, "hotels" phosphorescent with drug cultures, veritable cornucopias of garbage and dented double-parked Cadillacs.

Is that lovable? No, and yet the balloon speaks my heart. Darkness marched through the Thelemanngasse, as it now falls across West 83d, even if only as shadows from the frolic of jet fighters. But in my childhood street the darkness was absorbed blandly, sweetly, silently.

Silently. What saves West 83d (and what might yet redeem America) is its disquiet. The gutters are growling. You can't pass too many street corners without a gaudy-locked youth passing out pamphlets against the Bomb. I bought my balloon at a deafening block party for the benefit of a ghetto employment program. A storefront off Columbus Avenue yells out impatience, through the announcements of a tenants' union officed there.

When you've ducked past the doorman into the gentlemanly lobby of my own building, it is no haven either. Right by the elevator a poster accosts you from an apartment door: "In God's name, stop the bombing!" This is one turf which doesn't candy the national malaise but smolders and screams against it.

And that's much better than the poisoned euphoria of my European nook thirty years ago. West 83d may be rude, inequitable, filthy, abrasive, but it is not yet silent. Silence will make me pack up and run once more. Meantime, thank God, things are still loud on my block, louder even than the sanitation trucks. I love West 83d Street.   [2/17/68]

BROOKS ATKINSON

The Drama of Life in Kip's Bay

Although the apartment houses are choked with people, the neighborhood supplies the personality. In this instance, the apartment houses are the two lofty filing cabinets designed by I. M. Pei, called Kips Bay Plaza and located between First and Second avenues in the lower Thirties. (Note: The name should be stated as Kip's Bay or Kipp's Bay. The area is not named for

a kip but for Jacobus Hendricksen Kipp, a Dutch farmer who
lived there in the eighteenth century.)

Since the two buildings contain 1,130 apartments, the total
population is more than 1,130, including the children who explode with excitement in the lobby or in the wide arcade and
playground out of doors. Like most New Yorkers, the adults are
inclined to be reticent and suspicious, particularly in the
mornings. When they go off to work they look hopeless, resigned
to the belief that today will be intolerable, like yesterday, which
was unbearable.

But the neighborhood is congenial. None of the shopkeepers
is bored, suspicious or hopeless. Take, for instance, the four
Affronti sisters on Second Avenue near Thirtieth Street. They
are the third generation of an Italian family that has been
baking succulent pastries in the neighborhood since 1905.

Josephine and Mary, who preside over the daily routine (assisted by Victoria and Gina on weekends, enjoy people.
Everything moves fast in the Affronti shop because the girls are
in a state of constant excitement.

"We miss the big families," Josephine says ruefully as she
thinks back to the bountiful days when Kip's Bay was choked
with tenements. For the inhabitants of high-rise apartments
are frugal eaters. People who pay high rentals can't afford much
food. But the Affronti shop, with old Signora Affronti seated
like a queen in the rear, radiates personality.

When Fred Feldman opened his newspaper and stationery
store (Cards 'n Sweets) in May, 1964, Roz (Mrs. Feldman)
agreed to help for a year until he was established. You couldn't
drive her away now. She loves it. All day she is where the action
is. Roz, a slight woman with a flip sense of humor, and Fred, a
successful merchant who wears swinging sideburns and likes
to have people around him, have inadvertently created an information center.

From about five to about seven every morning Fred and Roz
deliver more than 500 newspapers. (Their nephews help them
with the 800 Sunday papers.) Keeping their newspaper route

up to date, they know most of the important things about the neighborhood. They know who is where and when. If he is out of town they know whether or not he had a good time when he comes back. Although the Feldmans seldom leave headquarters they are constantly in touch with Florida, California, Hawaii, Europe and other parts of the world. When he returns every resident reports to them.

The merchants in the old family stores tend to lead restricted lives. Across the street is the A & J Super Market that has been a family operation since before World War I. It opens with an exhilarating blaze of light at six and remains open until midnight, except on Thursday evenings, when it closes at nine. Jack goes to the races on Thursday evenings. Abe and his wife, Miriam, seldom get out except on Sundays, when they like to take a dip in a YMHA swimming pool on 14th Street and dine at Chandler's uptown.

The A & J Super Market is such an essential part of neighborhood life that the customers were dumbfounded a few Saturdays ago to find it inexplicably closed. All day long they came and stared in disbelief at the locked door and speculated on the awful things that might have happened. The explanation was simple. Wayne Robbins, son of Abe and Miriam, was having his Bar Mitzvah. Naturally no one in the Robbins family could be distracted by keeping store on a day like that.

These are not the only community centers where you can meet many of the strangers who live under your own roof. Joseph Behar, your neighborhood druggist, a notary public as well as a certified orthotist, knows everyone and what ails him. Joe is a weekend painter; there will be an exhibition of his paintings in May. Chris Laskar, who operates a captivating flower shop, knows who likes big sprays of forsythia, and who is content with a small spray of freesia. Mrs. Norah Lieu, hostess of the Golden Coach Chinese-American restaurant, weighs about ninety pounds. But every evening is a social occasion when she moves from table to table.

There is no personality in Bohack's, which tolerates customers but hates people, or in the branch of the First National City Bank, which mails all kinds of courtesy and credit cards to the depositors but looks suspicious if they come in. Corporations are never much fun.

But the family shops give Kip's Bay the character of a community. Although Mr. Pei won three high honors for the design of Kips Bay Plaza in 1964 and 1965, the informal good nature of the neighborhood was not an item on his drawing board. Like everything human, it is invaluable.   [4/6/68]

ALFRED KAZIN

The Holy Flame of Learning

I come from Brownsville, an unlovely Brooklyn neighborhood that has been much in the news lately. Whenever I see the word in print, I automatically think that I still have homework to do, for we were hot for education, our teachers expected to educate us, and our parents worshiped before the holy flame of learning. The greatest danger to life and limb in my day came not from that well-known Brownsville firm, Murder, Inc., but from not looking up from your book as you crossed the street.

The other day I went back to Brownsville to sit in on some classrooms and to hear supervisors and teachers talk about "our experiment," "our demonstration," "our children." Hopkinson Avenue near Atlantic is grimier and more full of boarded-up stores than it used to be, and old P.S. 178, which was old even in my day, has not improved in looks and comfort over the years.

There was no heat on this cold autumn day: The children in the music room, singing "Little children, come on board, little children," were in their overcoats. The halls were being swept by parents, and one hefty father was carting the school rubbish out the front door. The music teacher was young, pretty, enthusiastic and firm, and had the large group cheerfully "interacting," a word they use a lot in this school district.

At one point she got a little Puerto Rican boy to translate her English to a group of Puerto Rican girls who were sitting, slightly lost, in a little group of their own. And I suddenly remembered that one of the most famous literary scholars in America, on his first week in a Bronx school, did not know the English word for fork when the teacher held one up.

In the two Brownsville schools I visited, 178 and beautiful up-to-date 55, Brownsville has not changed, and the flame burns hotter than ever. I had forgotten how loud kids can get in the echoing halls, and how much physical stamina, deft coordination and loud, piercing enun-ciation it takes to keep a lesson going. I would never have imagined that a principal would be all over his school, running after and scolding every noisy child like the strictest of fathers. The same principal, when a visitor asked permission to visit still another classroom, said impatiently: "Walk in anywhere! We're not trying to look good!"

The teachers I saw were mostly white, young, and they looked very good indeed to me in their quiet steady concentration on the students. The intentness all over the place audibly vibrated in my ears.

The high point for me was a poem, "My Friend, Leona," that a teacher had clipped out of a magazine and that was being studied with considerable gravity in one English class.

Leona knows the alleys/Where people eat and sleep/In helter-skelter houses/And the company they keep./She knows a hump-back beggar/And a Welfare man./A lady who tells fortunes/With a peacock-feather fan/And she can raise geraniums/In a tomato can./She says she has ribbons/Wide as my hand/But she fastens her hair/With a rubber band./She says she has dresses/Too sweet to be seen/But the ones she wears/Are scrimped and mean./She says her home/Is huge and fair/But at present she's not living there./She says it's beautiful/Grand and neat/With seven white pillars/Set back from the street/With willow trees

*arching/The elegant drive/Silvering people/As they arrive.
. . . /That her father's the captain/Of a ship/Off on a long mysterious trip. . . .*

Despite Leona's obvious pretenses and lies, this fact was not
getting as much attention as *helter-skelter, scrimped, mean,
grand, arching, silvering.* There was a lot of practical stuff. *Can
you raise geraniums in a tomato can?* Nobody knew, not even
the teacher, who said she would have to ask somebody who did.
Arching was a lot of trouble, and so was *grand,* which when you
get down to it really means the way you feel and is not always
put next to *neat.*

I wanted to know who the author was but the teacher didn't
seem to know or care, while the kids, intent on the hard words,
didn't seem to think much of Leona. What an obvious character, this Leona! What a dreamer!   [11/9/68]

LAURA Z. HOBSON

1,200 Miles by Bike in Central Park

About a year ago the eminent cyclist and cardiologist Dr.
Paul Dudley White looked straight at me from the TV screen
and said, "Whenever anybody asks me if he's going stale or losing his creative ability, I feel the muscles of his legs."

Next day I rented a bike in the park—British made, three
speeds, hand brakes, $1.25 an hour. I had had a bike as a child,
but that was indecent decades ago, so I started where there were
no witnesses.

Then I plodded around the special bike path, an oval tape
of pavement 1.7 miles long, from 72d to 59th and back, from
East Side to West. Six or eight times en route I dismounted just
to breathe.

But my outraged muscles and I went out the next morning
and the next and the next. On the Sunday, with the roadway

closed to cars, I had my first sight of a New York on bikes, on skates, skate boards, trainer wheels, soapbox scooters, tricycles, tandems. It was a marvel, but all 500 rentable bikes were already gone. That week I bought my own, complete with speedometer, to measure whatever miles I might manage.

It took days to get to 10, then 20, then 30. I still did only the one orbit, still got off repeatedly to breathe. I had no ambitions about distance, no prescribed stint. I just liked it.

It was October, the golden time, and I began to look forward to the swish and brush of the leaves as my wheels slipped through them. I crossed 40, then 50, and one morning I did the oval twice and knew a triumph. It grew colder, but I went right after breakfast.

I don't keep a journal or diary, but once I start writing a book I do keep a work log. For November 13 it says, "Pages 90, 91, 92," and up above, "100 on bike, 5 wks." The next bike notation doesn't appear until January 9. "First bike since big snow at Xmas. At 243."

Somewhere along in there I began to wonder for the first time how many miles you could do in a month once you were really fit and the weather really good. How many in six months? In a year?

And also somewhere in there came lawlessness, civic sin, at the very least civil disobedience. I had never, not in four months, not in 300 miles, ever disobeyed the park ordinances that bound me to the 1.7 with its faded yellow stencils: BICYCLE PATH—PEDESTRIANS KEEP OFF. Now the word treadmill would pop unwanted into my mind; I began to look about. Visible everywhere under the winter-bare trees were the pedestrian paths, all but abandoned in the morning hours, inviting, beckoning, unknown.

One morning I did it. Delight! Change and exploration! What graceful arcs and dips and rises those paths made, how charming each new vista. But their stencils sternly said: PEDESTRIANS WALK—NO BIKES.

A little research showed that Central Park has 6 miles of bridle paths, 6½ of roadway for cars, only 1.7 for bikes. And it has 58 miles of pedestrian walks.

If only, I began to think, if only those 58 could be marked, Never on Sundays, Never on Saturdays, Never on any Afternoon, but Weekday Mornings—Bikes Welcome. Mayor Lindsay, Mr. Heckscher, retroactively, Mr. Hoving—if only!

One day in April I did 5 miles without getting off once. From then on it was 5 every morning, often 6 or 7. I crossed 500, then 600 and wondered, 1,000 by Labor Day? (I made it four days ahead.)

My bike anniversary came in October and fitness and work weren't the whole story. I had grown to know the park as I had never dreamed of knowing it, I, a born New Yorker, living only a few feet from it for years. I got to know every pond and lake and wading pool, every playground and playing field, every unexpected statue (would you believe Beethoven?)

I found out that squirrels will scamper aside at the ring of your bell but that a whole carpet of pigeons will scarcely riffle; what sends them is a sharply aspirated Wheee. I saw the Mall marked off for kids' races and hopscotch, and smelled new-cut grass again, and clover. I got to know which puddles would dry an hour after rain and which needed a full day, when ponds froze over in winter and when they thawed in spring.

I had grown up in a small town in Queens; this, in Central Park, was the feeling once more. It was an urban Walden, lying out there green and gray in cloudy weather, green and bright in the sun, bronze in fall, white in winter, but always there. I never knew before that I loved it.   [10/21/67]

MARIANNE C. MOORE

Crossing Brooklyn Bridge at Twilight

Assets tempt comparison, but I realize that my venerations are tinctured with materialism.

When I arrived in Brooklyn from New York in 1929, the first submarine—or, say, an early submarine—entitled *The Intelligent Whale*, weighing about ten tons, lay inside the Cumberland Street Gate of the Navy Yard. It was a shapely little cylinder of clamshell gray, like a pig.

The Squibb Laboratory was in use—memorialized later by Squibb Park, with a tower and lighted clock, an accommodation greatly welcomed by motorists, marking the end of the Brooklyn Bridge. Dr. Squibb was a Quaker but had been assured by an aunt that it was permissible for him to be a Navy doctor since he would not be killing anybody.

Brooklyn has been called the City of Churches and, one might add, of preachers. Lyman Abbott was pastor of the Plymouth Church and editor of *The Outlook*. Dr. Phillips Elliot, pastor of the First Presbyterian Church of Brooklyn, in a vesper series of lectures, Great Preachers of the Past, included Dr. S. Parkes Cadman, who, when asked what conduces to happiness, said, "A chance of happiness is better if we want to do something than if we want to have something."

The Brooklyn *Daily Eagle* was hospitable to writers resident or on the wing, and quick to detect talent. . . . The evening classes at Brooklyn College attract lively attendance. The Williamsburg Savings Bank clock tower has minutes on its face a foot wide that are visible for miles. . . . High school boys, my neighbors, acquired out-of-date tennis technique from me, on the Fort Greene tennis courts, which are free.

Brooklyn has trees—a group of massive English elms in Fort Greene Park, and sycamores arching over South Portland Avenue; but its crowning curio is the Camperdown Elm in Prospect Park, not far from the boathouse, planted in 1872. It has eighteen cavities, is in need of cleaning and bracing under its heavy horizontal limbs. Funds could make it serve as an outdoor classroom, demonstrating techniques of tree care. Will it be here in 1972? (Camperdown Fund, 171 Congress Street, Brooklyn, Mrs. Graff.)

New York has a waterfront. It has a Mayor of Presidential caliber. It has books: Rizzoli's of international Old World grandeur, and the Gotham Book Mart's New World compactness with Miss Steloff, Philip Lyman and Don Smith in charge on 47th Street. WISE MEN FISH HERE the sign says, and they do.

I have food nearby—a family of relatives named Montvori who wrap the items and buy the best. They may be praised or not. They are businessmen and not vain.

There is the unicorn tapestry in the Cloisters of the Metropolitan Museum; the Museum of Primitive Art on 54th Street; Audubon's cross fox is in the Museum of the City of New York. Some time ago the museum exhibited white sapphires, woven wind scarves and Tipoo's tiger with victim, the Victoria and Albert's automaton.

Brooklyn had a ball team. Roy Campanella and Dazzy Vance. The Mets to begin with had Casey Stengel—a master of restraint and elegant comportment when I made his acquaintance.

The Yankees are having an off season, but their timber is there. As the Boston *Transcript* said of the Harvard crew, "Win or lose, their speed is marvelous." The club with princely food and ball field to match should enable them to flower.

The Pierpont Morgan Library is directed by Frederick B. Adams. Its corridor of notable drawings, calligraphy, illuminated manuscripts, its lectures and music make it exceptional. The Museum of Natural History has a blue whale weighing sixty tons. Asked, "Can I take the Ninth Avenue Elevated to the Museum of Natural History?" the policeman on duty said, "Don't take it. The city needs it."

I like Santa Barbara, Vancouver, British Columbia; have an

incurable fondness for London. But of any cities I have seen, I like New York best. [8/5/67]

MARIANNE C. MOORE

The Library Down the Street in the Village

Jefferson Market Courthouse at the southwest corner of West Tenth Street and Sixth Avenue—now the main Greenwich Village branch of the New York Public Library—stood for two years with the hands of the clock at twenty minutes after two. Then devoted and persistent citizens saved the building from threatened demolition, transforming a particularly awkward architectural elephant into the mascot of Greenwich Village.

Never was there a Village project that had such unanimity. Mrs. Margot Gayle was chairman of the committee of neighbors to get the clock on Jefferson Market Courthouse started. Philip Wittenberg was chairman of the Committee for a Library in Jefferson Market Courthouse. The Honorable Eugene E. Hult was the Mayor's deputy when the library was officially opened on November 27, 1967.

The Jefferson Market Courthouse was built in 1876 and designed by Frederick C. Wither and Calvert Vaux, who with Frederick Law Olmsted was codesigner of Central Park.

The saga of Jefferson Market Courthouse is a true fairy tale of the transformation of our Venetian High Victorian Ruskinian Gothic relic into our chic Village Square Library. Cleaned, or rather "refreshed," was the word of the architect, Giorgio Cavaglieri.

In 1963 the Committee for the Clock paid off their $3,400 debt, having provided the clock with an electric motor. The clock was given new hands, its four faces were repaired, each face 8 feet in diameter. As the clock struck twelve Greenwich Villagers on the balcony of the Jefferson Market Courthouse tower could be seen throwing streamers and waving flags.

There is an extensive reference room in the library basement. Precaution was taken that the air-conditioning equipment at the top of the building would not be visible from the street and spoil the skyline. What was the Second District Court is now the Children's Room. A staff lounge and workroom are connected by a catwalk balcony above the east end of the main reading room. The underside of the spiral stairs to the first floor, simulating an unfurling fan effect, is worth more than a glance—reminding one of the medieval cathedral fan vaulting.

A further reason for pausing when descending the stair, a reminder of Jefferson Courthouse days, are the following sharply chiseled words in Gothic script on the curving stone of the wall: "The precepts of the law are these: to live correctly, to do an injury to none and to render everyone his due."

The liberality of the library staff affords a counterpart to these statements, although who knows what correctness is? The foregoing item could not have existed if two much-incommoded librarians, Miss Smith and Mrs. McCullough, in custody of frail clippings, had not trusted the public and rendered users of Old Jeff a great deal more than their due.

Leaving the building, I saw a long line of children, each with a book to be charged. Every book was protectively covered by cellophane or plastic. They were ideally neat by comparison with the library books in 1923, when I advised boys asking advice in the Hudson Park Children's Room, and might suggest John McGraw's *How to Play Baseball* and Christy Mathewson's *Pitching in a Pinch*.

The young readers did not incommode me or one another and I like my neighborhood very much; whereas in other libraries or city museums I have frequently had to avoid schoolbooks made use of as missiles or shields for the head.

I recalled from my recent Village reading that in early days children glanced up at old Jeff tower clock and got to school on time, and I wondered if Paul Freeman, Assistant Secretary of the Neighborhood Committee and Clock-keeper, may still not have become weary of fund raising. I felt that it would be the final triumph of the restoration of Old Jeff if the big bell on the Courthouse tower could strike the hours again, serving tradesmen, postmen, drugstores and laggards like me who neglect mealtimes when under pressure.

If only the clapper of the great clock on the library tower would continue to afford us its sonorously encouraging harmonies, and go on vibrating through the sometimes quiet streets of Village Square. [5/4/68]

KENNETH CAMPBELL

The Village of Other Days

Plans are afoot to rearrange traffic in Greenwich Village and there is always talk of vigorous methods needed to improve the moral tone of the place. No doubt reform is needed in both sectors. However, all this makes the old Villager exclaim, "What! again?" for somebody has always been taking out after illegal parking, sin or something else in the Village. There are many who love the Village, although it must be admitted that some of them are older members of the great Village alumni body who can think tenderly of the place although they haven't lived there for a long time.

An older generation recalls that when you arrived in New York a complete stranger from, say, the Middle West, with a copy of *Jurgen* and the unshakable conviction that H. L. Mencken knew everything, there really wasn't any place to go but Greenwich Village. Broadway was raucous and crudely unaware of James Branch Cabell. It was the Village that beckoned.

The public image of Greenwich Village in the twenties was formed by the Brevoort crowd—people like Sinclair Lewis,

Nina Wilcox Putnam, Rose O'Neill of the kewpies and perhaps
Edna St. Vincent Millay. Not every newcomer managed to get
into this group any more than he got to know the sometimes
mildly posh people who lived in the so-called "front Village"
—the streets just west of Fifth Avenue. His Village was the
"back Village": Charles Street, Bank Street and thereabouts.

There was an inexhaustible supply of young men and women
from the provinces seeking to escape from having to enter the
family business in some place about which Sinclair Lewis was
writing. There were dozens of places to hang out: the Black
Knight on Macdougal Street and the Stone Wall and the Liberal
Club. Bobby Edwards played his cigar-box ukulele at such
places as the old Pepper Pot in West Fourth Street and sang
his own songs. He sang "The Sultan's wives have got the hives,
Allah be merciful" or pledged himself in song that he "would
bring thee gems from Far Rockaway."

The young women who came to the Village from the provinces were, if memory serves, lovelier than dreams. Betty from
Vassar was working as a fashion designer. Ruth from Ohio Wes-
leyan was writing advertising copy. Esther from Brooklyn was
a dietician. They had a small apartment where the atmosphere
was heavy with art. A small trunk covered with a black cloth
served as a coffee table. They ate by candlelight from a card table. There was an iron bridge lamp with a plain parchment
shade and a square of batik to enliven the wall. A small bookcase set forth Michael Arlen, Dreiser, Carl Van Vechten and
others.

It was the time of prohibition, which rested lightly on Greenwich Village. The first bootlegger was somebody called Spanish
Willy—at least that is the legend. The Italian grocery stores
put a couple of tables in a back room and served *punchenos*
—Italian rum and hot water, an authoritative drink, at 35
cents a glass.

Public balls at Webster Hall and other Village dance places
were fixtures of Village life.

Various Villagers organized them and it was erroneously reported that with a little luck you could make enough out of one of these affairs to live for a year until the next festivity was due. These occasions had such names as The Pagan Route or The White Rabbit. Daring posters promised a frenzied bacchanalia for all ticket holders. But anyone who went expecting something resembling the frantic goings-on at one of the bigger Paris Latin Quarter balls was doomed to disappointment. The quarrelsome reveler was more in evidence than the reveling reveler.

The testiness of the merrymakers was due in part to the quality of the prohibition bathtub gin and to the use of near beer that had been spiked with ether. This last beverage anesthetized rather than intoxicated the drinker. His first act after "coming to" was to count his limbs. Occasionally stout, blue-clad men would arrive from the Mercer Street, or was it the Charles Street, station to remove a few embattled Pagan Route participants in the patrol wagon. But for the most part the Village ball was good fun. Sometimes it was sparsely attended, sentencing the amateur entrepreneur to a spell of dodging an angry printer who had not been paid in full.

But the organizer of the revel always hoped for better luck next year. Many remember the Village as the great national gathering place of the eggheads, as they would now be called, or those who aspired to such status. Many of them came from the provinces and remember a saxophone at the Greenwich Village Inn wrenching agonizing sentiment from "A Sheikh of Araby" far into the night. [3/27/65]

JOHN P. CALLAHAN

Farewell to Coastal Steamers

There is a sadness along the waterfront these days. Once upon a wintertime many of the Hudson River piers echoed the rumble of handcarts toting baggage to the gangplanks of white-hulled coastal steamers that tugged at their hawsers to be off for ports down along the Atlantic and Gulf coasts.

There was a special kind of excitement, a wonderful sense of abandon, when a coastal steamer weighed anchor up through walkable ice floes around the piers; reason enough for a cruise to ports south along our own shores. Just the mention of the ports of call took some of the chill out of a winter day: Richmond, Charleston, Savannah, Jacksonville, Mobile, New Orleans, Corpus Christi—cities that have a nice lazy summer sound to their names. A sail to Florida took two nights and part of a third day, and Norfolk was two and a half days—never long enough.

For nearly half a century the piers along the downtown section of the Hudson River saw the arrival and departure of close to 100 different coastal steamers the year around—165 sailing a month, coming and going with nearly half a million passengers a year. In 1939 this was more than a third of the total number of passengers carried on the transatlantic liners in and out of the port of New York.

Nor was the coastal vessel only a winter lure. In summer, when tar along the city's streets was footprint-soft, the blast of a coastal steamer's whistle meant the start of a cool overnight sail up to Fall River, where in the morning a train would be waiting for the short run to Boston. Twenty dollars covered everything.

Summer and winter, the names of the lines stirred romantic thoughts—Colonial, Clyde-Mallory, Fall River, Morgan, Old Dominion, Savannah—and for many, the luxury of the trip began long before they reached the pier.

It began in the moment of decision, and continued all the way through until the abrupt, inevitable moment of letdown when one walked reluctantly away from the wonderful world of make-believe that was reality for a little while.

It began for some in cozy indolence in a red velvet salon, in a mahogany-paneled dining room, or in the privacy of a stateroom where the push of a button brought a trayful of food and drink. Sleep came easily to the rhythmic throb, the mechanical lullaby of the engines.

But they are all gone now, the great coastal steamers, and when one walks past the old dilapidated piers, north from about Rector Street to 14th Street, a discarded coffee container rolls in a dirt-laden wind to emphasize the hurrying shabbiness of the area. They are gone, victims of war and victims of "progress." Immediately after Pearl Harbor the government requisitioned or bought practically the entire fleet of coastwise freighters and passenger ships. Of the eleven steamship lines that were in the cargo trade, five of them operated freighters that also carried passengers.

Some of the ships went to war as troop carriers, others as hospital ships, and some carried cargoes of war. Few of those that survived the war returned to their former assignments; they were sold abroad or scrapped.

For most of the owners of the coastal steamers, war's end meant the end of that colorful era of travel, an era that began before the turn of the century and, until the late 1920's, was an era of prosperity. But early in the 1930's the inroads of rail competition began to hurt, and operations often were recorded in red ink.

A 1946 study of coastwise shipping by the Port of New York Authority showed that between 1931 and 1940 nine steamship companies operating coastal services lost more than $4,000,000 —not because there was a lack of business; rather, because operating costs had risen beyond income. This was also the reason given the other day for ending the Furness Bermuda Line's forty-six years of cruises between this port and Bermuda.

Coincidentally, and steadily thereafter, the coastal lines went out of business while the railroads expanded their freight service. The airlines increased passenger service. The coastal passenger trade was dead. Who would think of spending a night getting to Boston when a plane could get you there in an hour?

The answer probably is thousands of persons, but apparently the stringent economic law of little or no return dissuades steamship operators who might want to revive the service.

[3/5/⁶⁶]

JAMES TUITE

The Sounds of Manhattan

New York is a city of sounds: muted sounds and shrill sounds; shattering sounds and soothing sounds; urgent sounds and aimless sounds. The cliff dwellers of Manhattan—who would be racked by the silence of the lonely woods—do not hear these sounds because they are constant and eternally urban.

The visitor to the city can hear them, though, just as some animals can hear a high-pitched whistle inaudible to humans. To the casual caller to Manhattan, lying restive and sleepless in a hotel twenty or thirty floors above the street, they tell a story as fascinating as life itself. And back of the sounds broods the silence.

Night in midtown is the noise of tinseled honky-tonk and violence. Thin strains of music, usually the firm beat of rock 'n' roll or the frenzied outbursts of the discotheque, rise from ground level. This is the cacophony, the discordance of youth, and it comes on strongest when nights are hot and young blood restless.

Somewhere in the canyons below there is shrill laughter or raucous shouting. A bottle shatters against concrete. The whine of a police siren slices through the night, moving ever closer, until an eerie Doppler effect brings it to a guttural halt.

There are few sounds so exciting in Manhattan as those of fire apparatus dashing through the night. At the outset there is the tentative hint of the first-due company bullying his way through midtown traffic. Now a fire whistle from the opposite direction affirms that trouble is, indeed, afoot. In seconds, other sirens converging from other streets help the skytop listener focus on the scene of excitement.

But he can only hear and not see, and imagination takes flight. Are the flames and smoke gushing from windows not far away? Are victims trapped there, crying out for help? Is it a conflagration, or only a trash-basket fire? Or, perhaps, it is merely a false alarm.

The questions go unanswered and the urgency of the moment dissolves. Now the mind and the ear detect the snarling, arrogant bickering of automobile horns. People in a hurry. Taxicabs blaring, insisting on their checkered priority.

Even the taxi horns dwindle down to a precocious few in the gray and pink moments of dawn. Suddenly there is another sound, a morning sound that taunts the memory for recognition. The growl of a predatory monster? No, just garbage trucks that have begun a day of scavenging.

Trash cans rattle outside restaurants. Metallic jaws on sanitation trucks gulp and masticate the residue of daily living, then digest it with a satisfied groan of gears.

The sounds of the new day are businesslike. The growl of buses, so scattered and distant at night, becomes a demanding part of the traffic bedlam. An occasional jet or helicopter injects an exclamation point from an unexpected quarter. When the wind is right, the vibrant bellow of an ocean liner can be heard.

The sounds of the day are as jarring as the glare of a sun that outlines the canyons of midtown in drab relief. A pneumatic drill frays countless nerves with its rat-a-tat-tat, for dig they must to perpetuate the city's dizzy motion. After each screech of brakes there is a moment of suspension, of waiting for the thud or crash that never seems to follow.

The whistles of traffic policemen and hotel doormen chirp from all sides, like birds calling for their mates across a frenzied aviary. And all of these sounds are adult sounds, for childish laughter has no place in these canyons.

Night falls again, the cycle is complete, but there is no surcease from sound. For the beautiful dreamers, perhaps, the "sounds of the rude world heard in the day, lulled by the moonlight have all passed away," but this is not so in the city.

Too many New Yorkers accept the sounds about them as bland parts of everyday existence. They seldom stop to listen to the sounds, to think about them, to be appalled or enchanted by them. In the big city, sounds are life.   [8/6/66]

H. I. BROCK

Anniversary of an Obelisk

The seventy-fifth anniversary of the setting up of New York's oldest monument, from which more than thirty centuries look down on Central Park, comes at a time when the land out of which that hunk of red syenite was quarried for a busy builder called Thothmes III is giving cause of concern to a world divided, and one side of it, at least, not sure where it is going next. It is not irrelevant, therefore, that while the present ruler of Egypt seems to aim at a leading role in a Near Eastern concert, the giver of that monument is the man who said: "Egypt is no longer in Africa, it is a part of Europe."

He was Ismail, Khedive, or Viceroy there, of the Sultan of Turkey. But he had been partly educated in Paris, and had introduced into his satrapy many European practices and devices —including the institution of credit for floating loans—and measures for advancing progress on the European model. He spared no pains to contrive for himself—though his country was only one of Turkey's provinces—rank among European sovereigns, and so far succeeded that he was received by Queen Victoria and welcomed by London's Lord Mayor.

International importance was lent to his adventures by the fact that the Suez Canal was in process. Begun in 1854, when his uncle and predecessor Said had granted the concession to

Ferdinand de Lesseps, the formal opening in 1869 provided opportunity to claim the rank he coveted and give and receive royal honors. The Empress Eugénie was on board the *Aigle* leading the procession of sixty-odd vessels of many nations assembled at Port Said for the ceremonial first passage, and one account says Francis Joseph of Austria was also present. In any case it was a big international show for Ismail.

Not long afterward, Ismail's extravagance, and especially his lavish use of credit, resulted in the taking over of Egypt's finances by representatives of France and England. He was invited to resign, and when he refused was deposed in 1879—made ex-Khedive by the Sultan, with the title passed on to his son Tewfik. It is an item of interest that when he had to sell in 1875 his block of Canal shares—44 percent of the lot—and they were bought by England, it was Benjamin Disraeli who assumed responsibility for the transaction, and thus, like Thomas Jefferson in the case of the Louisiana Purchase, consciously assumed a power he knew was not his. For the record the price paid for the shares was nearly £4,000,000.

This corner some years ago told the story of how the obelisk—Ismail's gift to us along with another to England—had been first set up about 1600 B.C. in Heliopis and taken to Alexandria by Augustus, and how it was brought to New York by a distinguished naval officer with the unlikely name of Henry Honeychurch Gorringe, who volunteered for the task. With W.H. Vanderbilt footing the bill, Gorringe had taken down the hunk of stone, 69 feet tall and weighing more than 200 tons, rolled it on cannonballs into the hold of one of the Khedive's ships, had it transferred to pontoons at Staten Island, towed by the steamer *Manhattan* up the Hudson to 96th Street and thence conveyed across Central Park and down Fifth Avenue to the knoll behind the Metropolitan Museum where it now stands.

If you ask why it is called "obelisk," that's Greek for "spit," the thing used to roast meat by the fire. The word refers to the shape—a long, narrow object tapering toward one end and pointed. Curiously, it means "little spit"—in spite of the size of the object to which it is applied. Our familiar name for the monument—"Cleopatra's Needle"—disregards history but keeps in mind the same shape on an even more reduced scale.

[1/24/56]

FRED M. HECHINGER

What the Taxi Panel Overlooked

The Mayor's Taxi Study Panel has come up with many recommendations which the cab-riding public will not contest. More taxis will mean less waiting in rain and snow unless all the new cabs are to be equipped with permanent OFF-DUTY signs, as the majority of old ones appear to be. The search for a vehicle that can be entered and left without spinal injury or indecent exposure will also meet with widespread approval, though few will understand why that search must venture beyond London's perfectly designed taxis or America's tolerable Checkers.

What the commission has failed to come to grips with is the human factor. What does it intend to do about the problems posed by the psyche of that man behind the wheel?

The most ordinary variety is the Common Misanthrope. He is no bigot. He does not focus his dislike on any minority. He just hates people. Without regard to race, color, creed or nationality.

This prototype also hates his wife, and without the slightest encouragement he will enumerate her foibles. She is the only reason why he drives a cab. To get away from her.

The people he hates more than all others are those who ride in his cab. "I remember," one of them said recently, his voice thick with nostalgia and Brooklyn, "when all them clowns used to go home on the subway instead of fighting for cabs."

Then there is the Music Lover. His radio is permanently turned on full blast, and the only sounds louder than "Why

Ain't You Lovin' Me?" are the commercial "messages" that follow. A request to reduce the volume is met with so constant a flow of inadequately suppressed grumbling about "people who think they own the cab just for a lousy 50-cent tip" that the guilt-ridden passenger is likely to ask the driver's pardon, sing along with The Animals and offer to pay handsome indemnity in the end.

A different kind of problem is raised by the Bookkeeper. Whenever it seems quite feasible to pass the green traffic light comfortably, he slows down or stops altogether to cope with elaborate bookkeeping operations on his work sheet. In the process he not only misses the light but forgets the current passenger's destination.

Another variety is the Social Philosopher who, just as the passenger relaxes in his seat, launches into a lecture on the follies of humanity as seen through the rear-view mirror. "The things I could tell you," he begins, and he tells them. Usually the monologue is directed at the moral depravity of passengers—especially female. Even so moral an agent as he finds it impossible to do justice to the topic without the use of the kind of profanity best remembered from the barracks.

A variation on the same theme is the Political Analyst, probably the cousin of the cabbie in Damascus and Danzig who is so regularly quoted as an incontestable authority by foreign correspondents. He finds evil everywhere—in Democrats, Republicans, Liberals, labor and management. "They're all the same," he sums up. "They all stink."

There are the innumerable subcategories. There are the Cigar Chewers who lay down a smoke screen between themselves and the passenger. There are the Cigarette Flippers who thrust smoldering ashes out their front window into the passenger's compartment. There is the Downtown Specialist who mutters angrily for the duration of an uptown fare, and vice versa. There is the cabbie who treats a $5 bill as if it were unredeemable Soviet currency. And there is the frustrated comedian who breaks into the crucial moment of a business conversation with a story you have heard—as did he—on television the night before.

None of these fundamental issues has been faced by the Mayor's commission. It is all well and good to call for bullet-proof glass between driver and passenger to protect the cabbie. But what, unless the glass is sound- and smokeproof as well, is to protect the passenger? Clearly the answers are to be found in the one-way speaking tube of yesteryear and in the creation of the brand-new position of fleet psychiatrist.   [2/11/67]

RICHARD F. SHEPARD

Putting a Foot Down on the Lowly Pedestrian

Is it time to put the pedestrian under control? He's been getting away scot-free for centuries, walking on public and private pavement, crossing streets that are built with money from gasoline taxes, living the life of an Indian cow. Automobiles are not allowed to touch him, whatever he does. He has no responsibilities. Is this right? Is this responsible?

There is a feeling among automobile clubs, and similar groups dedicated to Americans who are too proud to leave driving to them, that the American driver is much too harassed and can't stand for much more. As a matter of fact, he can't because he will be towed away from a no-standing zone if he does.

He is lured into town by new highways and, on arrival, accorded a welcome of the sort reserved for the bubonic plague. He has to dash into his friendly bank to borrow money to feed up-priced parking meters and he is warned to be off the streets by sunup. It's time to find another patsy.

We can't bother trucks, buses and taxis. They are too busy servicing us. No, wheeled traffic has about had it. However there is the American pedestrian, an unorganized, pressureless group that is, to be sure, dwindling in the footless move toward automobiles. But it certainly is still there as an annoyance. There are controls that simply cry out to be imposed.

First of all there is no constitutional guarantee of freedom to walk in the streets. Americans may assemble, demonstrate, print newspapers, store arms and refuse to quarter troops. But nobody has ever said a word about pedestrianism.

No civil liberties group has ever questioned the right to control the walker, even when New York City made it a crime to cross a street against a DON'T WALK sign, without regard to whether a pedestrian was blind, illiterate or crippled. In other words, the pedestrian is made responsible for observing traffic as much as the driver who has to buy his license and pay for being controlled even more stringently.

Oh, there are the visionaries who will lament that walking is the last uncertificated liberty left to man, but this bleeding-heart philosophy is as *dernier-siècle* as the idea that people should be left to starve on their own initiative. It doesn't fit our modern era.

Control need not be negative. For instance, mandatory licensing of pedestrians can bring great revenue to government. It will also require an administration that will make the Motor Vehicles Bureau seem like a ma-and-pa candy store—after all, most drivers are also pedestrians when they get out of the car, although many never do.

This would stimulate great employment and jobs for underprivileged pedestrians. The fee schedule could be based on a number of factors. Perhaps on weight, because it takes a fat pedestrian longer to waddle across a street than it does for a thin, fast model. Perhaps on traffic volume in the home neighborhood, although expressways in the backyard would have to be exempted because they are not supposed to be crossed. Or a special tax on shoes could be levied with a special assessment when old shoes go to the cobbler for new heels and soles and government inspection.

Pedestrians would have to take tests to be licensed. Those with slower reflexes and an inability to dodge a car moving at thirty miles an hour would get special licenses requiring them to use certain corners, where government guides would take them across every ten minutes or so.

Parking meters for pedestrians who stand and chat on sidewalks, that are designed to move foot traffic might also be helpful in relieving midtown congestion. There are plans downtown to revive walk-in banks, and a new walk-in movie house, the first in many years, is going to be built in midtown. The concept of pedestrian controls opens up entire new vistas for urban government. It is not often that civic responsibility may be nurtured by renouncing liberty for license.

There are a number of traffic regulations that could be forced upon pedestrians. They would have to be insured, of course. With all the small cars around, it is not inconceivable that a sturdy pedestrian could do incalculable damage in collision with a vest-pocket model. Ill-lit pedestrians are the cause of many accidents. Therefore, walkers should illuminate themselves from a half hour before sunset until a half hour after dawn.

This all cries for a foundation study. A grant would have to determine whether one white light would be sufficient or whether a pedestrian should have red and green port and starboard running lights. Obviously, we are not yet ready for taillights.

[7/13/68]

RICHARD F. SHEPARD

Fat Men of the World, Unite

There's a new design in buses and usually well-rounded circles are wondering whether there shouldn't be a civilian review board for the Transit Authority.

The board would, of course, include members of that large minority, the people of healthy girth who find that the new look ignores their well-being. The buses have side seats only, so that the passenger sits with his back to the windows. Not only are they modified bucket seats, but someone has thought to put a metal bar separating the row into two-seat compartments.

There are questions being asked. What lean Cassius perpetrated this design that forces the well-fed either to stand or to intrude their bulk boorishly on their partner? At times, the squeeze borders on molestation. In the old buses, where some seats were at right angles to the side, the man of great girth could overhang in the aisle and avoid the opprobrium that others, perhaps silently, heap upon him.

Does this restrictive pattern, asked one man large in spirit and body, indicate that the Transit Authority is thinking in terms of a depression in the belief that people, instead of growing with the era, are in for a period of malnutrition? Are the buses by chance made in Japan, where people are smaller? Was there a survey of size before the design went to the factory? If so, was the decision based on an average size, which is no help at all to the man who pulls the average up?

Obviously, the question goes deeper than buses. The affluent society has apparently spawned its Reformation, a reaction against the well-fed and a campaign for physical fitness just at the time when American life is at the point when people can eat, drink and be slothful. We are told that the world is full of thin men who threaten us, probably because they too want to get fat. There are times, as one muses upon it all while enjoying beer and potato chips, when it is reminiscent of *Kraft durch Freude*.

The paradox is that while the overweight, the really overweight, are a minority, they don't speak up in their own behalf. They are the victims of deep-seated inferiorities and want to be thin, like everybody else. They feel rootless because they have learned that it is thin men who have done everything worth doing in the world. Of course, this historical distortion is easily refuted by anyone who remembers Benjamin Franklin, Oliver Hardy, William Howard Taft and Santa Claus.

There is a crying need for a new program, federally subsi-

dized if need be, to fill the fat men with as much pride as cal-
ories. Avoirdupois must be encouraged. Underweight people
don't like being skinny, and this knowledge could be exploited.
Perhaps the trim majority may yet be induced to join with the
minority against the new busing practices.

At a time when transit fares are heading up, it is unfair to
put the pinch on the plump, especially when it puts a squeeze
on the thin. Let down the bars, the cry is heard. Let passengers
in a free society realize their full measure. Compression is oppression. Fat men of the world, unite—don't arise, sit down.
You should have a seat in the great society.   [7/23/66]

RICHARD F. SHEPARD

A Word for the New York Accent

They've been trying to abolish it for years. Teachers attack it. Students resist it. Users regret it, but it's harder to give
up than smoking. It and obscenity may often keep you off the
air. It's altogether unforgivable.

It, of course, is the New York accent. It's probably the city's
longest-lived landmark and it is the one that everyone is trying
to stamp out.

A fine German accent may bolster a psychiatrist's fee. A crisp
British accent simply cries for a lecture tour. Regional varia-
tions across the city line command affectionate toleration. To
speak as they do in Dixie—as long as it's intelligible—is a sentimental plus. The New England twang conjures up visions of
democracy in the raw, small townsmen going to meeting and de-
bating about raising money by lottery. The pioneer spirit in-
fests the Western drawl, even when it emanates from a mouth
that never shouted at a cow. Modified Midwestern is to us what
Florentine is to Italian, the standard, the stated norm that few
from elsewhere can more than approximate.

But they abominate the New York accent. New Yorkers abominate it, too. In school, patient teachers, with frustrating results, try to extirpate local aberrations, such as *oi* for *er, er* for *oi*, the *dese, dems* and *doses*, the *whatcha* for *what are you* and the lamentable, mystifying disappearance of the *r* that makes *Noo Yawkers* rush to *fi-uhs* when the *alahm* bell rings.

Add to this, ethnic variants with rising intonations and brutally misemphasized consonants and the city emerges as a linguistic disaster area, a desperate zone of pear-shaped poverty, in which even sizable federal aid will show no pronounced results. There are many degrees of disability; many New Yorkers have contrived to color their diction with accepted resonances and inflections, along with such critical minima as clear expression of *th's* and careful avoidance of caricaturelike vocal extremes.

Now, is the New York accent really all that bad? The answer, doubtless, is a resounding yeah. But it need not be so; that is a culturally bred reaction and nothing that a little positive thinking can't cure.

Happily, we have become a great nation and our immigrants have turned into true-blue Yankees, looking for roots. There is a passion for antiques dating back to Colonial days and homes with Ol' Virginny columns. We are in a preservation mood. We want to preserve old buildings. Why no old accents?

It is not as if the New York accent doesn't suit the environment. It is a rough-cut affair, matching the jagged skyline. It is as noisily slurred as a subway rush. It is as guttural as a traffic jam. If New Yorkers speak loudly without opening their mouths, it's not only a physiological triumph, it also avoids inhalation of the polluted air.

It is the dialect that unifies the fastest town in the world. It wastes no time on colorful metaphors and drawled verities. It runs toward a deed, a deal or a dollar, anything that has a goal from the most concrete transaction to the most abstruse research. It is not a time waster. It is the hurry-up, short-order accent of America.

This doesn't make it the best. But it doesn't make it the worst, either. Granted, New Yorkers should vocalize so that they may be understood by other English-speaking peoples (who have their problems, too, as anyone who has looked in on the Midlands can attest).

But must our accent be rooted out? Under New York's landmark laws, certain ancient buildings may be built anew inside but not a brick on the outside may be touched. Is there no way to harness the accent and its vigor, to reach a happy medium that will allow for some internal refurbishing while preserving the rugged exterior? Something between Mayor Lindsay and Zero Mostel?

It's one of the few things left to us that is untaxed and that we may call our own.   [11/5/66]

RICHARD F. SHEPARD

A Passion for Place Names

Talk about new nations assuming new names, they are doing it right here in New York. The Lower East Side, for instance, has been renamed East Village, much as a Broadway play comes back as a Broadway musical under a new title. The general layout is the same, but the tone has changed.

Why East Village? The Lower East Side was as strong on beards as East Village, but they hang differently somehow in East Village. The beards used to be the last link with the old country. Now they are the first break with the new country.

The young creative spirits populating East Village are displaced persons from West Village, better known as Greenwich Village. The word "village" is the key word. It indicates a closed, quaint world where the locals may conduct their own affairs without submitting to the pressures of the Outside.

The spirit of Greenwich Village—and in New York, all place

names refer to states of mind and status rather than to geography—was, of course, free-flying and unbound. It's where people go when they get disgusted enough with back home and look for a place to write about where they come from.

Such a conglomeration of intellectual, artistic and literary talents was certain to attract attention. People wanted to splash in the creative caldron and moved in, more people than the old neighborhood could handle. With the pressure of population hungry to share the quaint and narrow precincts with the thoughtful, buildings started to go up, sometimes replacing the tumbledown houses that were the flavorsome backdrops to the scene.

Other housing was renovated, rents went up, and where could a young fellow in from the provinces set up his angry shop in New York? No room in Greenwich Village, and the young man went east, bringing the paraphernalia of his generation with him, the coffee shop, the discotheque, the Off-Off Broadway. As a testament to the hegemony of the Greenwich Village spirit, the name East Village was foreordained.

As a matter of fact, the case could be made that East Village has become a Greenwich Village, while Greenwich Village—shades of Macdougal Street and its bizarre bazaar!—has become a Coney Island. Coney Island, where one can hear Spanish and English in almost equal volume, has become, perhaps, a Miramar.

And, meanwhile, what of the Lower East Side? It is still there, its natives as uneasily cheek by jowl with the invaders as the natives of Greenwich Village have been for many years with their transients. Many Lower East Siders of the past have broken through to the Upper East Side, another condition of life, a high-rent one, and will be able to tell their offspring of hard days in East Village.

The passion that place names evoke is typified by Harlem, that euphemism for a Negro neighborhood. Where Harlem once concentrated in an area north of Central Park and to the east of the island, it has spread north, south and west, mingling with

Washington Heights and the West Side. Some Negroes have
complained with justice that when an event long on civic virtue, whatever its color, occurs, it is said to happen in Upper
Manhattan. When it is something controversial about the Negro
community, there is no hesitation about placing it in Harlem.

These are the changing tides of the city that have kept Riv-
erdale apart from the Bronx, and Brooklyn out of Long Island
for so many years. Perhaps since the Hudson has become polluted, it is no longer necessary to distinguish the lordly uptown
reaches of the stream from the workaday downtown stretch
of North River. It is comforting at least to know that lo mein is
still in Chinatown and that the money is still in Wall Street.

[5/13/67]

A. H. RASKIN

The Commencement Day Uprising
(Class of '31)

The members of the Class of 1931 at City College read
with a certain nostalgia the threat of some members of the
Class of 1968 at Columbia to boycott their own Commencement
exercises.

The CCNY class—best remembered by this generation of
student rebels because it gave them one of the New Left's most
revered gurus, Paul Goodman—saw a good many middle-class
values go down the drain in the stock market crash of 1929.
When the sons of the furriers, the garment workers and the
candy store owners came to St. Nicholas Heights in 1927,
Calvin Coolidge and Herbert Hoover were assuring the country
of eternal prosperity.

By the time the class was ready to graduate, a quarter of the
work force was jobless, and disappointed dabblers in people's
capitalism were leaping out of Wall Street windows.

The class didn't take out its frustrations by seizing campus buildings, but it found plenty of other ways to bedevil the college administration. A few weeks before Commencement, the college president, the late Frederick B. Robinson, retaliated by informing the senior class president that he could not exercise his traditional role of marshal in the procession.

The class head had managed to make himself a special irritant as editor of the student newspaper—a premature Mark Rudd, agitating for everything from edible food in the college cafeteria to closing the brand-new School of Business as a misbegotten hatchery for malefactors of great wealth.

Dr. Robinson sought to take the edge off his ukase by persuading some less obnoxious class luminary to take over the vacant post as marshal. The intercollegiate one-mile champion—the first and last in City College history—was among the first to be tapped. He said no. The heads of undergraduate organizations, the captains of athletic teams, all the other big men on campus were called in, one by one, and asked to lead the graduation march. All said they would not scab on their president. Solidarity forever.

Finally, the administration found its man—a dreary grind who was slated to become a tutor in classical languages at the college. He was summoned away from Virgil and Horace long enough to be told he would be marshal—or else. The Sanhedrin of campus rebels met the appointment by calling on the Class of '31 to go on strike against its own Commencement. The class would march behind its president or it would march on a mass picket line outside Lewisohn Stadium in cap and gown with yellow armbands saying WE PROTEST.

Came the fateful night. The administration did not budge. Neither did the class. An hour before the ceremonies all the black-robed graduates gathered under the quizzical eyes of the gargoyles in the marble entry hall of the main building on Convent Avenue. The mission: issuance of the armbands and assignment of picket posts.

But, first, a brave gesture in the spirit of *morituri te salutamus*. The class officers had received from the uniform shop that rented out the caps and gowns the time-consecrated kick-back of something over $200, a sum that customarily vanished into the officers' pockets. No such trafficking with Mammon this time.

By vote of the class council, taken then and there, the money was turned over to the college as a scholarship fund. The class president tore a page out of a loose-leaf notebook and scribbled a message to Dr. Robinson asking that the gift be announced at the exercises. The graduates would cheer from outside the gates.

That still left thirty minutes to kill before the funeral parade for academic freedom. A small voice of defeatism began to emerge in the throng. After all, said someone, we've spent four years here. A lot of us plan to go to medical school or law school. The college doesn't have to give us our degrees. What's more, it probably won't. We won't be able to take the License Number One examination for teacher in the school system. We won't even be able to work in the post office. The Depression has put our parents in hock; they can't support us. We'll be derelicts, Bowery bums; life ends at twenty.

The small voice became a panicky roar. Suddenly, everyone broke and ran. The gargoyles giggled down on a marble floor littered with torn WE PROTEST armbands. The class fell in behind its apostate marshal. Even I, class president, was in line.

Of course, none of it has much relevance to what's happening in this era of mink-cushioned rebellion. Now the campus heretic has no end of outrages to crusade against—Vietnam, the draft, turmoil in the cities, hypocritical adult standards. And who need worry about such mundane distractions as working or any other bond of enslavement to the corrupt system? It all helps keep the mind clear so that a rebel can see how rotten things really are.   [6/1/68]

LEWIS NICHOLS

Chowder, Two Types

As they wander along the Eastern Seaboard this summer, vacationers from unspecified outer spaces will come upon an item of diet called clam chowder. Residents of the seaboard will find it, too, and more familiar with it, will go to endless lengths in order to track it down. Indeed, one of the best vacations of all is to move slowly, not just from place to place, but from chowder bowl to chowder bowl. To the uninitiated, however, let there be a note of warning this morning. There is a type of clam chowder named Manhattan. Beware it. It is not the true chowder. Manhattan is the name of an excellent song and a cocktail, and a borough that is nice to visit and to live in during the summer, and it is possible to enjoy these down the length of a lifetime. But not Manhattan clam chowder. If the menu says only clam chowder, demand to know which type. If the waiter won't say, remember that the markings of Manhattan are as distinct as those of a copperhead snake or a rattler. It is reddish, the result of adding to real chowder an alien substance called tomatoes.

Let it be understood at once that no attempt is being made here to denounce tomatoes, per se. They have a great many uses and values, one of which is that they will grow practically anywhere, thus assuring even the most wretched of gardeners a visible, tangible crop. Tomatoes are excellent in salads, and sliced and gently treated with a little sprinkle of salt, pepper and sugar. They are good stewed, mixed with bread to give body, and when separated from the pulp, the juice is fine of a morning. They can be used to stretch out a meal, when unexpected guests drop in and give no sign of leaving at suppertime, and they are used to stretch many a meal when the budget is a little weak toward the end of the month. It is possible that some cooks rely on them a little too much, and when thinking of a casserole dish immediately and by instinct reach for the tomatoes and the rice. This does not matter, for the casserole virtues of tomatoes exceed the cook's one vice. In short, tomatoes are worthy of the lyricist's best songs, the poet's most thoughtful muse. But tomatoes do not belong in clam chowder.

The only real chowder is, of course, New England clam chowder, although to sit here in Manhattan and say so has all the ugly markings of betrayal. Sorry, but a fact is a fact, and there it is. New England chowder is so made that each ingredient— the potato, butter, bacon, onion, cream, paprika, whatever else —does no more than delicately point up the wonderful taste of clam. Smother this unique combination of ambrosia and nectar with tomatoes, and you have a kind of tomato soup, little else. When making the real chowder, even the cans containing tomatoes should be turned so that the labels face the wall—or removed from the kitchen altogether—lest even a hint of tomato get near the clams. It even is advisable that all cookbooks containing recipes for tomatoes be carried elsewhere until the chowder is finished, for even a fleeting idea is enough to wreck the chowder. It must be remembered that a clam has delicate little edges, and nothing can curl these quite so fast as a tomato.

The best type of New England clam chowder is, of course, the one which takes a good part of the day in preparation. Anyone can buy clams, for the supermarkets are filled with them, but these are not the ideal chowder clams. The ideal ones are those detected with bare toes, as little bumps in the smooth sand. Dig there with the fingers, and if the bump is not caused by an empty shell, it may well be a couple of tablespoons of the evening's chowder. The sun warms the back and the water of the bay is soothing as bump after bump yields up its treasure, and as the pile of clams grows, so does the appetite. Pay no attention to this; let the appetite howl in anguish, for a good chowder must not be hurried, everything must go into it just so. Probably it was the notorious impatience of New Yorkers, hearkening to appetite, which brought about Manhattan chowder in the first place. Someone just opened a can of tomatoes as the easiest handy thing to stretch out an insufficient number of clams, and to do so quickly. So the great deception began. [7/11/63]

CHARLES SIMMONS

Egg-Boiling Variables

To sit down in a New York restaurant and order a three-minute egg is the act of an improvident man. He might as well ask for a boiled egg, or simply an egg. For some reason, casual egg eaters feel that specifying the time an egg is to be boiled will give them a certain result. This notion is based on the fallacy that since the temperature of boiling water is constant the only variable in egg boiling is the duration of cooking. A moment's consideration reveals a second variable: the size of the egg. A small egg will achieve a given consistency much more quickly than a large egg. Therefore the egg eater of discrimination should ask for, say, a two-and-a-half-minute small egg or a four-minute large egg.

Even when the two variables of time and size are given due attention the egg eater still can never be sure of the outcome. A strange and perverse phenomenon occurs inside some shells which leads imaginative egg eaters to suspect a vindictiveness on the part of certain eggs. In these eggs the yolk is not centrally suspended in the white, not evenly insulated by the albumen, and since the yolk virtually touches one side of the shell it congeals, while the white at the egg's center remains fluid. To open such an egg is a disconcerting experience for the egg eater who delights in hard whites and soft yolks. The hard-boiled-egg eater, of course, rarely notices this occasional displacement or, if he does, looks upon it with no more concern than on a prize discovered at the top rather than the bottom of his Cracker Jack box.

Hard-boiled-egg eaters are, on the whole, an insensitive bunch. But the type sometimes produces a mutant of extreme refinement who demands that the egg be hard-boiled to a certain point—a pretty conceit. Seven minutes, a member of this effete group may maintain, produces *the* egg; eight minutes, a horny object not edible by civilized human or domesticated beast. There are those, too, who claim that the cold egg taken from the refrigerator must be immersed in cold water and warmed gradually as the water is warmed. The sudden shock, they feel, of dipping a chilled egg into boiling water shatters the delicate overtones of taste.

But, however the egg's temperature is to be raised, precautions must be taken. Letting the egg slip through but a quarter of an inch of water to the bottom of the pan may crack the shell. A boiling egg with a cracked shell, as every egg boiler knows, emerges a monstrosity. Albumen escaping from the egg will congeal and form a benign tumor of grotesque contour on the shell. This hardened excrescence is both nourishing and tasty, but fastidious egg eaters shudder at the sight and turn to their cornflakes. Gentle deposition alone will not ensure against cracking. Vigorously boiling water often tosses an egg about enough to break the shell. Tranquilly moving water seems to be the safest and kindliest environment the egg lover can provide his egg with during its trying time of change.

Given a boiled egg of known consistency, the exacting egg eater, to ensure the fullest pleasure, will always demand a certain setting for his morsel. Egg eaters tending toward sensuality prefer their egg shelled and alone on a flat saucer. This type has the highest regard for the egg not pocked by careless peeling. And the sag of the egg, for them, tells immediately if the egg has been cooked to their specifications. The real test, of course, is always the first tender incision of the spoon. Eggcup users stand their eggs small end up. Most prefer the tap-and-peel method of shelling. But crueler temperaments will gouge off the crown, egg white and shell together. The end thus opened, this type proceeds excavation-style.

Boiled-egg eaters, whatever their crudities or decadent refinements, are, broadly, a loyal lot. They will eat an occasional fried egg or two at a friend's house for the sake of the bacon, or give in to a specialty at a restaurant featuring poached egg on corned-beef hash, even put away a barbarously homogeneous omelet once in a while. But one thing an orthodox boiled-egg man will never do—he will never lay fork on scrambled eggs. Scrambled eggs is a dangerous and ill-advised diversion. Boiled-egg eaters of long and honorable tenure have been known to have their sense of taste so perverted by scrambled eggs that they never enjoyed a boiled egg again. [5/7/52]

HERBERT MITGANG

Garden Spot of America, Sort Of

A street in Brooklyn renamed for the Honorable Peter J. McGuinness? Well, why not? Time has a way of making statesmen out of rogues, especially charming ones. And he certainly done a lot for Greenpoint, with its Newtown Creek serving as a small harbor on the East River, which the Honorable used to call the "garden spot of America." Greenpernters are in his debt.

When McGuinness served his neighborhood in the late 1920's and early 1930's, he did so as part of a remarkable Brooklyn Democratic machine which lived in a barony of palship protecting its own Our Thing. The three musketeers there were McCooey, McQuade and McGuinness. "Uncle John" H. McCooey was the Democratic boss of Kings County for more than two decades. From his post as clerk of the Surrogate's Court, he named Supreme Court judges, including his own callow son. The Honorable James A. McQuade, a county register, ran a horse parlor in his clubhouse, and managed to accumulate more than a half million dollars in six years. It was really not a gambling house, McQuade said; it was a "library." However, the only literature ever discovered in McQuade's library was "Armstrong's Scratch Sheet."

The Honorable McGuinness had been an alderman before stepping up to the post of assistant commissioner of public works. He doubled in brass as "executive member of the Greenpoint People's Regular Democratic Organization of the Fifteenth Assembly District," which made him a political rival of the Honorable McQuade, who came from the same neighborhood. McGuinness used to call McQuade "Payroll Jim, the Jesse James of Greenpoint," because there were so many McQuades on the city payroll.

But McGuinness considered himself a servant of the peepul. When he left his job as alderman for public works, he said: "I drove nine gypsy bands out of Greenpoint, as well as three hundred Chinese coolies and all the cats and dogs that used to run down the streets. One of the best things I done was to establish a farm garden so children could learn the real value of vegetables. I got Greenpoint three playgrounds, the subway, the one-and-a-half-million-dollar bridge on Greenpoint Avenue, and two million dollars' worth of paving. I done good. I thank you."

In the course of his investigation in 1931-1932 into the affairs of the City of New York, Judge Samuel Seabury put Greenpoint's benefactor on the witness stand and thereby received a lesson in semantics. McGuinness was describing a midnight police raid on his political clubhouse. He said that he hid behind a pillar when the knock came and yelled a warning to the gamblers in the club.

Judge Seabury inquired, "Did you say, 'Here comes the police' or 'Cheese it, the police'?"

"No, Judge," McGuinness said. "Cheese it, here comes the cops!"

Judge Seabury bowed and said, "I stand corrected."

The street named for McGuinness will bear the name of an authentic character, a sort of Honey Fitz of Kings County, who laid it on with a trowel and left them laughing while taking care of McGuinness.

He certainly was among New York's greatest defenders. "You can't find a more moral race of people on the face of the globe, I bet you can't," he declared. "There is no more profanity here than anywhere else in the country. New Yorkers may swear on impulse but never from the heart. New York has the healthiest air in the country. What if the girls go for few clothes? The good air gets to their bodies easier and makes 'em healthier."

When a police commissioner in the 1920's called McGuinness a "two-cent politician," the silver-tongued Greenpointer answered, "When I am attacked as a two-cent politician, the police commissioner don't realize that the pictures of Lincoln and Washington and Grant and Harding are on the two-cent stamps of the nation. I am proud to be rated with Lincoln and Washington. I thank you."

Well, maybe just a *small* street near Newtown Creek will do.

[2/24/64]

HERBERT MITGANG

Draw One Concentrated Beer

At the Third Avenue-type saloon on Eighth Avenue a couple of the regulars were discussing a subject close to hand—namely, beer. A rumor flew up and down the long mahogany bar that next month automation was going to hit the kegs. Or, rather, a first cousin of automation called concentration. The United States Treasury Department has approved the concentration and reconstitution of the stuff with a label saying: BEER —MADE FROM BEER CONCENTRATES. How the Feds get into the act is that the Alcohol and Tobacco Tax Division puts the arm on beer and thus on the gargler himself.

Anyway, the barflies wondered, was this another blow to

those who believed in beer for beer's sake? Here it was four
o'clock in the afternoon, perfect beer-drinking time—too
late to go back to work after lunch and too early to go home
to dinner—and how many such hours of quiet wonder remained? It was bad enough when they took down the El on
Third Avenue, pouring in light that could blind a man, put up
all those fancy buildings and let anybody into the saloons, turning them into public instead of private places. Now the search
for anonymity drove these honest beer drinkers west to Eighth
and Ninth. If the saloons served up a concentrate, would the
bartender pass you a jigger of beer mix if you asked him to
draw one?

Not likely. For 6,000 years beer has been the brew that made
some places famous. It has survived voting beauty contests,
baseball announcers, Prohibition's 3.2, warnings 'alfway through
a pub pint of, "Time, gentlemen, please," bottles, cans and tab
tops. It will survive concentration, too.

Beer concentrate is noncarbonated with about 75 percent of
the water removed; it is reconstituted by adding the water and
carbon dioxide.

But beer isn't just beer. It's place and mystique, too. The
delicate balance of the beer drinkers pressed against the bars
of the country depends on certain constants. It begins with a
size-up of bartender or barmaid and ends in silence or conversation. But not plain silence: bar silence. A man at the four
o'clock bar isn't kidding. If his glass hits bottom, it is refilled
without a word, before a look of terror crosses his eyes.

And what about those hard-boiled eggs, stacked like cannon
balls, behind the bartender? They are a vital part of the rit-
ual, for the man who drinks his lunch of beer, to put a little
lining on his insides. Beer or beer concentrate, that hard-
boiled artillery has got to stay.

The approach to the concentrate raised an interesting point.
Would it be possible to do some do-it-yourself mixing? For example, take a nip of concentrate, follow with half a glass of
seltzer, then jump up and down in place for two minutes. Would

the result meet a brewmaster's delicate proportions? Might the stomach be used as a lager tank, with leftover yeast added to the wort, and occasional ice bags applied to cool the hops?

Anyway, there might be an immediate advantage: no more of those Coney Island heads. The strange bartender who shot the beer into the glass so quickly that the top half became slowly sinking foam might not be able to pull his fast ones any longer. On the other hand, would it still be possible to enlist the sympathy of a friendly bartender filling the request, "Put a little head on it"? Meaning, "I've run out of money, so fill the top half of the glass and I'll be able to make it home better."

What it all added up to, said one of the four o'clock barflies, was the synthetic way things were going all over. Zip codes. Frozen orange juice. Digit dialing. Pre-crinkle-cut French fries. Instant coffee. Checks that talk back: "Do not fold, spindle or mutilate." Prerecorded answering services. Artificial flowers. Powdered eggs.

"You name it," said the talkative man to the bartender, peeling his second hard-boiled, or supper, egg, "they got it."

His silent companion nodded, repeated his favorite phrase, "Draw one," then added, "unconcentrated." [11/10/63]

HERBERT MITGANG

New York Athenaeum

After dark, below the marble dovecotes of the New York Public Library, the lights lower in the modified French Renaissance building at Fifth Avenue and 42d Street, and this common of steps and greensward at the crossroads of Manhattan Island becomes a haven for weary scholars, wanderers and lovers. In the daytime, the second-most-important building in New York (isn't the UN the first?) resounds to a more deliberate tread: The footsteps of all the world's scholars come to this friendly athenaeum that is the city's most precious vault.

Two new book discussion series—Significant Modern Books and Exploring the Universe—are on the library's roster of fall-winter activities for adults in the neighborhood libraries. Like other changing events originating here, everything's free. This despite the fact, unrealized by most New Yorkers, that the main public library is really private.

It is a treasure trove of information and surprise. Look at the building with the fresh eye of a visitor. Come upon it on a bright fall day: spread out a weekly news magazine and sit on stone; let a book drown out the cacophony of angry bus motors; see the college students pursuing themes and each other; old men bent on lifetime research coming out to smoke; Bohemians climbing the side entrance to Parnassus; follow the tapping heels of secretaries gathering up best sellers on a lunch hour. Notice, as you enter the high halls, a pride of lions stalking the marble fringes overhead.

They come here at the rate of 8,000 a day. Meeting them are hundreds of librarians—the cream of the caretakers of the world of books. If they cannot come, they call OXford 5-4200 (the 5 is for Fifth Avenue, the 42 for 42nd Street). By telephone, by mail and by personal query the people ring up 10,000 times a day.

The library has a split personality—reference and circulation. On the main floor is the headquarters branch of CC, central circulation, one of the eighty branches plus bookmobiles in and around the boroughs. These branches of the New York Public Library, which permit books to be taken out, have 900,-000 cardholders.

The reference books, the library's main wealth, number 4,500,000, plus millions of more pamphlets, newspapers, photographs, prints, maps—the whole realm of man's accumulated wisdom in all forms. Room 315 is probably the most famous room in the city. It is the library's public catalogue and has more than 7,000,000 cards. The Dewey decimal system, used by libraries around the country, won't do here—the New York Public Library has its own system.

It is a magic system compounded of equal parts of mystery and efficiency, charm and luck. When a reader fills out a call slip here, it flies away in a chute, disappearing into the hidden archives of the building where dispatchers, knowing exactly where the 4,500,000 books are located on the 80 miles of book-shelves, send the brass tubes to the proper stacks, where books are picked out and sent by pully up to the call desks. Matching odd numbers sit on one side of the reading room, even numbers on the other—waiting for their assigned book numbers to flash on a light board. Odds or evens, *faites vos jeux,* and, invariably, your book comes up.

The biggest surprise of the many to be found here, one dis-covers, is that the New York Public Library is a private library. New York City pays for the circulating branch upkeep, but the main library itself is a private corporation primarily main-tained by income from endowments and gifts. The statistics of daily existence are frightening. It costs the library $10 to put one book on the shelf; 80,000 books are added annually. It costs the library about $3.50 every time a reference book is called for and goes through the system!

But such matters need not disturb the visiting reader on a fall day: The dignified stone lions will be here for a long time, an invitation to enter. And, inside, these words from Milton's *Areopagitica* inscribed over the door to the Main Reading Room: "A Good Booke . Is the Pretious Life-Blood of a . Master Spirit, Embalm'd and Treasur'd. Up on Purpose to a Life Be-yond Life." That's the idea of this beautiful place, a book.

[3/15/64]

DAVID KARP

A Lost Angeleno Looks Homeward

Some time during the 1960's the population banner passed from the hands of New York into those of California. Third in physical size (some things won't change), California became first in people. Who pushed them over the top? I like to think that it was a group of New Yorkers. Perhaps my own small family of four, huddled in the steerage section of a Boeing 707, as we first peered with startled eyes on the milky soup of Los Angeles International Airport.

Two years in California qualify us as Los Angelenos. Earlier arrivals still ask the same question, "How do you like it here?" It is a sure sign of the uncertain provincialism of Californians. New Yorkers never cared whether you liked New York or not. You could attack New York for its heat, its crowding, its vulgarity, its inconveniences, its ten thousand shortcomings and New Yorkers nodded appreciatively and added some esoteric plaints of their own.

But in the end New York was New York and while it withstood censure, it never needed praising. California (Los Angeles subdivision) is a different state of mind. People anxiously ask one another how they like it.

To avoid arguments and recriminations from other ex-New Yorkers, you hit on the formula response, "Well, I'm getting to like it." You imply that it is an acquired taste, like having your salad before you have the main course (a culinary oddity which the Californian accepts as an article of faith). A California salad, by the way, looks like a mountain of rubbish on the great seas of garbage in New Jersey. Having eaten the salad, you don't need the main course, or a job, or a hobby. It can take up most of an energetic man's day.

The response to, "Well, I'm getting to like it," is always the same from fellow expatriates, "Wait until you go back to New York for the first time. You'll *hate* it." The implication is not that New York has grown more uncomfortable since you left, but once you have experienced the paradise of what local TV newscasters call "The Southland," New York, by contrast, becomes truly unbearable.

Emma Lazarus's poem on the dear old Statue of Liberty doesn't ask Europe for its rich, its titled, its comfortable, its successful. It wants the flops, the "wretched refuse of your teeming shores." Well, let's face it: The successful stay at home where they are loved and well known and have lots of going investments. The losers pack up and leave. And California is the biggest collection of losers who ever met on one piece of real estate.

This is a sociological fact which is recognized by businessmen in the coldest and quickest terms. The credit in California is about as easy and interminable as the salads and the sunshine. But the rates are close to usury, and the states of grace are only split seconds for the financially hesitant or forgetful.

If you miss a month's payment on the phone bill, the computers at General Telephone get frantic and write you preprogramed insulting messages to the effect that they will cut off your phone service. They know what kind of losers use their phones. The good old New York phone company took a casual attitude when I missed a month or two. They just toted it up and didn't raise a sweat. They knew we were winners.

Under all the sunshine and jollity and friendly financing there is an uncertainty in the people which, now and then, gets transmitted to the earth, and parts of Lower California get the shakes. Windows are cracked, dishes fall from shelves and chandeliers sway. You get the readings on the Richter earthquake scale along with the ball scores on the eleven o'clock news.

They can call it the San Andreas Fault if they like, but it is really the collective shakiness of the losers, one foot out the door, one eye out for the repossessor, the phone from General Telephone having already stopped its operative humming when the phone bill ran five days overdue.

California is going to mature and settle down and Los Angeles is going to be a great city one day when the Sunset Strip stops being sold as the Papeete of the credit-card delinquent.

They used to boast that the influx of migrants to California forced them to build a public school every three days. They gloss over the fact that they had to keep the bankruptcy court open Saturdays, Sundays and holidays to take care of the boom. As soon as the losers find themselves another paradise to go to, I am going to be able to say of an evening, on my patio, with the sun settling into the Pacific Ocean, "Yeah, it's terrible, but I live here and I wouldn't go any place else."

Then I'll know that I am, at last, a strayed New Yorker who found a home. [8/17/68]

IV
Arts, Especially the Literary

ORVILLE PRESCOTT

The Magic of Words

When sleep is slow in coming several choices are open to the wakeful. One of the most popular is to worry about one's problems, or about the problems of mankind. This is not recommended. Another choice is to turn on the light and read a dull book. There is a risk in this because the occupant of the other twin bed is not likely to approve. Some people tell themselves romantic adventure stories in which they cast themselves as hero. This is fun, but it can become monotonous. After you have brought peace and prosperity to the entire world, have written the greatest book of all time and have knocked out Cassius Clay with one casual punch few worlds are left to conquer. In such an emergency I like to think about words.

Sometimes I think about English proper names and compile a list of those based upon occupations: Abbot, Baker, Bishop, Brewer, Carter, Carpenter, Clark, Cook, Farmer, Fletcher, Hunter, Mason, Miller, Shepherd, Tailor, etc. There are hundreds more. As often, I think about beautiful words and why they are beautiful. Some are beautiful only because of their musical sound, many more because of their combination of musical sound with romantic, heroic and exotic associations. One man's beautiful word, of course, may not be another man's. For instance, cellar door is often cited as beautiful and I think it is. But its sound alone is beautiful. Its meaning may have so unpleasant an association for some that they cannot recognize its melodious charm.

A good example of a beautiful word with no beautiful association is caramel. The candy may be delicious, but the memory of its taste adds nothing to the music of the word. Consider tantamount, a very trumpet call of a word with only a sadly prosaic meaning. Or forlorn, one of the loveliest words in English and that in spite of its meaning of misery, desertion and grief. Here are five more whose sound, if the meaning can be forgotten, enchants: Gorgonzola, luminary, myrmidon, panorama and vermilion.

We tend to forget how much a sweetly chiming word can do. Kashmir, for instance, has romantic associations by itself. Vale is a mildly pleasant word. But the two words in combination, the Vale of Kashmir, are magical.

Rose is an attractive word, although perhaps an overly familiar one. But a Rose of Sharon is irresistible to the imagination, not because the Biblical word has any notable remembered association, but because of the music of the phrase.

In the same way, mountains is a pleasing word; but the Mountains of Morn are luminously lovely. And it is the sound which does it, for the actual mountains near Dublin are unknown to most people.

Many geographical names superbly combine beauty of sound with romantic, dramatic and glamorous associations: Coromandel, Rarotonga, Samarkand, Famagusta and Cathay. Many others are more specific in their ability to conjure up memories of ancient sorrows, legendary heroism or undying beauty: Troy, Karnak, Marathon, Persepolis, Taj Mahal and Parthenon. Such glorious, golden words are part of the imaginative heritage of all educated men.

Although many contemporary poets prefer to ignore the music of verbal sound in their intellectualized poetry, the beautiful sound of words (sometimes the beautiful but almost meaningless sound) has enriched poetry for 2,500 years. Poe's "Ulalume" may be hollow and bombastic, but its alliteration and resonant words can still delight:

> It was in the dank tarn of Auber
> In the ghoul-haunted woodland of Weir.

The coining of imaginary proper names can add a rich vein of beauty to prose. One of the great masters of this was the late E. R. Eddison, author of a masterpiece of heroic fantasy called *The Worm Ouroboros.* Here is an example of Eddison's zestful play with stately words:

> Before them the mountains of the Zia stood supreme: the white gables of Islargyn, the lean dark fingers of Tetrachnampf nan Tshark lying back above the Zia Pass pointing to the sky, and west of it, jutting above the valley, to the square bastion of Tetrachnampf nan Tsurm. The greater mountains were for the most part sunk behind this nearer range, but Koshtra Belorn still towered above the Pass. [4/9/66]

NADINE GORDIMER

The Word, Too, Falls Victim of Apartheid

The South African as a writer faces problems peculiar to his time, his place and his color—whatever that may be. They are the limitation by law of the freedom of expression, and the limitation of human experience by the compartmentalized organization of South African society.

All the work, past, present and future, of an individual writer can be erased by a ban on his spoken and written word. The ban not only restricts his political activity, which is its avowed intention, but negates his creativity—he becomes a nonperson, since his form of communion and communication with the society in which he lives is cut. This has happened to almost all black and colored South African writers—Ezekiel Mphahlele, Lewis Nkosi, Alex La Guma, Dennis Brutus, Can Themba, Bloke Modisane—with the 1966 blanket ban on forty-six South Africans living abroad.

The Publications and Entertainments Act of 1963 can ban a book under any one of ninety-seven definitions of what it classes as "undesirable." This act and the one it superseded have banned 11,000 books, many of them pulp fiction, but others the work of Faulkner, Moravia and Sartre, along with books by serious South African writers.

The writer may also be deprived of his passport. Apologists for the seizure of Alan Paton's passport (no book of his is banned) pointed out that he was the leader of an opposition, if perfectly legal, political party, as well as a writer. Not even this justification can be scraped up for the seizure of playwright Athol Fugard's passport.

Afrikaner writers, using the Afrikaans language, so far have not felt the whip. Their *avant-garde* hasn't yet ventured outside the *laager* (ring of covered wagons from within which Boer frontiersmen defended themselves) of conformist thinking in South African politics. They have merely taken the risk of shocking the Afrikaner church and literary establishments, somewhat in the inspiration of the two avatars of Virginia Woolf —the sexual frankness of *Who's Afraid* . . . and the mild experiments in literary form made, long ago, by the writer herself.

Yet Afrikaner writers are inextricably cross-linked with their fellows in other language and race groups. The necessity for curbs on freedom of expression in a rigid, dogmatically conformist society must enclose its creative people in a series of concentric circles from which, in time, not even the group closest to the ruling establishment can escape.

With this legal cutlery poised overhead, the writer in South Africa faces problems inherent to the structure of the society from which he draws his material—from the point of view of his potential as an artist, the most serious ones. George Lukács says that all writers present the world of their immediate experience from the inside, and the world beyond that experience from the outside.

The extent and depth of their grasp of the human situation are limited by the confines of their own social situation, at once a personal and a group situation, bounded by class, both social and economic, and, in certain societies, by color.

How deeply, how widely into the life around him does South African society let a writer go? The writer himself cannot experience everything he writes about; yet he cannot write meaningfully about what is shut off from his own *potential* experience. White writer and black in South Africa live in the same society, but it is compartmentalized in such a way that for each the potential of experience in that society is strictly limited.

There are things that can happen to a black man that can't ever happen to a white man. And there are things that can happen to a white man that can't ever happen to a black man. The black writer can speak for the ordinary people because the color bar keeps him steeped in the circumstances of their lives, confined to a location and carrying a pass, from the day he is born to the status of pickaninny to the day he is buried in a segregated cemetery.

The white writer, perforce, belongs to an elite, and, from the day he is born *baas* to the day *he* is buried in *his* segregated cemetery, cannot share the potential of experience of the 15,-000,000 on the other side of the color bar.

I believe that white writers will have less and less to write about as their inside view of the total society they live in becomes more and more restricted. And so long as our society remains compartmentalized, our literature will be stretched on the rack between propaganda, on the one side, and, on the other, art as an embellishment of leisure.   [8/31/68]

JOHN B. STARR

Thaw Before Reading

It is frequently the case that some of the most sweeping changes in modern life are presaged by those little articles on the back pages of newspapers which appear to have been included more on account of their brevity than their subject mat-

ter. Just such a portent was contained in an announcement by
a group of scientists in Glasgow who have been looking carefully at an old book which, from their description, would probably appear to the untutored eye very much like a novel left out
in one's favorite garden chair during a late-afternoon thunder-
shower. This book, however, had been left in the Antarctic by
an explorer some fifty years ago, and was recently recovered
and taken to Glasgow so that these scientists, through diligent
research, might attempt to postulate with some degree of accuracy what will become of the next book left out for fifty years
in the Antarctic by a careless explorer.

As a side effect of their investigations, the scientists discovered
that the fact that the book had been frozen for a half century meant that its pages were, when thawed, in better condition than a similar edition from a local bookshop, if one were
willing to overlook a slight waterstain or two about the edges.
This fact itself probably flabbergasted no one, given the worldwide currency of frozen peas and TV dinners nowadays. The
article closes, however, with a hint of ominous days ahead. Libraries, the scientists aver, will be interested in these findings
in order to better preserve their collections. The more a library
can be made to resemble the Antarctic, if one may be permitted
to paraphrase their conclusions, and the less it resembles a Glasgow bookstall, the longer the books will last.

Visualize, if you will, then, the Low-Temperature Library of
tomorrow. Entering from the balmy out-of-doors, one moves
across the gelid foyer where intrepid librarians pore Eskimo-
like over card catalogues while others hastily pop overdue books
into quick-chill boxes. One reaches at last the checkroom,
where parkas and mittens are available for rent at a nominal
sum. Moving briskly on to the stacks, one pulls one's hood
tighter about one's ears and, feeling a sudden camaraderie with
Jack London's unsuccessful fire builder, checks instinctively
one's match supply.

Proceeding down the banks of shelves, one glances at the
titles, which have been made conveniently legible by the timely

advent of the frost-free refrigerator. Gone, however, are the days of browsing about in the works of one's favorite author or leafing casually through the tomes on one's favorite subject matter, for the sign plainly indicates that the books are not to be opened before having been thawed at least forty-five minutes. Gone, too, are the afternoons of yore which one spent browsing randomly through the shelves, moments and hours slipping by unnoticed as one proceeded from book to book guided only by fancy. This becomes evident rapidly, for one's nose and ears soon begin to manifest a foreboding of advancing chill.

Having made our selection, then, we emerge from the library, in Matthew Arnold's words, "frozen up within and quite/The phantom of ourselves," clutching under our arm a book which is reported to be in infinitely better condition than its companion volumes in the bookshops of Glasgow.

But this will be only the beginning. There is a chain of reasoning prevalent among merchandizers that runs somewhat as follows: Any product that works well in the institutional or business world will work equally well in the world of the private consumer. Hence that product is desirable to the consumer. Hence that product is necessary to the consumer. Think of the marketing possibilities for the home version of the Low-Temperature Library. Preassembled walk-in freezers to replace one's cozy but outdated study. Chill boxes for display purposes at bookshops. Fur-lined reading gloves. Quilted library coats.

If the life of the man who reads for pleasure is in for some changes as a result of the negligence of an Antarctic explorer, the life of the scholar is in for a veritable revolution. Condemned to conduct the pursuit of knowledge at subzero temperatures, his only recourse will be to cultivate that state described by Thomas Carew, for whom

> The torrid or the frozen zone:
> Bring equal ease unto my pain;
> The temperate affords me none.

One can even foresee the day when scholars will come to regard the scars of frostbite as the badges of academic achievement. [11/20/65]

NONA BALAKIAN
Style and the New Economy

Gore Vidal's article in a recent *Book Review* explaining why he had lately felt the need to overhaul three of his early novels contained a passage on punctuation which no student of literary style—and we don't mean simply usage—can allow to go unnoticed. Wrote Mr. Vidal:

> I was startled to find how much I—and others—used the colon in the Forties. Like a blare of French horns introducing a significant theme, the colon was used almost as much (and as irritatingly) as Sterne's dashes. The semicolon was also fashionable then: it is seldom used nowadays in the best prose but I am still loyal to it. As to commas, those of us brought up on Fowler used to allow them to swarm like gnats upon the page. Now the comma is used sparingly and I prefer the new economy.

Mr. Vidal's suggestion that punctuation is largely arbitrary and hinges on fashion would doubtlessly have disturbed the great Fowler; it would probably not trouble at all a more recent expert on usage, Theodore M. Bernstein, who, in *The Careful Writer*, speaks of punctuation marks as "traffic signals" on which "traffic engineers" do not always agree. The tendency these days, adds Mr. Bernstein, is to eliminate as much punctuation as possible, especially commas.

Well, we are all for the "new economy" of course when *all* that's involved is clarity of meaning. But punctuation is perhaps more art than science, and we cannot but feel dismayed at the prospect of losing all that interesting variety and commotion which commas, colons, dashes, parentheses, yes and even periods (artfully spaced) afford a printed page—lending signature and style to what has been communicated.

Take the maligned comma. José Garcia Villa, the poet, some years ago set off each word with a comma—apparently to achieve a staccato effect. But apart from such extremes, what can a writer do without this "signal" when his thoughts run in short takes that connect like slurred notes in an uninterruptable series of cadences? What would Proust have done? Or Dylan Thomas?

> Earth, air, water, fire, singing into the white act,
> The haygold haired, my love asleep, and the rift blue
> Eyed, in the halloed house, . . .

And what of the semicolon? Is it really ready to be scrapped? Not, surely, while there are writers around whose ideas follow a lateral pattern, who no sooner finish a thought than they feel another of equal weight emerging, and still another; all leading to a final note of elucidation.

Nor does it seem fitting to treat the colon with contempt when, if properly employed, it is the punctuation of definition, the precise thinker's tool. It is especially favored by literary critics (T. S. Eliot) and philosophers (Jean-Paul Sartre).

More than fashion, then, it seems to be the particular bent of a mind and the quality of the thing it wants to create that determine the amount and kind of punctuation used. One of the most eye-catching "signals" is the dash, used chiefly and dramatically to imitate the spontaneity of speech—the sudden hesitation, the switching of controls that give the emphasis of gestures. Emily Dickinson (who hoarded so much drama) was full of dashes. And so was Conrad: "Mistah Kurtz—he dead."

As for those sly or humorous asides, the afterthoughts, scrupulous modifications and studied counterpoints—how could they be expressed, effectively, without the parenthesis? They couldn't—not by Cummings or Faulkner or Seymour-Salinger, at any rate.

Even the exclamation point and the period have their artistic uses. "It was a gorgeous day. Lolita!" writes Nabokov, and the final punctuation brings home the poignant intensity of his desire. In the same way, the period, which stands for silence, has its own eloquence when used to convey emotional states. The short but pregnant sentences of a D. H. Lawrence or Anais Nin reverberate with what is left unsaid.

True, one of the greatest artistic uses to which punctuation was ever put—in the work of Joyce—called for its near elimination: But the stops in *Ulysses* were taken out not for greater clarity but to suggest a continual internal flow. And finally there are the pure prose stylists—like Flaubert and Katherine Anne Porter—whose writing is so translucent and thought process so structurally sound that, though the punctuation is there, it is all but invisible. They remain outside the problem, their "economy" being the art that conceals art. [11/27/65]

CHARLES SIMMONS

Author Trouble

The trials and tortures of writing a book do not end with the delivery of the finished, bound product, or possibly with reading the reviews the book might receive. Actually the trouble then begins. Letters arrive. The nature of the book, of course, largely determines the nature and the number of the letters. If the author has been so foolhardy as to write a self-help book, the chances are a handsome percentage of purchasers will find, after reading the book, that they still can't help themselves and need further individual instruction from the author. "I don't quite understand this part on page 48," or "You say on page 69 thus and so, but on page 201 you say. . . ." Letters like this the author is apt to spend considerable time answering, since by doing so he is explaining and defending not only his book but himself. And most authors love doing that.

Then there is the type of letter which was obviously inspired
by an urge to receive a personal answer from a bona fide author.
The writers of these letters, as well as feeling that there is
something definitely godlike about anyone who has written a
book, also feel that such a person could not possibly reply to un-
solicited correspondence unless it was either provocative or
provoking. In consequence, these letters tend to be archly cute,
daringly antipathetic, or just incisive as all get-out. These are
the letters the author finds most irritating to read and to answer.
They are not sincere (and the author is always interested in
how his book has really struck his readers), nor appreciative
(and all authors deeply appreciate appreciation), nor even interested (this type of letter writer is much more taken with himself than with what he purports to talk about). Fortunately for
the author, though, he can forget completely and in good conscience about these communications.

The most disconcerting are the letters from crackpots. Edmund Wilson, somewhere in his recent *The Shores of Light*,
mentions that no one can turn out a book so bad that someone
won't write to the author to say that it has changed his life. The
reason this kind of reader response is so upsetting to an author
is that it comprises in a way everything the author was striving
for and didn't accomplish. The book he wrote, whatever it was,
did change his own life, and ideally he wanted it to change the
lives of others. But how many books in a century do that, and
to how many people? Even being aware that these responses
come from crackpots, they make the author uneasy—somehow suspicious that he has taken advantage of incompetents.
And as for answering and how to answer, there is no adequate
solution. He cannot disregard the letters. They are based on a
faith he alone was responsible for creating. And yet to go along
with the letters, accept their adulation, would be a piece of
conscious dishonesty of which he is incapable.

Another type is the correspondence trap. This is the missive
that is chatty, friendly and a trifle windy, but still rather nice to
receive. With these the author loosens up and writes back, put-

ting a good deal of effort into striking just the properly amiable note. But what happens? Three or four days after his reply has been mailed there comes an even chattier reply to his reply. The danger is immediately manifest, as are the difficulties. The author can hardly reverse himself and send a cold, short closer. And he can't ignore the letter either, since his own original reply asked for this. The only thing to do, then, is to wait. Wait an indecent length of time and then reply with a sparse apology. If even this letter evokes a return, the author best forget the matter and resign himself to being thought a boor or a dead man by the correspondent, who likely has a good deal more leisure at his disposal than the author and, like all incorrigible consumers of other people's time, must be dealt with firmly.

According to the temperament of the author, there is one particular problem attending readers' letters which can be either a fascinating game or an unsettling necessity. And that is responding to each correspondent in that tone which might justly come from the kind of person the correspondent imagines the author to be. It is appalling that from the most simple declarative and factual book different readers envision an author of utterly opposing characteristics. One reader will see the author as a cynic, another as an idealist; one as a clever and charming hypocrite, another as an earnest moralizer. The author who doesn't care much for epistolary histrionics finds it safest to extend the tone of his book, as he sees it, into all his replies. The ham, the mirror watcher, of course, charges forth and has a really gay old time for himself.   [1/7/53]

HERBERT L. MATTHEWS

Dante, the Seven Hundredth Milestone

Dante Alighieri was born under the zodiacal constellation of Gemini—the Twins—700 years ago. The true Dantologist is an extremist. He raves esctatically. He sees no flaws. He holds the doubters and the indifferent in contempt. But we cannot all be Dante scholars; in fact, they are a rare breed, like nuclear physicists—and about as interesting. You and I, living in a more prosaic world, must not allow ourselves to be cornered or shamed. We can find our simpler treasures.

Two works keep Dante alive—the *Vita Nuova,* one of the loveliest tributes paid by man to woman; and what is surely the greatest poem ever written in any language, the *Commedia,* known in English as *The Divine Comedy.* It was the *Commedia* that led T. S. Eliot to write: "Dante and Shakespeare divide the modern world between them; there is no third."

In any language the *Commedia* offers rich rewards, but those who cannot read Italian will miss the full measure of Dante's greatness, and miss it by a large margin. The best poetical translations—and there are many good ones—are the palest shadows of the original. The excellent prose translation in the Temple Classics seems more honest.

The *Vita Nuova* (*New Life*) is Dante's youthful and glowing tribute to Beatrice. His "love affair"—the most famous in literature—was mystical, unconsummated, unreal and yet charged with an emotion that reaches across seven centuries to touch our hearts today.

The *Divine Comedy* begins "in the midst of this our mortal life" in the year 1300, when Dante Alighieri was thirty-five years old. As no one needs to be told, it is the story of his journey down to the uttermost depths of Hell, up the mountain of Purgatory, to the Earthly Paradise, and from thence through the circles of the Heavens to the Empyrean and the vision of God.

Today, with all due respects to the scholars, it is the narrative, and the inspired poetry in which it is couched, that live for us. Libraries have been written about the allegorical meanings, but the average reader soon ceases to care about esoteric meanings. The long, philosophical and doctrinal passages, expecially in the *Paradiso,* become too boring, except for occasional lovely passages of poetry. On rereadings one learns to skip through pages and even cantos.

Few in our age, even this age of Auschwitz and Hiroshima, can feel anything but revulsion at the hideous tortures of Dante's hell. The *Paradiso* is too utterly ethereal and taxing to hold its attraction. Beatrice never stops talking in the *Paradiso* and one ends in time thinking of the once lovely girl of the *Vita Nuova* as a crashing bore. It is the *Purgatorio*, surely, that lives most vividly and meaningfully for us today.

I like to think that it meant most to Dante, because life meant so much to him. Consider the poignant passage in *Purgatorio* XXVII where Dante, fearful and coaxed by Virgil, walks through the wall of fire on the uppermost terrace and suffers so terribly that he would have thrown himself into boiling glass for refreshment. It was his farewell to life and to all that made him want to cling to this sinful and wonderful earth where he had been so happy and so sad.

Only much later, standing in the heaven of the fixed stars and the constellation of Gemini under which he was born, does he look back and see far, far down "the little threshing floor which makes us all so fierce."

He has put the earth in its place, but his heaven, purgatory and hell were part of his world. He lived a full, passionate, combative life. He loved and hated that "little threshing floor" over which he, too, got "fierce." And out of his suffering he fashioned the most beautiful of all monuments to man's triumph over life and death.

The *Divine Comedy* lives for us in the twentieth century because the souls in torment or in bliss were real. Each generation since he finished the poem in the year of his death, 1321, relives the same torment and happiness, and it is because Dante Alighieri described them in words of such surpassing beauty and truth that he is honored seven centuries after he was born.

[5/22/65]

THOMAS LASK

Shakespeare Updated—Once Again .

A recent note in this newspaper described a new version of *Hamlet,* prepared by Rouben Mamoulian. In it the stage and screen director has substituted modern equivalents for some 2,000 Elizabethan words, rewritten lines, eliminated others altogether, provided fresh punctuation and otherwise satisfied his Thespian instincts. There is no malice in this. The idea is to make the play intelligible to others less gifted than Mr. Mamoulian. Robert Graves did something of the sort, though not so extensively, for a British production of *Much Ado* a while back. It is an impulse that has been with us for a long time. Dryden in the seventeenth century defended his revision of *Troilus and Cressida* by saying that language "in general is so much refined since Shakespeare's time," that many of his words, and more of his phrases, are scarcely intelligible. And he went on to describe Shakespeare's version as coarse and obscure.

At first hearing, such activity seems to be desecrating a public monument, and our instincts are to gather the citizenry and smite the miscreants hip and thigh. The chances are that if Shakespeare were alive he wouldn't join the posse. He would probably look at the whole Shakespeare hero worship with wry amusement. For Shakespeare took no sacrosanct attitude to his own plays. He was a craftsman, not a classic, as close to a play carpenter as to a divine reed. He may be for all time, but his plays were for his own age. They were vehicles to amuse the populace. They did amuse and they made money. By the end of his life, our Stratford man was a very solid citizen.

We know too that he meddled in other people's material. He borrowed plots, incidents, language. Since he refurbished the work of others, he wouldn't have been surprised to find others polishing his. We are also not quite sure how much he saw his plays as literary works. The feeling of the time was that plays had their life in the theater. Indeed had it not been for two friends, a good half of his plays would be unknown to us. A contemporary wit, asked what he thought Shakespeare's "Works" were worth, answered, "Not a farthing." His plays were worth a great deal but his works nothing.

Those who object to any sniping at the text might ask themselves, "What text?" The printed versions we have today represent the wrestlings of three centuries of editors, and they are a kind of consensus. (One of the incidental pleasures in reading in the Shakespeare literature is to see how the editors go about their work. Holy Writ could not call forth more vehemence and debate.)

Editors are not at all agreed as to how near we are to the poet's words. Between us and the bard may stand a scribe who copied his rough drafts, a prompter who put in his own markings, an idiosyncratic typesetter, the mechanics of the Elizabethan printshop and the usual gremlins. One scholar has estimated that the First Folio, the most considerable source for any edition of Shakespeare's plays, contains 3,500 serious errors and 2,000 minor ones.

Looking at a modern edition, Shakespeare might well feel like a Hollywood screenwriter who has just seen a film he wrote, with changes made by the director, the producer, the star, the censorship board, the distributor and the executive vice president of the bank that financed the film.

Even if we had his exact words, understanding would not come easy. Shakespeare's irregular spelling, different punctuation and grammar would complicate matters. Some words are no longer current; in others meanings have changed.

It is these things that Mr. Mamoulian is presumably out to clear up. His version might be successful too. Davenant's paraphrase (if that's the word) of *Macbeth* lasted some eighty years and pushed the original from the stage. Even worse was Nahum Tate's *King Lear,* a massacre of the original. Yet it was popular for more than a century, and four generations of play-goers thought it was Shakespeare himself. Now both of these are in the dustbin, curiosities only to the antiquarian.

In the end, readers, actors, producers, audiences try to get back to the historical Shakespeare, to see him in his own time, as the Elizabethans saw him. It is probably an impossible task, but it is better than settling for an updated version. That is why the scholars, full of flaws of their own, are still the best bet. Reading Shakespeare with their help may take effort, but is as close to the man as we can get. [2/12/66]

THOMAS LASK

That Strange Organism—the Audience

Peter Weiss's play *Marat/de Sade* aroused New York audiences from their traditional decorum. Evidently some of the paying customers to this provocative play were restless and dissatisfied and did not hesitate to show it. One member of the cast, nettled by the hubbub up front, was driven to scream, "Shut up!" And at another performance, Ian Richardson, who has a major role as Marat, and an anonymous playgoer discharged a flurry of boos at each other.

Would that we had been there. For the fact is that New Yorkers are too polite. They endure much and applaud everything. If they don't approve the creative part, they applaud the performers. And if neither satisfies, they applaud the scenery.

Especially are they cordial to what is familiar. At the Metropolitan Opera, a standard aria from a work done ten times a year for the last forty years will bring down the house. Ovations are as common as daisies in spring. At that, the *aficionados* never permit the music to finish. As the sustained high note is about to end, they break in with tumultuous approval. They have cut off so many arias and act endings that a man can truthfully say that he has attended the Metropolitan for half a century and hasn't yet heard a complete performance of *La Traviata.*

The customers do have a way of showing their disapproval. Borrowing a page from the UN (or vice versa), they walk out when displeased. Generally they are displeased at what is new. What is new may be something as old as Monteverdi's *Orfeo* or as recent as Busoni's *Arlecchino.* But between those who come in late and those who leave early, the concerts sometimes resemble a promenade rather than an indoor event of music making.

In the past, however, audiences were not so benign. In Dublin in 1907 occurred that splendid difference of opinion over John Millington Synge's *Playboy of the Western World.* The play evidently got past the opening night at the Abbey. After that, the audience behaved as if it wanted to take down the building brick by brick. The play proceeded in the midst of assorted catcalls, threats of fisticuffs and name-calling. Except for the brief periods when the police lined the walls and kept order, the play was a pantomime. Not a word could be heard. When the management offered to refund the money to the protesters so that those who wished could hear the actors in peace, the offer was scorned. Art was above commercial considerations.

In 1913 in Paris equal enthusiasm—on both sides—greeted the first performance of Stravinsky's *Rite of Spring.* The more conservative took Stravinsky's music as a personal affront. One lady, coronet and all, insisted that she had never been so insulted in her life. The audience hissed, spat, uttered animal cries and made specific suggestions as to how the ballet ought to proceed. Nijinsky, who had supplied the choreography, wanted to go out and take on the crowd single-handed. Diaghilev, the impresario, had the electricians flick the lights on and off, while in the pit Pierre Monteux tried to keep the music going. When we remember how significant and important a score *Rite* turned out to be, its birth pangs on that day were all the more appropriate—unplanned though they were.

Perhaps the art lover shows little indignation today because he does not know where to turn his fire first. What with Happenings, action painting, oils that drip, dancing in which the dancers worm their way across the floor, aleatory music and writers whose words flow through the typewriter rather than the mind, the poor fellow is in a state of inarticulate numbness.

Seeking a place of refuge, he is most likely to find it in concerts of chamber music. The audience is small and dedicated. No one comes to be seen. No photographers line the entrance, television takes no film. There is neither high couture nor high coiffure; no person present will turn up in the gossip columns the following morning. But the feeling of communion between the audience and the music is almost palpable. And in these small off-Broadway halls a miracle takes place. In the midst of megalopolis with its turmoil, its haste, its pulverizing pressure, an oasis of serenity is born that passes understanding. [4/2/66]

THOMAS LASK

Father and the Cultural Explosion

Every June there is a cultural explosion for a significant part of the populace, some of whom haven't put a foot into a concert hall all year. For most lovers of the arts the winter season has just ended, the summer festivals not yet begun, but for Father this is a month of such cultural activity that four weekends are sacrificed, including two fishing trips and one Sunday afternoon outing to the ball park. For this is the season in which all the artistic enterprises in which the daughter of the family has participated—music, dance and art—come home to roost. What we mean is that everything that has been learned is put on exhibit before a captive audience of parents and occasionally grandparents. No brother has ever been known to attend.

For some reason which Father has never been able to figure out this spiritual activity has a strong worldly side that consists of clothes, hairdos and matching accessories. Evidently the young lady in the house can't toot the flute without getting dressed up as if she were going to a graduation ball. Trips to the local shopping center, tears; trips downtown, more tears; purchases and returns and long telephone consultations with friends over what they are going to wear is part of the price paid for culture. At the end, there are enough clothes to furnish all nine muses and to provide a few changes of dress in the intermissions.

The dancing, split between ballet and "modern," is never given on the same afternoon. After all, the styles could scarcely differ more. Modern runs to austerity. There are no fancy tutus, no rhinestone coronets, no silks and satins. The young ladies wear black leotards and bare feet. The class bends, stretches, runs and leaps, and what Father thinks is only a warm-up turns out to be the first half of the program.

The second half is far more ambitious. The dance, on a cosmic theme, is explained by the teacher. The seriousness of the theme is underlined by the fact that the teacher bangs a tom-tom throughout and all the dancing is done with the girls lying on the floor. Since the improvised seating is not raked, and since all the mothers around him rise for a better view, Father finds himself blocked off from seeing anything but a crack in the ceiling. He gathers that it is cryptic but profound. Cookies and punch are served.

There's no trouble, though, with the ballet: "Alice in Wonderland," a ballet infinitely expandable to include everyone in the school. The characters are certainly familiar, especially the one who has a powder puff sewed on behind and the young lady with the tall hat marked MAD HATTER. The dancing is good, too, especially when dovetailed to the music.

The young ladies are a delight to the eye, even though they have some difficulty getting up on toe and staying there. Indeed, there is so much uncertainty that Father begins to develop a distinct pain in his own ankle—an anxiety syndrome, the calm lady next to him explains. Cookies and punch are served.

The most spacious of the exhibits, the art exhibit, is held on the lawn, the works themselves suspended on makeshift frames: a cornucopia of crayon drawings, charcoal sketches, watercolors, oils and linoleum blocks. It is difficult ferreting out the family product. Pitchers and apples have a tendency to look remarkably alike when drawn by sixth graders. Fortunately, names in the lower right-hand corner make any mistaken attribution impossible. Before long, some of the thumbtacks begin to give way; one frame collapses entirely. Greater disaster threatens when a sharp wind rises. As the fathers gather the exhibits, cookies and punch are served.

The most weighty of the projects—a festival in itself—is the annual school musicale. Here the year's work is really on view: the seventh-grade winds, the eighth-grade strings, the seventh-grade chorus (not to be confused with the seventh-grade winds), the junior band, the senior band, and the crown of them all—the orchestra. The senior band, supported by at least ten trumpets, leads from strength, but the orchestra is all finesse as it plays Sibelius, Wagner, Tchaikowsky and Beethoven or reasonable facsimiles thereof.

For the finale the entire company returns. Choristers line the walls, instrumentalists fill the stage and a "Pomp and Circumstance" march by Elgar sends the audience briskly into the gymnasium, where the ladies auxiliary serves cookies and punch. Without trying to be ungracious about it, Father thinks that by this time he deserves something stronger.   [6/19/65]

KENNETH CAMPBELL

Songs That Shake the World

Now that the integrationists on the picket lines sing "We Shall Overcome" as their semiofficial song, they may prove the truth of the saying: "For three with a new song's measure can trample an empire down." Sometimes it is these simple songs as well as the great national anthems that move and shake the world. The integrationist song is gentle and meaningful. Often the songs of movements are harsh and sometimes the words are nonsense rhymes. The ghostly soldier in Shaw's *Saint Joan* hits off the improvised marching song very well when he sings, "Rum tum trumpledum/ Bacon fat and rumpledum . . . ,/ O my Ma—ry Ann!" He explains, "That don't mean anything, you know; but it keeps you marching."

One of the songs that helped shape history in the seventeenth century was "Lilli Burlero." With its scurrilous doggerel it became known as the song that had "sung a king out of three kingdoms." The King was England's James II and the kingdoms were England, Scotland and Ireland. The verses made sense of sorts, but the refrain went: "Lilli Burlero, bullen a-la./ Lero lero, lilli burlero, lero, lero, bullen a-la." It was a rousing march and in World War II the BBC revived it and played its opening bars daily in one of its broadcasts to the armed forces.

Sometimes movements have formal and serious songs, but it is often discovered that people on the march have a distressing habit of singing what they please whether it is sponsored or not. "The Battle Hymn of the Republic" was a noble song, but the Union soldiers were more likely to sing the song about "the girl I left behind me." The confederates favored a sentimental song about a girl named "Lorena."

Radical movements in the United States have called forth remembered tunes. The Industrial Workers of the World, the Wobblies, sang "Joe Hill" and a song in which workers were told to "Work and pray, live on hay."

In the Spanish civil war of 1936 the Loyalists sang "The Four Insurgent Generals"—new words to an old Spanish ballad about four peasant mule drivers. The Americans in the International Brigade favored a song about the Jarama Valley sung to the tune of "Red River Valley." On the Franco side the men of the Falange sang "Facing the Sun" to an old Spanish tune.

In Britain the Conservative Party uses the old imperial hymn

"Land of Hope and Glory." The Labor Party clings to "Red Flag" although its bowler-and-tightly-rolled-umbrella supporters are inclined to squirm at the words. The song is strictly for the cloth caps on the red Clydeside: "With heads uncovered swear we all/ To bear it onward till we fall./ Come dungeon dark or gallows grim/ This song shall be our parting hymn."

In the United States neither the Republican nor the Democratic party seems to have a song permanently associated with its public image, although Franklin D. Roosevelt made good use of "Happy Days Are Here Again." In France, De Gaulle often appears to the stirring tones of "The Lorraine March." France has been great for songs of political movements. For a time the Bonapartists had "Off to Syria." But it was heard with relative infrequency because it was scored for eight pianos.

Although it was not a political song, "Lilli Marlene," the song of Rommel's Afrika Korps in the western desert, touched many a sentimental heart. The German army radio often played it just as the soldiers settled down for the night. The British loved it and "Lilli Marlene" became known as the "song that sang two armies to sleep." After the end of the Tunisian campaign, "Lilli Marlene" was considered war booty—a "captured" song. [8/27/63]

LEON EDEL

Henry James in Today's Washington Square

People always ask me—since I happen to be his biographer —"What would Henry James think?" The other day, one of the editors of this newspaper put it to me: "That Picasso in Washington Square—what would Henry say?"

It takes courage to speak for the dead even if one can do so without contradiction. "He wouldn't like it," I said.

Since then I've had second thoughts. I remembered that

James did recognize the genius of the *avant-garde* of his time. He discovered Flaubert and Zola for America. And when he first looked at Whistler's work, he was forceful—"a picture is not an impression but an expression." Twenty years later he was writing with great affection of the Impressionists.

So I'm not altogether sure what he'd say about the 60-ton sculpture destined to stand on the grass plot bordered on three sides by New York University's 30-story apartment towers facing Bleecker Street (in the newly baptized La Guardia Place).

The pictures I've seen of this Picasso are alarming: the head of a woman rising 36 feet—to the third-story level—visible from Bleecker and Houston Streets and La Guardia Place. It will be a kind of visual coercion. Whether one likes it or not it will be there to say to us all, "I'm a woman and my name's Sylvette; and I'm by Picasso—and you can't avoid looking at me, unless you close your eyes."

Now that I write this, I think of precedents. James had a fascinating correspondence late in life with an American sculptor in Rome named Hendrik Andersen, who had a passion for huge statues. The novelist protested against "the Big, the Bigger, the Biggest, the Immensest Immensity, with all sense of proportion, application, relation and possibility madly submerged."

What would he think of Washington Square today? At one time he complained that the arch celebrating the deeds of the soldier and citizen George Washington, at the end of the Avenue, was "truncated," reflecting a kind of parochial view of "glory."

At another time he spoke of the Square nostalgically, remembering his childhood in the 1840's: "I know not whether it is owing to the tenderness of early associations, but this portion of New York appears to many persons the most delectable. It has a kind of established repose which is not of frequent occurrence in other quarters of the long, shrill city."

We linger over the words "glory" and "repose." And doubtless the present dwellers, along Macdougal Street particularly, would linger too, as they listen to the bongo drums and the guitars, the high, shrill voices and observe the general uninhibited behavior of the transient population. We can safely predict that today Henry James would look elsewhere for "repose."

Certainly the Square now is hardly the one about which he wrote his novel—*Washington Square,* he called it, relying on the simple evocative quality of the name. It had, 125 years ago, "considerable quantities of inexpensive vegetation, enclosed by a paling"; there was its "rural and accessible appearance," its ailanthus trees, which smelt strangely, but doubtless today would refresh the polluted air.

James's Washington Square was "the ideal of genteel and quiet retirement," for professional men who had lived hitherto "downtown," that is, near City Hall. The Square was uptown, almost suburban. The reservoir was at Fifth and 42d. In between the Square and the reservoir was farmland. The professional men built fine wide-fronted houses in the Square, with balconies and flights of white marble steps. The houses embodied "the last results of architectural science." Not many are visible today.

Henry James, wandering in the Square in 1968, might discover a plaque placed in his memory on the Brown Building of New York University, where his birth house once stood. And he would look curiously, but not altogether in surprise, at the hippies. For he himself once wrote a story (called "Mora Montravers") about a young girl who leaves a comfortable middle-class home to live with a little artist-man whose studio is "distinctly dirty" and who is himself "almost as spotty as the large morsel of rag" with which he wipes the paint off his hands.

But we have little to guide us as regards the forthcoming "Bust of Sylvette." A little large for a bust, one might imagine James murmuring, and of course "why this mania for the collossal?" When it comes to that, we know what James thought of the skyscrapers with their glassy eyes—and the American cult of impermanence.

"Dear Boy," he might say gently to Picasso, in his friendly, familiar way, looking up to the third-story level of Sylvette, "it's magnificent, it's sublime, it's heroic; only I feel as if it were let loose into space like a comet, with you dangling after like the tail. I must confess I positively yearn for the smaller master-piece." [3/9/68]

RICHARD RULAND

Recalling H. L. Mencken

This year marks the tenth anniversary of H. L. Mencken's death. A Mencken of seventy-five is doubtless impossible for some to imagine. They would recall an earlier date, perhaps that November in 1948 when he was stricken with the aphasia which left him unable to read or write. He was certainly lost to us then. Or did he die when the market crashed in '29 and we had no time to listen to the outrageous horse laughs that were, he quipped, worth 10,000 syllogisms.

Mencken claimed he had written some 5,000,000 words. He was the "prince of journalists," and yet he had little to say about the Depression.

"You know what I think of Hoover," he told Charles Angoff. "Turn him upside down, and he looks the same. Yet the fathead was right. Pretty soon every American will have a couple of ga-rages and a whole slew of chickens in his lunchpail. . . . All this talk of depression is nonsense. It's a mild upset, a cleansing process, a purge, and out of this mess will come a stronger economy and a stronger nation." He cried when Philip Good-man showed him a breadline, but he would not adjust the whimsicalities of his *American Mercury* to the world of the '30's.

He lived on for many in his regular coverage of the political conventions. (He predicted one FDR renomination on the grounds that "No one wants to change barrels while he's going over the falls.") But his stroke rendered final what might have been only a temporary loss of audience. Forty years before, in preparing a study of his idol, Nietzsche, Mencken had been moved by the fate which befell Nietzsche when a stroke deprived him of his powers. There is, Mencken wrote in 1908, "something poignantly pathetic in the picture of this valiant fighter —this arrogant *Ja-sager*—this foe of men, gods and devils—being nursed and coddled like a little child."

Walter Lippmann once called Mencken "The most powerful influence on this whole generation of educated people." And while Mencken was not directly responsible for the whole literary renaissance of the second and third decades of the century, he served a valuable function in his support of writers unwelcome in academe.

"Mencken was what we . . . call a cheer leader," Lewis Leary once told a British audience, "an energetic man who bounds boisterously up and down on the sidelines, shouting encouragement, and inciting an almost mindless mob of spectators in roars of properly placed approval." The figure is a good one. A large portion of Mencken's audience *was* composed of what Paul Elmer More called "the immature and the ignorant," and he captivated many of them by the mere motion and energy that are often confused with depth and insight.

But even more apt in Leary's image is its scene: In much of Mencken criticism of contemporary life and letters there is the unmistakable suggestion that he regarded the whole thing as a game—a serious game, it is true, and one with high stakes for the cultural welfare of the country, but nevertheless a diverting sport, never wholly out of season. It is in this spirit that Mencken rejoiced in the critical wars of his time.

"Today," he wrote in 1922, "for the first time in years there is strife in American criticism, and the Paul Elmer Mores and Hamilton Wright Mabies are no longer able to purr in peace. The instant they fall into stiff professional attitudes they are challenged, and often with anything but urbanity. The *ex cathedra* manner thus passes out, and free discussion comes in. Heretics lay on boldly, and the professors are forced to make

some defense. Often, going further, they attempt counter-at-
tacks. Ears are bitten off. Noses are bloodied. There are wallops
both above and below the belt . . . that melodramatize the
business of the critic, and so convince thousands of by-standers,
otherwise quite inert, that criticism is an amusing and instruc-
tive art. . . ."

We miss Mencken most because we miss this lusty spirit in
today's literary life.   [6/18/66]

MARYA MANNES

The Select Many

Not long ago the president of a major advertising company, suggesting a plan by which the commercial television net-
works could inject financial plasma into educational programing, said this: ". . . maybe it's unfair to force this mass medium
to contort itself to develop programing for the select few."

He was echoing a familiar theme. The broadcasters know
What the Public Wants. The Public is They, and They don't
want what the Select Few want. The Select Few are little knots
of intellectuals who go for Bach and Shakespeare and sixteenth-
century madrigals, and of course they have no buying power.
They want only serious programing that is above the heads of
People.

One wonders how the broadcasting powers can explain certain things. Like the crowds, for instance, who have been filling
the ANTA-Washington Square Theatre seeing *Man of la Man-
cha.* They are not few and they are not particularly select, but
when they are not holding their breath in the silence of total
attention they are cheering and applauding and weeping at a
story of an aged Spanish squire who dreams impossible dreams,
fights unbeatable foes, pursues an unreachable quest of Honor
and Right, and dies a failure except to those who—however
briefly—were touched by his vision.

Among them are the audience, and it is impossible not to feel that they—we—shared this elevation, that at last something was being given us to make us grow after the relentless stunting of mind and emotions by commercial trivia and the cold anarchy of pop culture and the pseudo arts. Oh yes, it was a musical—not a tract. There was plenty of song and action and dramatic effect that anybody—yes, anybody—could understand.

But there were things long denied us, too: a hero, a cause, an incorruptibility that restored man to his potential stature after fashionable abandonment in the gutter. We were permitted compassion.

When Arthur Miller spoke to an interviewer about the surprising success of *Death of a Salesman* on television (it was seen on CBS by nearly 17,000,000 people) he said:

> The thing that bugs me about TV is that the people who control it [TV] have no respect for the audience. Whenever I hear a producer say that "they"—the public—are not capable of appreciating quality, he really is referring to himself.

It is more likely, and certainly ironic, that he believes himself to be one of the select few who can determine (by means of ratings and profits) what the many should have. Because *Gilligan's Island* and *Petticoat Junction* are commercial successes, these are what They want. To the broadcasters an audience of 5,000,000 people—huge by any rational standards—reflects only minority tastes and deficit programing.

Yet who are all these select "few"? Intellectuals? Hardly. Most intellectuals who think of themselves as such use television (if at all) as an opiate; they look elsewhere for stimulation. If there were qualitative instead of quantitative ratings, rest assured that the audience for the best that television has offered, in whatever field, has been seen by cab drivers as well as teachers, by salesgirls as well as doctors, by janitors as well as lawyers, by construction workers as well as architects.

Intelligence crosses the boundaries of education and condition. So does the yearning for the unattainable, not in goods so much as in good. The great majority of humans, whether they are aware of it or not, would like to be better than they are, know more than they know, feel more than they have felt.

Our answer to all these yearnings has always been, simply, education: a matter of learning certain things and passing certain tests. If you do this well, you get better jobs and you earn more money. But if this heightened level of living is not matched by a higher level of feeling, people will, inevitably, be let down.

This brings us back to that word "elevation." The Select Few are in fact the increasing Many in search of it. They crave for commitment to a higher vision. And until the powerful few who claim to satisfy our tastes become aware of this, they will—in the end—be in as much trouble as we are.   [11/19/66]

FRED M. HECHINGER

The Press Conference Game

The other day a reporter, chagrined by a press conference that had produced no news, asked the public relations director in charge why the statement could not simply have been delivered to the newspapers.

"You don't think we want to pass up the television cameras?" the PR man said.

This should not have surprised the reporter, who had recently witnessed a spontaneous protest demonstration stop dead in its tracks, only to be spontaneously reenacted. The PR director in charge of spontaneous demonstrations had noted the late arrival of the camera crews.

Television or not, the press conference has assumed epidemic proportions. It is replacing messengers and the mails.

Reporters shudder at the sight of the familiar telegram that summons them: no respectable press conference is convened without a shower of telegrams, even if the newspaper is located on the same block as the organization that is calling the briefing. "Briefing" is a more ominously compelling term for the same thing.

Most press conferences are called because the press agent must impress his employers by demonstrating his ability to line up a gaggle of reporters. In addition, he gambles on the reporter's Calvinistic horror of lagging productivity: Having wasted the time needed to attend the conference, he will try to persuade his editors that he had been witness to the news.

To underscore the festive import of the occasion, liquor and miniature hot dogs are served at some press conferences. While this brightens momentarily the reporter's view of the news, the glow wears off by the time he reaches his typewriter and the depression is deepened by the realization that, despite the elaborate folder with "background material," no news has been produced.

Press conferences are called by speakers before they speak, in order to explain what they plan to say, and after they have spoken, to explain what they said or, more often, what they might have said, had they thought of it in time.

Press conferences "launch" fund drives and subsequently issue interim, halfway and final reports on the progress of the campaigns.

Press conferences announce breakthroughs, milestones, thrusts and sweeping innovations—usually involving electronic equipment—designed to solve unsolvable problems.

Recently, during a press conference to announce a controversial new program, spokesmen for the opposition handed reporters invitations to attend a counter-press conference in a nearby hotel immediately after the press conference then in progress. Ultimately this practice can lead only to the permanent floating press conference.

A new version, the flying press conference, is held in an inaccessible place that can be reached only by private company plane (a status symbol designed to impress the media). This removes a maximum number of reporters from the nation's vital centers of communications and flies them to an isolated retreat in which to "release" the news.

Since secrecy has shrouded the news, with only telegraphed hints as to its revolutionary potential, few editors have the courage to ignore the summons. Following a dramatic landing and reception, the press conference is convened. Reporters are given a "complete package" of the news, but since they have no prior opportunity to read the 316-page release, they will not have any questions to ask until they have returned home.

The theory behind the airborne abduction is that: (1) an investment of two days of a reporter's time should compel the editors to recoup their losses by permitting something to be written and (2) that news becomes nationally important when it requires inconvenient travel.

It is clear where it will end. One day soon, all reporters will be attending press conferences all day and well into the night, long beyond deadline. In the morning the publisher will call a press conference to announce the news that would have been in the paper had not the press conferences prevented it from being written. [1/31/68]

FLORENCE JULIEN

Tomorrow's Problem of Leisure

Alexander, it is said, wept when he had no more worlds to conquer. Architects, if this feeling be universal in the successful, must be feeling tearful now that they have solved almost every problem of modern living; but here could be a fresh field of endeavor to cheer them: the home visual arts room.

In order that houses may be the complete machines-for-living of the late Le Corbusier's dream, the ideal home should contain a space where members of the family could practice their favorite creative arts. There, too, is a new challenge for lighting engineers: to re-create that lovely watery light of Holland, the light of Vermeer and Rembrandt; or, for painters of another genre, the light of Paris in gay or sulky mood; or even a golden Aegean light. The recent findings at Saliagos of marbles of great antiquity and white painted pottery of a hitherto unknown type will surely spark off new interest in the plastic arts; the bold, simple lines of Cycladic marble figurines, now so highly prized by museums and private collectors, look easy to imitate—yet connoisseurs have commented on their analogies with the work of Brancusi and Modigliani.

Now would be the moment for some enterprising manufacturer to bring out mold-your-own marbles, on the lines of assemble-your-own antiques. For beginners who dare not aspire to create their own designs, there could be patterns and instructions for functional shapes such as vases, and for curios like the early Cycladic "fiddle idol," the violin-outlined flat figurine which was the rarest of the neolithic finds.

Never was sculpture so simple: "Pure" art need not represent anything, nor tell a story; its purpose is purely visual tactile enjoyment. Even without a blueprint, anyone can produce a piece of abstract sculpture in baked clay or welded metal for a spot of form and color in the living room; if it looks rudimentary, no matter; it is high style in fine arts to look prehistoric.

Modern stone sculpture looks fascinatingly easy to do. Recent prizewinners were "Not in Central Park No. 3," by Jerry Rothman of Paramount, California, and "Retreat No. 5" by Win Ng, San Francisco, in the twenty-third Ceramic National Exhibition at the Everson Museum of Art, Syracuse, New York. Both might serve as models for the home stonecarver with a leaning to the abstract, while for the practical minded, a functional prize-winning piece, "Casserole" by Richard Leach of Albion, Michigan (or even Mom's saucepan), might fill the bill.

Heads are currently popular. At the International Biennale of Sculpture being held in Athens, Greece, from September to

November, "Tête de Monserrat" by Gonzalez and "Tête de Femme" by Modigliani enrich the display. Another exhibit, "Développement d'une bouteille dans l'espace" by Boccioni, might provoke the thought "I could do something along those lines." As for the mammoth Moore in Manhattan, though she has not the archaic simplicity which would make her a model for the home craftsman, at least this behemothic bather will ram home the fact of sculpture in its modern manifestation, neither tame nor conventional.

This bronze maiden reclining in her vast pool might even inspire the would-be Michelangelo to try his hand at a small scale model for the pond in the back garden. Even if the masterpiece turns out like a scarecrow (the ideal of art is so exalted there are bound to be failures); or—even more depressingly—if she looks more like a slipper when the puppy has finished playing with it than a water nymph, its creator can solace himself with Heine's thought: "I find it more moving to accomplish something bad than something empty," or sigh, with that other poet, "a poor thing, but mine own."

A garden ornament no longer need resemble a pixie or an urn: A mushroom, easy to model in metal or marble, is a natural, and if it should fail of the classic shape, its architect can always save it with a stylish title . . . "Crushed mushroom."

Molding in clay, metal and marble has been man's esthetically satisfying pastime from time immemorial; to carve and paint is a primitive urge; these are the ideal hobbies for over-mechanized moderns; and one good way of coping with that problem of leisure that looms just around the corner might be the sculpt-your-own-stoneware (or mold-your-own-marbles or fashion-your-own-fiddle-idols) outfit in the home atelier. And here is a motto for over its doorway: "I, too, will something make, and joy in the making." [9/11/65]

FLORENCE JULIEN

What Do Fine Feathers Make?

It is said that Picasso invented Pop Art—at least, he was the first eminent painter to use trashcan objects in collages. But surely the vogue for slashed doublets, shoes, hats and gloves, which reached its peak in the 1530's was Pop-inspired. It all began when the Swiss soldiers won a battle against the Duke of Burgundy in 1477 and mended their ragged uniforms with strips of tents, banners and furnishings left behind in the flight of the Burgundians. German mercenaries adopted the slashion, and shortly thereafter, clothes all over Europe were being slashed to reveal puffings of contrasting fabric and color.

Over a century ago ladies of fashion were flaunting Pop-designed outfits, if Pop can include a walking garden as well as a walking ashcan. Readers of the society column of 1846 learned, for example, that Miss Snobky's *habit de cour* of rich pea-green corduroy was trimmed with bouquets of Brussels sprouts, its pink train festooned with white radishes. And Lady Snobky's court gown trimmed with spangles, tinfoil and red tape, with underdress of sky-blue velveteen trimmed with knots of bell-pulls, and headdress of a bird's nest with bird of paradise over a rich brass knocker *en ferronnière,* must have served as conversation pieces for many a day to those privileged to feast their eyes on the radiant spectacle. Even if Thackeray was writing with tongue in cheek, still—can there be smoke without fire?

Extravagant fashions have always been grist to the mill of satirists. Addison in England, Molière in France, used the rapier of ridicule to point out the folly of certain styles of dress. In France, at the height of the Sun King's glory, etiquette demanded that a man of fashion sport ribbon bowknots, jeweled buttons, gold lace, fringes, tassels and braid loops. Mascarille, in Molière's comedy *Les Précieuses Ridicules,* crashes his way into society decked out like a mercer's shop. Even Shakespeare took

a potshot at Pop, with Malvolio's yellow stockings, cross-gar-
tered, in *Twelfth Night*. Olivia could not bear the sight of
them!

Grave scholars have written volumes on what Ruskin called
the "great and subtle art of dress." There are Carlyle's *Sartor
Resartus,* and Ruskin's own treatises on the political economy
of dress, in which he calls on leaders of fashion to give the people
simplicity and economy to imitate. Ruskin reserved his most
eloquent prose for the fabric designers and garment manufacturers, whom he held responsible for molding public taste and
manners. Their wares should be educational: "You may literally become more influential for all kinds of good than many
lecturers on art or many treatise-writers on morality." Theirs
was the power to further the arts by creating a truly beautiful
style of dress, without which no nation could ever possess a living art concerned with portraiture. Designers and manufacturers should aim high, and not rest content with being merely
the thriving merchants of a state when they might be its guides,
counselors and rulers, wielding powers of subtle but gigantic
beneficence. The loom's role was equally sublime: to bestow
comfort on the indigent, civilization on the rude, and dispense
through the nations the grace of simple adornment and useful
possessions.

Ruskin, historian, art critic, sociologist, had studied the rise
and fall of nations and traced their histories in stone, and art,
and architecture. He believed that national character was revealed by the clothes people wear: "The plain chequers of the
tartan fold over true, brave, and noble hearts," he writes in *The
Two Paths,* 1858.

But which comes first, the character or the dress, and which
influences the other more? Is there some magic in the plaid that
makes its wearer stiffen the sinews, summon up the blood—or
does that type of person instinctively reach out for squares?
Should a wise government, desirous of having all its citizens
true, brave and noble, order a general wearing of plaid, as in
feudal times government regulated the length of a merchant's

shoe? Or should it give credence to the old proverb about the habit not making the monk? What was the effect on the moral character of medievals of particolored hose and little silver bells? Or did these merely arise out of the moral climate of the times? Must we worry about the spiritual state of a nation that goes in heavily for beatnik modes and Pop styles? Would not plus fours, glengarries and Sherlock Holmes hats be safer and steadier? Designers and manufacturers of garments, cognizant of their responsibility for the welfare of the commonwealth, might find this a good time to examine the question, *au fond.*

[12/4/65]

MARYA MANNES

Unaccustomed to Her Face

By now a good many of us will have listened to solemn groups of correspondents telling us on the small screen what last year meant and what this year will bring. It will probably occur to few to wonder why they have always—with single exceptions—been men. Most of them are mature, perceptive, and experienced journalists of national name who have been describing and interpreting the news of the world for many years. And what the younger men lack in experience they compensate for with firsthand knowledge of where the action is and of what it consists.

The fact remains that in a world of men and women where this action is of equal concern it is the man who brings us the message.

Is it simply because there are no women of equal knowledge and stature to speak with authority on politics, economics, technology, or the social condition? Possibly. Regardless of their qualifications, there is still a reluctance, no matter how disclaimed, to groom women for the high echelons of journalism and editorial interpretation, both printed and electronic.

The press is more hospitable to them than television, which permits young and personable females to report news (in the afternoon), women's feature material, and weather, but shows a marked disinclination to allow the expression of opinion from more seasoned minds. These are occasionally displayed on serious panel discussions understandably avoided by the mass of viewers.

Behind this disinclination runs a persistent argument: that women, in the nature of their being, cannot be objective and therefore cannot be trusted to recognize facts. Opinion has long been considered unbecoming to a woman except in areas directly related to her "role." These areas presumably do not include the matters of life and death, war and peace, truth and falsehood examined and judged on year-end roundups. Women, it goes, might not be able to view them dispassionately.

But there are other supportive and seldom expressed factors in this argument which have less to do with what a woman thinks or says than with how she looks and sounds. If it is reasonable to assume that a mature mind very often resides in a mature body, could it be that she is not attractive to a public geared to the package rather than the content, the Bunny rather than the Brain?

Yet many of the male pundits of our television roundtables are over fifty and even sixty, and although some are handsome, a number are not notably so. We listen to them for their views, not for the firmness of their jawline or the size of their waists. Women have long and enviously observed that men of vitality and intelligence can retain their attraction regardless of age or girth. But can women, even in this biocosmetic era?

A high-ranking broadcaster was once heard to say "People don't want to look at a middle-aged woman, particularly if she's serious." That may be one answer, which in turn leads to a second: This woman speaking with authority reminds men of their wives or mothers. They just don't want to hear that voice in their ears; and, alas, they may have a point. They have had to develop an automatic shut-off to the inconsequential chatter and the high-pitched or saw-edged voice of too many of our sex.

As for women, it has become a truism that they would rather listen to men than to members of their own tribe. The soothing male voice in commercials selling them everything from cake mix to laxatives would bear this out. But if this is true in products, is it equally true in world affairs?

Other countries don't seem to think so, among them Sweden and the Soviet Union, where a woman broadcaster and commentator is a familiar sight. The facts of her sex and age are irrelevant so long as she is qualified for the job. Possibly it is assumed (except in those states where opinion is dogma, regardless of gender) that as the maker of life she is entitled to have some views on its quality and disposition.

It could also be suggested that when facts seem to make no sense—and they don't to a growing number of human beings including commentators—objectivity makes no sense either.

But that, of course, is a typically feminine argument. It just goes to show. . . .   [1/7/67]

WILLIAM M. SPACKMAN

Turning On the Human Spirit with the Classics

The cracks in our educational walls may be easier to see today, but our colleges of education will still tell us they're not cracks at all, they're the latest linear design.

A sardonic humanist has proposed "Nothing but the best is too good for our children" as the educationist's real motto (and never mind what the best is). In fact, this nation shambles from quagmire to quagmire in great part because the electorate no longer has a solid enough education to decide for itself which way is out.

For education is the way a society unifies itself, learning enough common assumptions so that it can argue with itself in a single context, whereas we are now so split by haphazard and pointless miseducations that even on subjects like Vietnam the two main sides are hardly aware that they're not discussing the same topic.

How, then, get back to educational sense? The new math did it; could the humanities too? I should argue that they can, if two trends of the last half century are reversed.

First, our liberal arts colleges must bluntly take back from our teachers' colleges the control of what high schools teach. In 1900 we were a fairly well-educated nation. The educational ideal was clear: just train the child, and leave his God-given limitations to God. But God, left to Himself, is careless about preventing dropouts, and naturally our education mongers know better than that—if a curriculum produces dropouts, obviously what wants dropping is the curriculum.

So our educational ideal was remodeled inside out: train the dropouts, and let God provide the education of everybody else. The first duty of a modern curriculum is therefore to be so soft-minded that children no longer flunk—they merely "experience a temporary lack of success in the daily learning situation."

Passing from high school to college today is thus as automatic (and hence as meaningless culturally) as passing from the fourth grade to the fifth was in 1900. Insert your child in the slot at age five and at age twenty-one out he plops BA—very possibly as ignorant of what the human spirit is all about, of what an educated and responsible citizen can be, as when you inserted him.

The second trend that must be reversed is to restore literature—the one great cultural artifact that is both universally teachable and culturally unifying—to the place it had before language departments shriveled to mere multimillion-dollar language laboratories.

This means, for a humanist, first of all repairing the strategic mistake that classics made, in the years after 1900, of keeping

Latin and letting Greek go. That reasoning looked sound—Latin doesn't make you learn a new twenty-four-letter alphabet or all those irregular Greek verbs. (Of course students now learn thirty-one Russian characters without a murmur, and willingly choke down the indescribably wilder Russian verb.)

But the reasoning made two bad oversights. First, Latin literature is largely boring, even unteachable, while Greek literature sets a young mind on fire. Secondly, whereas Greek is a fluid language, with sentences often so like our own that they can be rendered word for word, Latin is so compressed and compact that a child has no natural approach to translating it.

Thanks to the mistake, the classicist today is hardly more than a kind of hominine computer: He stores vocabulary and syntax, publishers punch a key, a learned mumbling ensues, and out slides a translation. Translation is not literature but only the content of literature, the crude "meaning." Homer in English bears no resemblance to Homer.

Young men who have studied the classics recently can see that a great literature is an antidote to provincialism. Why on earth, then, not take advantage of all this? Why not a new classical investigation—and this time the right one at long last, the reintroduction of Greek in quantity? The new mathematicians have emphatically shown the way.

And the way would be toward a reunified culture. No one is quite sure why the classics unify; but the fact is that they always do. The old days of a classical education did not mean that there were fewer sonorous dupes or beef-witted heroes running things than run things today. But at least many more people were educated enough to know it.   [2/3/68]

HERBERT MITGANG

Doing It the Hard Way for Book Critics

Seldom do we find anything in the political arts with a Madrid dateline worthy of possible praise, but the other day an item caught our eye. It said that the state prosecutor wanted to sentence a book critic to two years in prison because he wrote a review without reading the book. Those who write books instead of about them must have had a fleeting thought of revenge at the prospect of giving the works, for once, to the enemy.

Of course, the facts disclosed that the book happened to say some unkind things about Generalissimo Franco. Obviously the only way the book critic could save his skin was to admit that he had not read the book. If he said that he had, and failed to point out this fatal flaw in any book published in Spain, he would have been hung by his thumbs instead of his head. Either way, he was on the horns of an Iberian dilemma—and we still don't know if the critic read the book or not.

In the perfect state, criticism is not necessary. In the near-perfect state, it is welcome. "You may be free as you like in your criticism of our laws," Plato declared, "for there is no harm in knowing what is wrong; that is the first step to improvement, if a man receives criticism in no resenting or hostile spirit."

But none of the rules apply—in dictatorships or democracies —when a man's book or play or performance is placed before the public. There is hardly a creator alive who can separate criticism of the work from personal criticism. Give him a dozen adjectives of praise for his book; his eye will run down these and light upon the one or two of qualification.

Do book critics read books? An interesting question and, no doubt, a trade secret. Play critics see plays; they are right out in the open and if they smile, or grimace, producers' hearts flip-flop. Even their wives are watched for knowing nudges or cackles. Movie critics in private screening rooms are visible, too;

they usually have even less excuse to leave a show early because they can doze unseen. Art critics may or may not appear at galleries; in retrospective shows, some have been known to look at the reproductions in an art book instead of legging it to the gallery. TV critics can do their work at home; or have their children do it for them.

But book critics are engaged in a private communication between the author and the reader; it is one of the last two-person artistic encounters left. In this country, skilled hands see to it that summaries of the book are inserted as releases with the book itself. Jacket copy here (less so in England and on the Continent) often provides the necessary plot, plus the author's meaning, plus the adjectives of praise about the book's importance. Quite often, the authors themselves are allowed to take part in the writing of jacket summaries and praise—in effect, their first reviews (invariably favorable). So the book critic who lifts a few perceptive lines from the book jacket may not be a villain; he may be getting as close to the theme as any author could hope.

Many an author suspects that the book is not read because, reading the reviews from around the country, he finds that there is a bland sameness of language. Very often, the review is little more than the opening paragraph or two from the inside front jacket. But what really raises eyebrows is when the same tired adjective turns up from newspaper to newspaper. Syndicated reviews appear in publications, large or small, anonymously ordinary. Sometimes these canned reviews include a mistake of fact or a typographical error in the original and, sure enough, the author sees the error repeated a score of times, uncorrected.

And yet, the suspicion exists that serious book critics really do read the books they review. One this corner knows has a standard straight-faced reply to the question: "I wish I didn't have to, but I find that if I read the book, it helps me write the review." [5/11/64]

HERBERT MITGANG

The Creative Process

When pundits who normally tell us what we are thinking, or how governments should behave, run out of their
weekly quota of suppositions, sometimes they go to the movies.
Or read a book; or, worse, write a political novel.

The real danger comes on rainy days, when they attempt to
apply journalistic standards, as writers or critics, to the creative
process. The results usually are appalling. They praise an ordinary film or novel purely on grounds of factual content, not
artistic intent; or condemn a superior work for its point of view,
ignoring its artistic level.

With a keen ability to pull things together, make a sweeping
generalization, and see major events through the egotistical eye
of personal experience, the political pundit makes it look easy.
This special talent might work with a ministry, but it does not
work with a movie. Nor does it work when the roles are reversed: The movie or book critic who judges a film or novel
by how closely it matches life in Washington, or at a convention,
or in the Defense Department, also can be a fish out of water.
For the creative process is its own creature.

Once a work of art reaches the canvas, or rolls along as a musical composition, play, novel or film, it assumes a life of its own.
A work of art, in whatever form, acquires its own tensile
strength. When right, it begins to work from the inside out.
Art then grows, multiplying its seedlings. If these come out
properly, they can be pruned and reshaped. As brush strokes
succeed each other, as film frame follows frame, as characters
meet in obligatory scenes, and as notes become harmonious,
they ideally master their human creator.

Having created them to begin with, he then must follow the
course art itself takes. The creative process works not by mere

observation, the journalist's method; or interpretation, the columnist's; but by implosion, the artist's.

Leonardo's "The Deluge" was not a sketch in the sense of a "sketch from life," but certainly a sketch in which he strove to jot down all those features of the image as it passed before his inner eye. "This," noted the classic film theorist and director Sergei Eisenstein, "accounts for the profusion in his description not only of graphic and plastic elements, but also of sound and dramatic elements."

Ordinary minds demand mere communication. Black and white. Proof positive. Facts. There is little room for humor, hardly any for satire, and none for the absurd. Stanley Kubrick's *Dr. Strangelove or: How I Learned to Stop Worrying and Love the Bomb* is attacked by serious observers in Washington and elsewhere who regard it as untrue, unpatriotic and unheard-of.

Similarly, *Seven Days in May* is subjected to abuse from the radical right because it suggests the possibility of a military takeover of the government. The improbable book *Fail-Safe* leads to a heavy-handed book reply of its own, written by a professor who with straight face says about the novel, "If the influence of *Fail-Safe* grows and the hysteria it germinates affects public policy and American defense efforts are curtailed, the Communists will become progressively emboldened." Our republic still stands.

What these critical defenders of the American establishment fail to realize is that they are reasoning like the Soviets they deplore. For it is the Soviet cultural amateurs who demand literalness coupled with heroic and romantic treatments.

What the journeyman observer fails to comprehend is that the creative process makes its own demands and that the greatest of these is upon the work itself.

Joyce Cary, a modern renaissance man of arts and letters, said that audiences had an obligation to educate themselves so they could comprehend the artist's form of communication.

On the relationship of art and fact, he said: "Only art can convey both the fact and the feeling about the fact, for it works in the medium of common sympathies, common feeling, universal reaction to color, sound, form. It is the bridge between souls, meaning by that not only men's minds but their character and feeling."

In the creative process, art is often antifact and fact antiart.

[4/6/64]

V
A Backward Glance

WILLIAM LIVINGSTON ALDEN

The First "Minor Topics"

It is a common practice of the engineers of steamboats on reaching the wharf to "blow off" steam at full pressure. The sudden noise first startles, and then deafens, man and beast. The other day a pair of horses were frightened into running off at the foot of Harrison Street by the engineer of the steamer *Seth Low*, and Mr. Stephen V. W. Jones was knocked down and mortally injured. The Coroner's Jury in the case recommended that the steam-blowing nuisance should be stopped by the authorities. We heartily concur in the recommendation. There is another grievance which is growing to be insufferable, and which is a direct violation of a Corporation ordinance. We refer to the blowing of tin horns by peddlers of stale fish. These fellows disturb the slumbers of the weary and prevent the departure in peace of the dying by their uproar. Their blasts are strong enough to topple over stronger walls than those of the ancient City of Jericho. Blows of suppression ought to be dealt against these town blowers of steam and tin.

• A recent amendment of the copyright law makes it incumbent, under a penalty of $25, upon every proprietor of a book, pamphlet, map, chart, musical composition or photograph, for which a copyright shall have been secured, to deliver a copy thereof within a month from the time of publication at the Congressional Library. The publication may pass through the Post Office free, the postmasters are required to give a receipt for it, if a receipt be demanded. This amendment does not bear very

hard upon the owners of the copyrighted article, but it certainly
does upon the Congressional Librarian, when the enormous
quantity of such matter produced yearly is considered. The
wonder is where the room will be found to store, even temporarily, the good, bad and indifferent material which goes
through the copyright mill in the clerks' offices of the United
States District Courts.

• The Police are moving in a lively manner toward enforc-
ing certain ordinances against emptying ash boxes into the gutters, allowing goats and pigs the freedom of the streets, and last,
not least, the failure to remove snow and ice from the sidewalks.
The office of the Corporation Counsel is clogged with thousands of such complaints, and due notice is given that they will
all be pressed. Considerable dissatisfaction is felt by the defend-
ants, especially in suits growing out of the last-mentioned offense, that a great deal of time has elapsed since the period of
the alleged violation, and that it is impossible to remember
distinctly now whether they are guilty or not. The fine in each
case is $3, and the costs $2.50. Where judgments are obtained
there will be a prompt levy to satisfy them.

• Colonel Emmons Clark, nominated by the Governor to be
Fire Commissioner in place of M. B. Brown, resigned, is a
young man of practical ability and energy, and will make an ef-
ficient officer. He served through the war with credit, and is
connected with the Seventh Regiment. His selection encour-
ages the hope of a thorough reform in the Board of Fire Com-
missioners. The Governor's original selections were unfortunate, and did much to discredit the new system and impair
its efficiency. If we can have new men, practical, energetic and
competent, the Paid Fire Department will speedily become as
popular and useful as the Police.

• The "East Side Association," which has just been established, has for its object "the promotion of the general welfare

of the City lying north of Fifty-ninth-street and east of the Central Park." It proposes to take cognizance of legislation of the opening, grading and sewerage of streets, or ordinances and laws, of taxation and assessments, and of finance. Such an organization can hardly fail to be of great service to that part of the city which it represents; and, upon the principle that a just benefit to any part of a community is a benefit to the whole thereof, will be of service to the entire island.

• We had occasion some time since to expose in *The Times* the extortionate practice of the Inspectors and Sealers of Weights and Measures. A correspondent again brings to our notice an attempted imposition on the part of these officials, and asks information as to the law in the case. The fees of the Inspectors and Sealers are fixed by a city ordinance, the details of which we print in another column. We are satisfied that the legal rates are often exceeded by the officials, and therefore give the public the knowledge which will enable them to resist overcharges. [3/16/1867]

WILLIAM LIVINGSTON ALDEN

Smiting the Heathen

It is undoubtedly true that mobs are inexcusable, and that riots are not to be tolerated in any civilized community. And yet it sometimes happens that the law is unable or unwilling to suppress some public and gigantic evil. In such case mob violence becomes the only alternative of degrading submission, and to this alternative a courageous and high-spirited people will usually resort. It is evident that this is the true explanation of the frequently threatened popular risings against the Chinese in California, and however much we may deprecate unlawful massacres perpetrated by unauthorized rioters, it cannot be denied that the conduct of the Chinese has provoked and invited public hostility.

When the earliest Chinese immigrants arrived in California they were not regarded with any serious dislike. On the contrary, much innocent amusement was derived from them by that frank, free, and manly class of the American population locally known as the "hoodlums." To drag a Chinaman backwards by his cue was considered a wholesome and enlivening sport, and children too young to be trusted with revolvers were taught to cultivate accuracy of aim by throwing stones at the timid heathen. At that period the Chinese were too few in number to compete in any way with resident Christians, especially as they were allowed to search for gold only in claims which had been previously worked out and abandoned. This happy state of things was, however, of brief duration. The Chinese immigration increased with alarming rapidity, and it is now estimated that in the Chinese quarter of San Francisco there are fully 20,000 so-called souls.

That these alleged men—for even in California there are Americans who unblushingly assert that the Chinaman is a man—should incur the hostility of the hoodlums, was inevitable. Their want of manliness and morality is simply disgusting. The Chinaman is not only always willing to work, but he does his work with mean-spirited thoroughness, and for wages which a hoodlum would refuse with loathing and contempt. He has no conception of the manly joy of intoxicating himself on bad whiskey and of engaging in spirited "difficulties" with his friends or with casual strangers. Though he may have resided for several years in a Christian country, the Chinaman is seldom able to swear with fluency or originality. It is true that in his own quarter of the city he gambles with other Chinamen for preposterously small stakes, and it is not impossible that he blasphemes in his own intricate language, and in a feeble, heathenish way. It is nevertheless undeniable that he lacks the courage or the ability to practice those virtues in public, and right-minded men cannot do otherwise than despise those who are manly and chivalrous only in private.

There are other and, if possible, worse vices to which the Chinamen are notoriously addicted. They wash themselves and wear clean clothing. This loathsome practice naturally renders them hideous in the sight of the hoodlum, and it is not surprising that it is generally regarded as a direct insult to voters. Equally heinous is the frugality practiced by these depraved heathen. The Chinese actually save money out of their meager earnings; and while they affect to scorn the free lunches provided by beneficent liquor sellers, it is currently reported that they dine on carefully fattened puppies, and even prefer that unnatural diet to the wholesome flesh of the still-fed hog.

It will hardly be credited by persons unfamiliar with Californian law that there is not a single statute which prohibits the revolting pagan practices above described. Not only is this true, but certain Californian courts have deliberately decided that if an American citizen playfully shoots a casual Chinaman, or if an American small boy fractures a Chinese skull with a paving stone, the injured Chinaman can cause the arrest, and in rare instances the punishment, of the aggressor. The law, so far from declaring the Chinaman to be *ferae naturae,* and thus placing him on the same plane with the umbrella, as an object which can be stolen or smashed without fear of punishment, shamelessly proceeds upon the absurd assumption that he is a man, and has thus certain natural and inalienable rights. It is therefore worse than idle to appeal to the law to suppress the Chinaman; and it follows that either the hoodlum must submit to the degrading presence of thousands of industrious pagans, who corrupt his moral nature by the open parade of their heathenish vices, or he must rise above the law and cure the Chinese ulcer with knife and pistol.

The latter is the course which he is apparently resolved to take, and though we may not approve of rioting in the abstract, it cannot be denied that an industrious, orderly, and frugal heathen is a sight adapted to goad the average hoodlum to

frenzy. San Francisco has evidently made up its mind that the
time has come when the resident Chinamen must be taught
that this is a free and Christian country, where they and their
pagan vices cannot be tolerated. The massacre of the Chinese
can be easily accomplished, and as China has no fleet with
which to bombard San Francisco, in imitation of the American
and European custom of exacting satisfaction for the murder of
a drunken sailor by a brutal mob of bloodthirsty Chinese, the
hoodlums need have no fear of punishment. Of course, the municipal authorities of the city will nominally object to the
threatened riot, but inasmuch as the Chinese have no votes,
while every hoodlum polls at least a score, no very vigorous interference with the popular will need be apprehended.

[1/1/1874]

WILLIAM LIVINGSTON ALDEN

The Hat Problem

Among the most fascinating questions upon which profound and subtle thinkers are in the habit of speculating is the
question, what shall a man do with his hat in church? Great men
in every age have grappled with this problem without reaching
any satisfactory conclusion. It is true that the Jews have tried to
solve it by wearing their hats in the synagogue, but this is a sub-
terfuge unworthy of Christianity, and not much better than
Spinoza's plan of evading the issue by not going to church at
all. We, in this enlightened and Christian age, recognize the
necessity of going to church, and the duty, while in the sacred
edifice, of putting our hats somewhere else than on our heads.
Where to put them is still as unsettled a question today as it was
eighteen hundred years ago.

Of all the various expedients by which ingenious church-
goers have endeavored to safely dispose of their hats, there is

not one that has not been abundantly proved to be fallacious. To hold one's hat continually in one's lap is practicable only in a Quaker meetinghouse, where the worshipers remain seated during the entire service, and never use any devotional implements, such as prayer books and hymn books. No man could successfully balance a hat in one hand and find the Epistle for the twenty-second Sunday after Trinity with the other hand; while to stand up in order to repeat the Creed or to sing a hymn, with a hat under the left arm, would be the height of absurdity. The hat, then, must be laid entirely aside during divine service, and our churches, being constructed with exclusive reference to souls instead of hats, afford no resting places for the latter.

The extreme danger of placing a hat in the aisle immediately outside the pew is universally known. The first lady that sweeps up the aisle carries with her a confused mass of defenseless hats, which are deposited in the shape of a terminal moraine in the front of the pew which is her final goal. Of course the hats which have been subjected to this process are reduced by attrition to a rounded form and are covered with scratches, reminding one of the marks of glacial action on granite boulders. However interesting they may be to the geologist, they are of no further value as hats, and can rarely be bent into a shape that will allow their owners to wear them home. In the days when expansive crinolines were in fashion, the fate of the hat deposited in the aisle was still more appalling. When a well-dressed lady passed by in its vicinity, it disappeared totally from human sight. There are cases on record where one fashionable woman has thus caused the disappearance of thirteen separate hats during her passage from the church door to a pew in the neighborhood of the pulpit. What was the final fate of those hats was never ascertained. Their owners simply knew that they vanished at the rustle of crinoline, and left no trace behind. Whether they were absorbed by contact with soft kid, or resolved into their chemical elements by proximity to steel, is yet to be discovered. The boldest men shrank from making

248   WILLIAM LIVINGSTON ALDEN

investigations as to their fate, and preferred to bear their loss in sad and dignified silence.

Next to the aisle, the pew seat is the most dangerous position in which a hat can be placed. Statistics show that out of every one hundred hats thus situated, sixty are sat upon by their owners, thirty-five are sat upon by other people, and only five escape uninjured. It is a curious fact that more men sit down on their hats after repeating the Creed than after reading the Psalms or performing any other perpendicular part of the service; and another curious fact is the attraction which a hat thus exposed upon a seat exerts upon a fat person. Neither of these facts has ever been satisfactorily explained, although they are matters of general notoriety. A man may enter a remote pew in a strange church, and place his hat on the seat in a position where it is impossible that a fat man could perceive it on entering the church. Nevertheless, experience has shown that in six cases out of ten—or, to be exact, in 6.139 cases—the sexton will show a fat man into that precise pew within ten minutes after the hat is in position, while other and further fat men will from time to time hover about the locality, with the evident desire of ascertaining if the hat is still susceptible of further smashing. There is clearly a law of nature at work here which needs to be definitely formulated, and it is discreditable to science that this has not yet been done.

As to putting one's hat on the floor underneath the seat, no man who follows this reckless course can expect anything but disaster. If there is a small boy in the pew, he will infallibly discover that hat, and kick it to the farther end of the pew within the first thirty minutes of the service. If there is a lady in the pew, a surgical operation will be required to remove her boot from the interior of the hat, while in any event the hat is certain to absorb every particle of dust within a radius of eight feet, and to fasten itself to the floor with the aid of forgotten Sunday School gumdrops. Neither under the seat, on the seat, nor in the aisle can the wearied hat find rest, and the plan of establishing a hat pound in the vestibule, where hats could be ticketed and kept during service, would simply result in converting a church into a hat exchange, where the sinners would secure all the good hats, and the saints would be compelled to content themselves with wornout and worthless ones.

Thus a severe and exhaustive process of reasoning shows that there is no place in a modern church where a hat can be reasonably safe. But let us be thankful that we are at the dawn of better things. A clever inventor has just devised a plan for solving the problem that has so long baffled the acutest minds. He has secured a patent for what he calls "an improved pew hatholder." It consists of a sort of wire cage attached to the back of the pew, and intended as a receptacle for hats. When filled this receptacle revolves, and carries its precious freight into a safe and obscure recess, whence it is alleged that it can be withdrawn in an uninjured condition at the end of the service. Let us hope that the inventor is not too sanguine, and that his scheme will meet all the exigencies of the case. Who can tell how great will be the effect upon the spiritual welfare of the community when the masculine churchgoer can dismiss his hat from his mind and give his undivided attention to other, purer, and better themes.   [1/7/1874]

WILLIAM LIVINGSTON ALDEN

The Decay of Burglary

That the "hard times" have seriously affected that large and enterprising class of our fellow citizens, the burglars, there is abundant evidence. A marked change is plainly perceptible in the manner in which they do their work. Formerly the burglar was usually an artist in his profession, and showed a conscientious thoroughness and nicety in its practice. He effected his entrance into a house in a dexterous and workmanlike manner, leaving no broken glass or smashed panels to accuse him of clumsy incompetence. He knew what articles of value to select, and how to avoid disturbing the inmates of the house by rude and inconsiderate noises. In no circumstances would he be guilty of wanton and ungentlemanly destruction of property. If he found himself insulted with plated spoons, and mocked by oroide jewelry, he never showed his resentment by twisting the former and stamping on the latter. If he thus failed to meet with any adequate reward for his midnight toil, he simply withdrew quietly and inoffensively, and contented himself with pitying the selfish parsimony with which house-holders, rolling in plated teaspoons, ignored the hardworking burglar, and left him to suffer in silence the pangs of disappointed hope.

To this praiseworthy burglar of former days has succeeded the rude pretender to burglary, who cannot undertake the simplest job without showing his incompetence and vulgarity. He breaks into suburban houses by the primitive process of kicking out the cellar windows, and scratches the matches with which he lights his lantern on the spotless parlor walls. His first idea is to rob the refrigerator and make a hearty meal, careless of the annoyance which he thus inflicts upon the thrifty housewife, and of the disgrace which he brings upon his art by subordinating it to sensual gratification. After supper he makes an exploration of the house, soiling the carpets with tobacco juice and breaking the locks of desks and drawers. If he finds nothing that is worth stealing, he expresses his brutal anger by cutting the pictures, scratching the piano, and breaking the clock. Before he departs he usually manages to fall over enough furniture to awaken the proprietor, and to thus promote that want of harmony in the domestic circle which inevitably occurs when a husband hesitates to accept his wife's advice to go downstairs armed only with his nightshirt and capture a burglar. The contrast between this ruffianly housebreaker and the skillful and accomplished burglar is painfully forced upon our attention whenever we read the police reports, and thinking men naturally ask themselves what has been the cause of this sad deterioration which apparently involves the whole profession.

The root of the evil lies in the high prices which have prevailed since the Civil War. Formerly burglars' tools could be obtained at prices which permitted men of moderate means to enter the profession. Today a complete set of tools costs fully $400, and no one but a capitalist can equip himself for the practice of burglary in an artistic and creditable way. It thus follows that burglary has fallen into the hands of "shysters," who undertake to rob houses by the unaided light of nature, and without either burglars' tools or the knowledge of their uses, while men who might become able and accomplished burglars, were they provided with suitable tools, disdain to rob with their naked hands, so to speak, and prefer to become gamblers or statesmen, rather than to bring disgrace upon a more honorable profession by using clubs or paving stones instead of center bits and jimmies.

In order to improve the condition of burglars, and restore the profession to its earlier excellence, we need, first of all, to remove the restrictions which the law has unfairly placed upon the manufacture and sale of burglars' tools, and which necessarily increase their market value. Plumbers' tools are openly made and sold, and gas manufacturers are permitted to supply that heaven- and man-defying instrument, the gas meter, to their victims. The law which sanctions these things nevertheless makes an arbitrary discrimination against burglars' tools, and thus, while with one hand it protects the plumber and the gas manufacturer, with the other it hampers and oppresses the burglar. Take away those offensive restrictions and burglars' tools will fall 50 percent in price, while a substantial victory will be gained for the great principle of free trade.

Men who have the interests of burglary at heart will not, however, be content with merely securing the repeal of an obnoxious law. If we wish to be robbed in a skillful and artistic way, and to avoid the annoying visits of incapable and vulgar ruffians, we must encourage men with a talent for burglary by placing full kits of burglars' tools within the reach of the very poorest. To do this, a charitable society should be organized and a plan of action devised which should secure the end in view, without at the same time pauperizing the burglar. If this is done, the best and brightest days of burglary will soon return, and the householder will have the gratification of being robbed by accomplished artists, instead of the annoyance which he now experiences at the hands of the miserable pretenders who disgrace the profession.   [1/14/1874]

WILLIAM LIVINGSTON ALDEN

Pockets

A London magistrate lately told a woman whose pocket had been picked that if women would change the position and plan of their pockets, they would not so frequently suffer from the depredations of light-fingered thieves. This was a judicial opinion of remarkable acuteness and exceptional value, insofar as it indicated the true reason why women are the favorite prey of pickpockets. Still, it is one thing to point out an evil that deserves to be remedied, and quite another to designate the remedy. The court which denounced the present female substitute for a pocket did not suggest any practicable improvement upon it, and, indeed, it is doubtful if any man who is not a professional scientific person is fully capable of dealing with so difficult a question.

Man is marsupial, and herein he is broadly distinguished from woman. Nature has provided man with pockets in his trousers, his waistcoat, and his coat. The number is not always the same, some men having, in the aggregate, twelve distinct pockets, great and small, while others have only eight or nine; but a man totally without pockets would be a *lusus naturae*. It is remarkable that pockets are not congenital, but are slowly developed during childhood and youth. The trousers pockets, which are earliest developed, seldom make their appearance before the fifth year, and one of these usually comes to maturity ten or twelve months before its fellow. About the eighth year a male child develops two and sometimes three coat pockets, and two years later the lower waistcoat pockets appear. Nature then pauses in her work, and it is not until the fourteenth year that the small fob pockets of the waistcoat and the watch pocket of the trousers are developed. The appearance of the pistol pocket and the two coattail pockets is usually synchronous with the cutting of the wisdom teeth. When these have reached maturity, the normal development of pockets ceases—for the comparatively recent discovery of isolated specimens of men with pockets in the sleeves of their overcoats, apparently designed for stowing away female hands, does not as yet warrant any change in the scientific classification and description of human pockets.

Of the uses of the pocket it is unnecessary to speak, since we are all familiar with them. It may, however, be safely asserted that without pockets men would never have emerged from barbarism. Handkerchiefs, penknives, money, tobacco, latchkeys—those articles the presence of which is essential to civilization, and the absence of which constitutes barbarism—manifestly could not exist in any useful form had not beneficent nature endowed us with pockets. It is a significant fact that the higher a man rises in the scale of civilization, the more numerous become his pockets. The red man has no pocket whatever; the Turk has two pockets; the people of the south of Europe have rarely more than five, while the man of Anglo-Saxon blood has nine, or—counting those in his overcoat—ten well-defined and practicable pockets. Representative government, fine-cut tobacco, trial by jury, and revolving pistols are the precious inheritance of the nine-pocketed races. Ignorance, superstition, and a general assortment of miseries are the lot of those who have not developed more than four or five pockets.

Why nature constructed woman without true pockets it does not become us to inquire, although the fact might easily be interpreted as an evidence that women are not designed to become the military or civil leaders of mankind. It is sufficient for us to know that the pocket, in the scientific sense of the term, is the monopoly of the male sex, for it is not yet established that even Dr. Mary Walker has developed a really masculine pocket. Emulous of the more gifted sex, women have striven to supply the deficiencies of nature by art, and boldly claim that the mysterious and unseen bags which they carry concealed about their persons are virtually pockets. On this point the distinguished anatomist Cuvier says: "The capacious muslin organ generally called the female pocket has none of the essential characteristics of the true pocket. It is situated a little lower than the placquet, and forms a cul-de-sac, to which the placquet serves as the entrance. It may be removed by the knife without any perceptible effect upon the health, and it is plainly artificial and extraneous." The same opinion is held by all educated anatomists, and, though we may admit that the so-called female pocket is capable of containing a large amount of handkerchiefs, candy, hairpins, and other necessities of feminine existence, its real character as a commonplace bag ought not to be concealed under the pretentious title of pocket.

From the nature of its construction, this bag is so easy of access to the shameless pickpocket that he looks upon it in the light of a storehouse, in which is laid up for his especial benefit portable property of more or less value. No one will dispute the dictum of the London court, that women who place their purses in these pseudo pockets invite pickpockets to steal them; but what other device can they substitute for the inefficient muslin bag? To require a woman to develop pockets without a basis of trousers, waistcoat, or coat, would be more cruel than was Pharaoh's request that the Hebrews would make bricks without straw. Women who desire artificial pockets are limited to the use of the treacherous muslin bag, and the locality in which it is now worn is declared by competent comparative anatomists to be the only one where such an appendage could be securely placed, and remain at the same time easily accessible. The only way out of the difficulty is for women to abandon the vain effort to emulate marsupial man, and to lay aside their muslin bags. Thus will they remove temptation from the pickpocket, and prove themselves capable of accepting, without a murmur, the mysterious law of nature, which lavishes pockets upon one sex and withholds them inexorably from the other. [1/21/1874]

WILLIAM LIVINGSTON ALDEN

Dr. Schliemann

It is announced that the Turkish government has authorized Dr. Schliemann to resume his excavations on the alleged site of Troy and that the learned digger, having laid in a new copy of Homer and a large supply of spades, will immediately resume his labors.

Some misapprehension exists in the public mind as to the object of Dr. Schliemann's labors. It is generally thought that he has hitherto been digging in search of the alleged city of Troy. In point of fact, he has been trying to exhume the *Iliad,* and his success in so doing has been remarkable. There are very grave doubts whether there ever was such a person as Homer, or such a city as Troy, and granting the existence of the latter, its true site is wholly conjectural. There is, however, no sort of doubt as to the existence of the *Iliad,* as every college freshman sadly knows, and hence Dr. Schliemann showed a praiseworthy discrimination in digging for the topographical and biographical incidents of the latter. At first he was rather embarrassed with the richness of the ruined cities which he unearthed, for he exhumed no less than four consecutive buried cities, one above another. The lowest of these he decided to call Troy—throwing the rest away as comparatively valueless—and in this so-called Troy he found everything of interest which is mentioned in the *Iliad.*

The maps which the good Doctor drew were extremely ingenious. They contained a plan of Troy, showing the principal buildings and such localities as have interesting Homeric associations. Priam's palace, the town pump, the cottage occupied by Helen, the Lyceum, the spot where the Trojan horse disgorged its contents, the horse block on which Anchises perched himself in order to climb on the pious shoulders of Aeneas, the Post Office, and the prominent banking and insurance offices, were all duly displayed on Schliemann's maps, and gave the alleged city nearly as imposing an appearance as is presented by the map of some projected town in the Far West. As for interesting relics, Schliemann found them by the basketful. His method was a peculiar one. He would strive to put himself in the place of some respectable Trojan, and then imagine how he would have conducted himself in any given contingency. Thus, he said to himself, "If I had been Priam, I would have put my portable property in a small box, and as soon as the Greeks entered the city I would have slipped out of the back door, climbed the back fence by means of the stepladder, and gone out of the west gate, where a cab would have awaited me." Having thus satisfied himself as to what Priam actually did, he followed that respectable monarch's course until he reached the west gate, where he picked up the box of portable property which Priam had evidently found too heavy, and which the cabman had refused to carry except at an exorbitant price. In like manner Dr. Schliemann was able to divine where to look for Helen's hairpins, and where to find the blue spectacles with which Paris strove to disguise himself from the eyes of the private detective employed by Menelaus. Thus, the exhumation of the *Iliad* was attended with extraordinary success, and there is no doubt that Dr. Schliemann in his future diggings will find every sort of object not absolutely inconsistent with a liberal interpretation of Homer's immortal epic.

Great as is the interest which attaches to the hairpins of Helen, and the fine-toothed comb of Paris, there are those who feel that Dr. Schliemann has dug quite long enough at Troy, and that he ought to exercise his remarkable genius in other fields. He is just the man to dig on the site of the Garden of Eden, and to reclaim the articles of personal property which our first parents left behind in the suddenness of their departure. He would not have the slightest difficulty in determining the exact locality of the primeval paradise. All he would think it necessary to do would be to visit the plain of Mesopotamia; to pick out a good-sized garden spot, and to announce that he had fixed the exact position of the Garden of Eden. Then he would begin to dig and to discover with the energy and success which have hitherto characterized him. He would soon lay bare the asphalt paths over which Adam was accustomed to walk, and would find his lawn roller and sickle in a rusty but still easily recognizable condition. As soon as the excavations became large enough to warrant a map, he would construct one calculated to bring tears to the eyes of the most hardened geographer. On that map would be marked the position of the apple tree which Eve had such melancholy cause to remember, together with a dotted line, labeled "Probable route of the Serpent on entering and retiring from the garden." That same valuable map would also show Adam's Swimming Pool, the Birthplace of Eve, the Croquet Ground, and the Sartorial Fig Tree. As for relics, Schliemann would find them to order for the use of clergymen's families and Sunday Schools. Fig-leaf aprons would be picked up by the sharp-eyed searcher on every hedge. Small fish bones, "supposed to have been used as hairpins"; polished bits of tomato cans, labeled "hand mirrors," and innumerable quantities of agricultural tools and packages of Weathersfield garden seeds would be sent to Europe and America by the shipload, and if somebody were to order a slip from the original apple tree, Dr. Schliemann would send out more young apple trees in the course of two years than the united nurseries of Long Island could furnish in ten.

When such a field as this is open to the good German discoverer, it is a pity to see him wasting his time at Troy. Trojan relics are, of course, very well in their way, but the public has somewhat lost interest in them, and in any event they are less interesting than relics from Eden would be. After what Dr. Schliemann has found at Troy, there is not the slightest doubt that he could find anything at any other locality that anyone might desire. Let him go to Mesopotamia and exhume Paradise, and it may be safely predicted that his discoveries there will be precisely as valuable as those which he has made on the alleged site of Troy. [1/28/1874]

WILLIAM LIVINGSTON ALDEN

A Sad Case

The sea serpent has been seen again; this time in the Malacca Straits, and by the captain and surgeon of a British steamship, assisted, as they allege, by all the rest of the ship's company. The alarming apparition is described at great length in an affidavit made by the two officers aforesaid, and there is no doubt that it ought to be a terrible warning to them.

On the eleventh day of September last, at 10:30 A.M., the steamship *Nestor* was passing through the Malacca Straits, on her way to Shanghai. We need not inquire what the captain and surgeon were doing at that precise hour, but, as it was early in the day, we may assume there was merely a slight dash of brandy mingled with the soda water. Suddenly they saw on the starboard beam, at a distance of about 1,200 yards, an animal that filled them with horror and alarm. It was, of course, serpentine in form—as that style of retributive animal always is—and it comprised a body of 50 feet in length, together with a tail 150 feet long. At least, this is the way in which the two unhappy officers describe their vision, although it might be preferable to say that the serpent consisted of 150 feet of tail, with a 50-foot body attached thereto. In point of color, the animal could have given odds to Solomon in all his glory. Its head was of a pale yellow color, while the body and tail were encircled with alternate stripes of yellow and black. In fact, the surgeon was at first inclined to think that he was gazing upon a titanic mermaid, with yellow hair and a wealth of fashionable hosiery; but the conception of 200 feet of striped hose was too vast to obtain a permanent lodging in his wearied and excited brain. What was exceptionally remarkable in this portentous snake was its total want of either mouth or eyes. It is well known to all naturalists that the serpents usually seen by seafaring men in thirsty latitudes are provided with eyes of pure phosphorus, and are equipped with mouths of tremendous size, which they habitually wear wide open, in order to breathe out streams of fire. Still, there is no reason why we should doubt the appearance of an eyeless and mouthless snake; and, indeed, such an animal would have a weird look, which would startle and appall the beholder, because of its very novelty.

When the captain first saw this terrible creature, it was swimming parallel to the ship at the rate of 9¾ knots, and he felt a wild impulse to run it down, as though it were merely an American man-of-war in a Japanese harbor. On reflection, he decided that such a course might injure the blades of his screw, and that, after all, experience had demonstrated that the more one tries to slay a serpent of that particular species, the more apt it is to transform itself into a regiment of objectionable goblins. Moreover, the serpent suddenly ported its tail and ran under the steamer's stern. It kept company with the ship for some time, and why it did not come on board, and following the captain and surgeon to their staterooms, divide itself in two pieces and coil round their respective legs, we are not told.

So great was the shock experienced by the captain and surgeon, that as soon as the ship reached Shanghai they rushed to the office of a local magistrate and in his presence solemnly "swore off," or, as they preferred to put it, made an affidavit. It is from the descriptive passages in this affidavit—which are the only portions of it which the deponents have ventured to publish—that the facts above set forth are taken. It is unpleasant to charge two British officers with a lack of candor, but it is impossible to read this affidavit without recognizing its evasive nature. The deponents weakly imagined that they could conceal the true state of the case by refraining from calling the marine monster a snake. Not only do they assert that they "should not for a moment compare it to a snake," but they also allege that it resembled "the frog tribe." We all know that the frog is a reputable cold-water animal, which can be seen without gross cause for scandal by the most sober and abstemious persons, but the captain and surgeon of the *Nestor* cannot deceive the public by calling an animal consisting almost entirely of tail, and devoid of either legs or fins, a frog. They saw an open and undisguised serpent, and little hopes of their permanent reformation can be entertained so long as they attempt to deny the fact and to babble of innocent frogs.

If we may believe the testimony of these two unfortunate men, the sea serpent was also seen by their fellow officers and by all the passengers. As the latter were principally Chinamen, their testimony, even if we had it, would not be held to be of much value; but surely we ought to hear what the first and second mates of the *Nestor* have to say concerning the matter. Neither the captain nor the surgeon mentions the impression which the sight of the sea serpent made upon these two estimable seamen; and although the captain does mention that the third mate said the animal was nothing but a shoal, he omits to tell us how he thereupon took the third mate aside and explained to him that delirium tremens could not be tolerated in a subordinate officer, and that he must abandon the intoxicating cup and sign the pledge if he wished to remain the third mate of the *Nestor*. There is not the least doubt that the captain and the surgeon saw precisely the sort of serpent which they describe in their affidavit, but when they hesitate to call it a serpent, and suppress the evidence of the first and second mates in regard to the vision, they excite in the public mind a doubt of their strict honesty. [2/3/1874]

FREDERICK CRAIG MORTIMER

The First "Topics of The Times"

The London *Saturday Review* asserts that the war in Cuba is rapidly degenerating into pure barbarism, and makes the following interesting suggestion:

> It need surprise no one if President Cleveland does intervene, and that with decisive promptness, to save what is left of civilized life in Cuba. He occupies a personal position of peculiar independence, since from a politician's point of view the party which elected him to the Presidency may be said now hardly to exist. The Democrats have repudiated his fiscal policy, and the Republicans are, of course, at daggers drawn with him on the subject of the tariff.
>
> If he called "Halt!" to Spain, it is certain that the two rival parties now fighting for the Presidency would outvie each other in enthusiastic support of his action. Neither Mr. McKinley nor Mr. Bryan would dream for a moment of attempting to stem the popular torrent of hatred for the Spaniard which such a step would let loose in America; they would be forced instead to add to its impetus by all the means at their disposal.
>
> The effect of such a violent diversion upon the pending campaign it is impossible to forecast, but it would at least restore Mr. Cleveland to his place as the chief figure in American public life.

• The Albany *Argus,* recalling the Maynard convention, in which but a single delegate protested, although the people beat the ticket by more than 100,000 votes, has a word of counsel for Tammany in regard to its action at Buffalo:

> It is time for the leaders of Tammany to reflect: a time for them to think twice before they act. Much as to the future of Tammany herself may depend upon the decision, and this

year, as in other years, her unusual strength and facility of organized effort may mean much of benefit or much of harm to the Democracy of the State. Least of all should the leaders of Tammany, or the leaders of any other Democratic organization, be deluded into the belief that sentiment is all one way.

• The Chicago *Tribune* has discovered a new argument against William Jennings Bryan:

One of the comical features of the Presidential campaign is the showing made by the religious denominations. Gen. Palmer is a Baptist, Major McKinley is a Methodist, and Mr. Bryan is a Presbyterian. The Baptists and Methodists are making the point that as Cleveland and Harrison are Presbyterians, the country has already been under Presbyterian control for twelve years, and there is a manifest impropriety in making it sixteen by the election of Bryan.

• The Raleigh (North Carolina) *News and Observer,* a silver paper, tries its hand at refuting Mr. Carl Schurz's argument:

If Mr. Schurz has forgotten the cry of starvation that has been coming up from Ireland for 500 years; the distress of thousands in "Darkest England"; the gaunt faces of the half-fed peasants in every gold-standard country—if Mr. Schurz has forgotten the real conditions that confront the humble in "civilized Europe," the masses of immigrants have larger memories. They want no system perpetuated here that has driven them from their native land.

• The best that the Cumberland (Maryland) *Times* can find to say about the Indianapolis Convention is contained in this amiable paragraph:

A closer and more thorough reading of the platform adopted by the sham Democracy in convention assembled at Indianapolis but brings out more clearly and more forcibly the unmitigated check of the forces of plutocracy and their reckless disregard for truth which characterized this convention as a triumph of prodigious mendacity, as well as of astonishing irregularity.

• The Washington correspondent of the *Journal* sends the news that Li Hung Chang is confident that within twelve months a full remonetization of silver will take place. He adds:

> This information pleased Li Hung Chang, because he sees in the prospective advance in the price of silver and the coordinate reduction in the purchasing power of gold a great advantage to China, which has now that greatest blessing of Western civilization, a bonded debt, interest and principal payable in gold.

• The Louisville *Courier Journal* shares the feeling generally prevalent since the Indianapolis Convention that the Democratic Party of the future will be the National Democracy. As for Bryan:

> The Babylon of Popocracy totters to its fall. Come out of her, Democrats, that you may not be partakers of her sins, that you receive not of her plagues.

• The New Orleans *Picayune* hits it about right:

> The Indianapolis Convention represented the Democracy of the United States. The Chicago Convention intended to do so, but the children sent there were abducted by the Bryan combine and silverites, and are being brought up by hand in Colorado and Idaho.

• Noting Mr. Bryan's fondness for quoting Solomon, the Philadelphia *Record* suggests that he might profit by Solomon's advice:

Whoso keepeth his mouth and tongue keepeth his soul from troubles. [9/8/1896]

FREDERICK CRAIG MORTIMER

*Can War Be Endured Without Tea? . . .
Belligerent Pacifists . . . On the Making
of Mazeppa Fire Companies*

Among the restrictions on imports that were announced by the British Premier as essential to the safety of the empire was one that must have impressed his hearers rather more than did most of the others, as indicating the gravity of the submarine peril. Probably none of these others meant to so nearly every Briton a daily personal deprivation as does—or rather, as would—the shutting off of the tea supply other than Indian tea.

Though tea may not count as a necessity of life, it is not much different from one for those who have become accustomed to its use, and it is the practically unanimous testimony of men who, as explorers or otherwise, are forced to make great expenditures of energy under rigorous conditions that tea is a most important addition to their fare. They willingly take the trouble to carry it with them on journeys where every added ounce of burden receives careful consideration and all "luxuries" are left behind. Of course the great majority of human kind managed to get along well enough until comparatively recent years without this narcotic, or any of its near relatives, but the welcome it everywhere received when once known shows plainly enough that it met a want that is not the less real because not easy to define.

But the Premier's warning as to tea was not as terrifying to the Britons as it might have been, for the proposed exclusion is to be complete only as regards what he called "foreign" teas, meaning, in effect, those of China, and of those the English have not been great consumers since the raising of the precious herb has become an important industry in several of Great Britain's colonial possessions, notably Ceylon. Even of these "native" teas, however, the imports are to be cut to smaller amounts than have become usual in the regular course of trade, and it is apparent that a good many British teapots will have to be retired from present service.

Thereby will be appreciably increased the gloom of a situation that was already dark enough, and the endurance of the trials of the time will be made measurably harder. Taking everything into account, it is at least probable that Mr. Lloyd George might better have restricted the manufacture of intoxicants more than he now proposes and let the tea trade alone.

• As might have been expected, it was the "lunatic fringe," to use Colonel Roosevelt's happily invented phrase, that finally gained control of last week's pacifist convention in this city and took the definite action on which all who attended the meeting will be judged by the rest of the country. Nothing less than a formal declaration that war for any cause was wrong, which is the same thing as saying that peace is worth any price, would satisfy the ruling fraction of the delegates, and the more moderate, or less fanatical, of the men and women present counseled in vain against the adoption of resolutions that would emphasize and justify all that the foes of pacifism had been saying about it.

There is significance, too, though no real cause for surprise, in the fact that the convention was a disorderly one from beginning to end—that these professed worshipers of peace applied to each other epithets as harsh as are ever used at gatherings of unregenerate politicians, and that, if they did not come to blows as a means of settling differences of opinion, it was because the possessors of such common sense and ordinary regard for public opinion as had exemplification there yielded to the inevitable before the ultimate display of inconsistency could be made.

It would be interesting to know what the extreme pacifists would do if confronted with the alternative of fighting, and killing, if they could, a band of hungry wolves, or else of allowing themselves, their wives and children to be eaten up. That contingency differs in no essential degree from that which many a nation has had to meet, with bipeds instead of quadrupeds threatening destruction, and the moral elements in the two cases are precisely the same. In each, indeed, a third course is or might be open—that of running away betimes and leaving the wolves of whatever species masters of the field.

Several races, among them Eskimos, are said by the ethnologists to have done just that, though their flight into lands nobody else would take as a gift is ascribed to incompetence for war rather than a lofty disapproval of it. Wolves would have the same rights in any frontier village, and the same plea of "necessity" that the Germans had in Belgium, and, if no war is defensible, to make against wolves the only sort of resistance they understand would be wicked.

• A list of the bills passed by the present session of our legislature and signed by the Governor is printed in *The Law Journal*. It is a truly impressive showing, and one calculated to make the reader wonder how the minds of these statesmen stand the constant and varied strains to which they are subjected.

Prominent among the achievements on the record is "an Act"—well deserving the capital letter it receives—"to incorporate the Mazeppa Fire Engine Company, No. 2, of Nyack, Orangetown, Rockland County, State of New York," and settling the momentous question of how many men may join it. Another "Act" gives the Surrogate in Westchester County an additional clerk, and a third allows Onondaga County to have an auditor and tells him how to audit and what, while a fourth amends the charter of the village of Fredonia. Westchester County, too, graciously has been empowered to borrow some money and to erect some public buildings in which to house its paupers and criminals.

So the annals of this great law-making body run on. To the uninitiate by far the greater part of what it does would seem to be work which the several counties and towns were, or ought to be, quite competent to do for themselves without any outside advice or assistance, but, of course, that cannot be true. In some real, though mysterious way it must be that the establishment in Nyack of a Mazeppa Fire Company, No. 2, cannot be safely or well done unless Chautauqua and Richmond counties, and all the counties in between, have a voice in the matter.

If not thus controlled and restrained, Nyack might go on creating Mazeppa Fire Companies in endless succession and fall into hopeless bankruptcy as a result of its mad passion for this form of municipal activity.   [2/26/17]

SIMEON STRUNSKY

Strange New Tongue

Because it is the custom among male Americans to wear a derby for informal evening parties, while Englishmen put on a bowler, there has grown up a popular indoor sport in this country. It is called the American Language. The object of the game is to make believe that such a language really exists, or soon will exist, and that it is quite different from the English language in which the King James Version is written and which Stanley Baldwin still employs when addressing the House of Commons.

Mr. Mencken has dedicated a learned, amusing and successful book to the subject and is reported to be at work on a sequel.

Other hands have made lesser contributions. H. W. Horwill's new *Dictionary of American Usage* does not set up an American language, but the occasion has been seized upon by commentators whose ardent hopes do run that way.

Listening to the more excited philologists on the American language one would think that when an American citizen comes across "To be or not to be, that is the question," it is all Greek to him. Apparently he must have it translated for him, perhaps by a learned German scholar. Similarly, a modern Englishman who meets "Of the people, by the people, for the people" is compelled to look up the words in his pocket dictionary, edited very likely by an eminent Japanese grammarian.

By the American language hypothesis the man from Cambridge, Massachusetts, and the man from Cambridge, England, speak two different tongues for the reason that the American wears a derby and the Englishman sports a bowler. The American wears suspenders, but the Englishman depends on braces. One buys his railway ticket from a ticket seller, the other gets his from a booking clerk. One travels in a railway car and the other in a railway carriage. One buys his tooth powder at the druggist's and the other at the chemist's. And, of course, every child out of arms is aware that Americans go up to the tenth floor in an elevator, whereas Englishmen invariably take the lift.

This strange belief is based on the fact that readers of *The New York Times* walk on the sidewalk, whereas English newspaper readers walk on the pavement. If Al Smith had been born in the shadow of Waterloo Bridge instead of the shadow of Brooklyn Bridge, his favorite song would have been "The Pavements of London." Instead of running for President, the English "Al" would have stood for Parliament. Needless to say, his brown derby would have been a brown bowler.

But Al Smith happens to be an American speaking the American language. That is why distinguished English visitors when they go up to the top of the Empire State Building must bring along an interpreter to converse with Al Smith; probably some

brilliant young postgraduate student of linguistics from Man-
chukuo.

American usage and English usage are real things, and their
divergence may well produce occasional misunderstanding,
embarrassment, comedy. It is quite true that when an American feels indisposed he says he is sick, and he puts on his derby
and runs down to the drugstore. In the same circumstances an
Englishman feels ill, dons his bowler and visits the chemist.
Englishmen who want to make a lot of money in a hurry go
down into the City, whereas Americans go into the Street.
When they abolish the Corn Laws in England it means the laws
about the importation of wheat. Things may be even worse
than that. When the House of Commons tables a bill it brings
it up for discussion. Over here when we table a proposal we
bury it. A public school in England is a private school in the
United States.

The more moderate philologians do not claim that there is
already an American language. They do see English usage on
the two sides of the Atlantic going their separate ways, and some-
day there will be two different languages. The question is how
many hundred years are needed. People in Portland, Maine,
and Phoenix, Arizona, still have no difficulty in understanding
the English of *Gulliver's Travels,* 200 years ago, and *Paradise
Lost,* about 300 years ago. They can even get the drift of
Chaucer's English, nearly 600 years ago.

On the other hand, there is Hollywood. The American talkie
has made English household words out of "okay," "on the spot,"
"bull," and "highhat." In fact, many Englishmen say their
speech is being swamped by American movies. So there is
actually a chance that the language bond between the two nations will be stronger than ever in the future. Before Americans
need a dictionary to read *Alice in Wonderland* Englishmen
will be wearing derbies, eating quick lunches in the drugstore
and going up in elevators.

Perhaps there are a couple of hundred such instances of
different English usage on the two sides of the Atlantic. Since

the English language has a mere 400,000 words, it is plain that a gulf exists between the two languages.

It is an odd circumstance that the existence of such a language abyss seems to appeal most strongly to Americans with strong international sympathies and a worldwide outlook. They like to think of all men as brothers, but they also like to play with the idea that people in San Francisco and in Liverpool speak two alien tongues. They know how much in common Americans have with the ancient civilizations of China, India and Guatemala, but they like to think that the language in which *The New York Times* is printed is really a different language from that appearing in the London *Morning Post* and the Glasgow *Herald.*   [8/11/35]

SIMEON STRUNSKY

Baccalaureate with a Difference

Men and women of the Class of 1941: It is my intention this afternoon to upset as many precedents as I can manage in the short time at my disposal. And I propose to start right in by giving you my parting injunctions and counsel at the very beginning of my address instead of holding back the secret until the very end, as is customary on such occasions.

Consequently, with all the earnestness at my command, I beseech you, my dear boys and girls, to take with you into the great world which you are about to enter, as an inspiration and a guide to conduct in these critical times for America and for democracy, the following watchword and battle cry:

"Let us be complacent."

America's greatest need today is the very best opinion of itself that it can muster.

That is the reason why you may have noticed that I have this afternoon donned, beneath the academic black gown, a form-shaped tropical-weight suit in a snappy apple green. It will also strike you that the Persian color effects on my cravat are distinctly on the vivid side, not to say garish. In other words, I have resolutely discarded the conventional sackcloth and ashes in which baccalaureate orators since 1930 have regularly appeared before you. They have considered it the only appropriate costume in which to stand up before the college youth of the nation and to apologize to the young people for the awful mess which they, the old folks, have made of the world. They have regularly apologized for the sorry condition in which they are now compelled to hand over the country to you young people.

But this afternoon you will hear no apologies from me. I will not grovel. I feel that the sackcloth and the ashes and the breast-beating and the contrite tears have been tragically overdone. It hasn't done the country any good and it hasn't done the young people any good either. Many of you look about your America today and find nothing in it to love and nothing to believe in and nothing to defend.

You are really seeing America through the frightened eyes of the last dozen years of elderly baccalaureate orators. Your disenchantment is not primarily the result of bitter experience. You are only giving us back the pat phrases we have taught you. We of the older generation have done so much apologizing and repenting that you young people have naturally concluded that the facts are even blacker than we have painted them.

Boys and girls of 1941, there are two sides to every story, but you have been told only one side. Middle-aged or elderly baccalaureate orators have stood up before you every spring since 1930 and with hot tears running down their ashen cheeks have asked forgiveness for handing over to you an America devoid of opportunity.

And yet it never seems to have occurred to these crestfallen apologists or to their youthful hearers to ask why baccalaureate orators should be apologizing to huge multitudes of college men and women such as in 1900 or even in 1915 would have seemed incredible. In the year 1915 the baccalaureate orators addressed themselves to a college population of 300,000 men and women. In 1940 the orators were speaking to a college population of one and a half million men and women. For every boy and girl in college twenty-five years ago there were five in 1940. Yet it was obligatory on baccalaureate orators to tell their young people that they were a generation robbed of opportunity.

My dear young people, there are two sides to every story. If I have this afternoon been stressing the brighter side of the American story it is because that side has been so thoroughly forgotten.

But the American faith is here. It has always been here. It is only necessary to go back over the American record and free it of the distortions and the slanders. All we need do is simply to give up this latter-day habit of counting our failures and forgetting our victories. We simply must give up this pernicious habit of thinking of the American nation in terms of "one-third of a nation."

Otherwise, my dear young people, you will never have the faith to stand up against the new slavocracies of Europe and their so-called faiths. You must win back your confidence and your pride in an America without conditions and provisos. Altogether too many of us stand ready to defend America—as she might be. That will never do. You must learn to be proud of America as she is. It was recently observed by one ingenious writer that when men in the past have fought for their homes and their wives and their young they have not stipulated that the home shall be a duplex apartment on Park Avenue, that the wife shall be fairer than Garbo, and the children shall be a combination of Shirley Temple and young Mozart. People have fought for country, home and family as in the living average.   [6/1/41]

SIMEON STRUNSKY

This Social Insecurity

"And in this manner it has come about," a leading economic historian of the year 1976 will write, "that in the expansion of social security we have reached a point where the individual American citizen is secure against every conceivable mischance or natural ailment. The only victims exposed to the threat of insecurity are the American people taken as a whole. This seeming paradox can be explained in a few words.

"How the American people as individuals have attained the full measure of security which they now enjoy is familiar to everyone. Old-age pensions give them security against the onset of time. Unemployment insurance gives them security against the vicissitudes of the business cycle. Health and accident insurance, superimposed on the older life insurance, are self-explanatory.

"By appropriate legislation members of labor unions have been made secure in the right to strike," our future historian continues. "Other regulations, like the check-off and the maintenance of membership and the right of wholesale picketing, have made the position of the labor unions additionally secure. Seniority provisions have provided security inside the factory. Other guarantees and safeguards will no doubt occur to the reader. On the whole, it is no exaggeration to say that in this year 1976 the national system of social security offers the American citizen security against every conceivable challenge 'from the cradle to the grave,' to use the words of a celebrated British economist of a generation ago, by the name of William Beveridge.

"But now we come to the paradox suggested in our opening paragraph," continues our future historian. "The American people, as so many individuals, have been achieving more and more social security, but the American people as a com-

munity, as a public, has found itself growing less and less
secure every year.

"Because the aforesaid right to strike has become a recognized
feature of the wage earner's security a community of 10,-
000,000 people, like New York in the 1970 census, may have its
milk supply cut off by a strike of a few thousand milk drivers.
The city's coal and oil may be cut off by a few thousand striking
tugboat employees. Five million daily travelers on the city's transit lines may be stranded, and the city's life brought to a standstill by a few thousand striking transport workers. And the same
thing has come to pass with a city's—or a nation's—telephones,
telegraph lines, radio and television communications.

"It is not a question here," the argument proceeds, "of great
mass strikes involving hundreds of thousands or perhaps even
millions of workers, as in railroads, coal, steel, and the new
atomic industries. In such cases the numerical disproportion
between strikers and public is not so glaring. The strikers in
their own absolute numbers command a certain respect. But
here we are speaking of the so-called key industry strikers. They
are small in numbers but strategically situated to threaten the
public security. They are openly boastful of their power as key
men to impose their will on the community.

"In this manner it has come about," our economic historian of
the year 1976 will approach his conclusion, "that in the pursuit
of social security the American people have managed to
achieve the surprising result of making the part more important than the whole. It has been made easy for a comparative
handful of people to dictate terms to millions of their fellow
citizens. In this bicentennial year of the Declaration of Independence it often seems as if the American people are less secure in the matter of life, liberty and the pursuit of happiness
than they were a hundred years earlier in the heart of laissez-
faire under President Ulysses S. Grant.

"The average urban American today has no feeling of security that he will get his bottle of milk for the children tomorrow morning, that his heat and light will not be turned off,

that his telephone will not go dead, that he will be able to reach his place of work five or ten miles away, that he can get hold of a taxicab for an emergency trip to the hospital.

"But even worse," our future historian will conclude, "than the state of insecurity to which a community or a nation may find itself reduced by the fiat of a militant handful of organized workers is the spirit of the thing. The handful is proud of being a handful, an elite. It exalts the control of the many by the few. That explains why all over the democratic world the big problem in people's minds has become the problem of majority right —how to protect the majorities against the minorities."

[2/26/46]

The Contributors

WILLIAM LIVINGSTON ALDEN contributed the first "Topics" column under the heading "Minor Topics" in 1867. He became a regular editorial writer for *The New York Times, 1874-1885*. A journalist, lawyer and diplomat, he was a lineal descendant of John and Priscilla Alden.

ELIOT ASINOF, novelist and scenarist, frequently writes about the sporting world. Among his books are *Man on Spikes, The Bedfellow, Eight Men Out* and *Seven Days to Sunday*.

BROOKS ATKINSON, retired drama critic and critic-at-large of *The New York Times*, received the Pulitzer Prize for foreign correspondence about the Soviet Union. Among his books are *Once Around the Sun, Tuesdays and Fridays* and *Brief Chronicles*.

NONA BALAKIAN is a member of *The New York Times Book Review* staff. Her reviews and interviews have appeared in *The Kenyon Review* and other publications. She is coeditor of *The Creative Present: Notes on Contemporary American Fiction*.

CHESTER BOWLES, a longtime government official, has served as Ambassador to India and to Nepal. Among his books are *The Conscience of a Liberal* and *The Making of a Just Society*.

H. I. BROCK joined *The New York Times* staff in 1902, served in various editorial and writing capacities, and retired in 1959. He died in 1961. A frequent contributor to the "Topics" column, he was author of *The Meddlers* and *New York Is Like That*.

DENIS W. BROGAN is Professor of Political Science at Cambridge. Among his books are *American Aspects, The French Nation* and *The Free State*.

JOHN P. CALLAHAN served as a reporter for *The New York Times* from World War II until he died in 1967. As a foreign correspondent, he reported from Pakistan; in New York, his specialty was the waterfront.

KENNETH CAMPBELL served as a reporter for *The New York Times* in Europe and the United States until his retirement in the mid-1960's. His particular beat abroad was France.

LEON EDEL, writer and teacher, received the Pulitzer Prize and the National Book Award for his biography of Henry James. He is Henry James Professor of English and American Letters at New York University.

ANTHONY EDEN, Earl of Avon, served as Prime Minister and Secretary of State for Foreign Affairs of Great Britain. His books include *Full Circle, Facing the Dictators* and *Toward Peace in Indo-China.*

JAMES T. FARRELL is best known as the author of the *Studs Lonigan* novels. Among his many books is *Reflections at Fifty and Other Essays.*

J. WILLIAM FULBRIGHT is chairman of the Senate Committee on Foreign Relations. He has represented Arkansas in the United States Senate since 1945.

JOHN KENNETH GALBRAITH, Professor of Economics at Harvard, is the author of *The Affluent Society, The Great Crash* and *The New Industrial State.*

JOHN W. GARDNER served as Secretary of the Department of Health, Education and Welfare before becoming head of the national Urban Coalition. He is the author of *Excellence.*

MORRIS GILBERT served as a reporter and editor for the daily and Sunday editions of *The New York Times* for many years until his retirement in the mid-1960's. His writings frequently had a Paris background, where he lived and wrote before the Second World War.

ARTHUR L. GOODHART is a member of the English and New York bars. He was Master of University College, Oxford, and chairman of the International Law Association.

NADINE GORDIMER, novelist, short-story writer and foe of apartheid, lives in Johannesburg. Although she is not a banned person, her 1966 novel, *The Late Bourgeois World,* is banned in South Africa. Her books include *The Lying Days* and *Occasion for Loving.*

MARGARET HALSEY is a social critic and novelist. She is author of *With Malice Toward Some, The Pseudo-Ethic* and other books.

FRED M. HECHINGER is education editor of *The New York Times.* He is the author of *The Big Red Schoolhouse, Pre-School Education Today* and (with Grace Hechinger) *Teen-Age Tyranny.*

LAURA Z. HOBSON is the author of, among other books, *Gentleman's Agreement, The Celebrity* and *First Papers.*

FLORENCE JULIEN is an essayist and journalist who has reported from Canada and the United States. She now lives in Ireland.

JUSTIN KAPLAN received the Pulitzer Prize and the National Book Award for his biography, *Mr. Clemens and Mark Twain.*

DAVID KARP is a novelist and scenarist. Among his books are *One, Platoon, The Day of the Monkey, All Honorable Men* and *Enter Sleeping.*

ALFRED KAZIN, literary critic, teaches at the State University of New York, Stony Brook. Among his books are *Starting Out in the Thirties, On Native Grounds* and *A Walker in the City.*

ROBERT F. KENNEDY served as Attorney General of the United States from 1961 to 1964 and Democratic Senator from New York from 1965 until his assassination on June 5, 1968. He was author of *The Enemy Within, Just Friends and Brave Enemies,* and *Thirteen Days,* published posthumously.

JONATHAN KOZOL, a teacher, is the author of *Death at an Early Age,* which received the National Book Award.

THOMAS LASK is a daily book critic and poetry editor of *The New York Times.* He has frequently written about music, the theater and the cultural scene for *The Times.*

HAROLD LAVINE is an editor and writer in New York. He is the author of *Fifth Column in America.*

ARCHIBALD MacLEISH, poet, served as Librarian of Congress and Assistant Secretary of State in the Franklin D. Roosevelt administration. He has received Pulitzer Prizes in poetry and in drama. His works include *America Was Promises* and *J.B.*

EUGENE J. McCARTHY, the Democratic-Farmer-Labor Senator from Minnesota, challenged the Johnson administration's stand on Vietnam in the Presidential campaign of 1968, causing the new politics of youth involvement. He is the author of *The Limits of Power.*

MARYA MANNES, essayist and journalist, is the author of *More in Anger, Subverse, But Will It Sell?* and a novel, *They.*

HERBERT L. MATTHEWS served as a foreign correspondent and member of the editorial board of *The New York Times,* retiring in 1967 after forty-five years on the paper. Among his books are *The Education of a Correspondent, The Fruits of Fascism, The Yoke and the Arrows* and *The Cuban Story.*

MARGARET MEAD, anthropologist, is curator of ethnology at the American Museum of Natural History. Her books include *Coming of Age in Samoa, New Lives for Old, People and Places* and *The Golden Age of American Anthropology.*

ARTHUR MILLER, playwright, wrote *All My Sons, Death of a Salesman, The Crucible, Incident at Vichy, View from the Bridge, After the Fall,* and *The Price.* His short stories are collected in a volume, *I Don't Need You Anymore,* and he is the author of a novel, *Focus.*

HERBERT MITGANG is an editorial writer and member of *The New York Times* editorial board. His books include *The Return, Lincoln As They Saw Him, The Man Who Rode the Tiger* (recipient of the American Bar Association's Gavel Award), and *The Letters of Carl Sandburg.*

MARIANNE C. MOORE has received the Pulitzer Prize and the National Book Award for her poetry. Her books include *Tell Me, Tell Me, O To Be a Dragon, The Arctic Ox* and *A Marianne Moore Reader.*

JOHN A. MORSELL is assistant executive director of the National Association for the Advancement of Colored People, and a fellow of the American Sociological Association.

FREDERICK CRAIG MORTIMER became assistant city editor of *The New York Times* in 1886 and remained with the newspaper until 1926. In 1896 he began to write the column "Topics of *The Times*" and continued to do so until his retirement. He died in 1936.

FREDERIC MORTON, novelist and contemporary historian, is the author of *The Rothschilds, Asphalt and Desire, The Witching Ship, The Schatten Affair,* and *Snow Gods.*

HERBERT J. MULLER, Professor of English and Government at Indiana University, is the author of *The Uses of the Past, The Loom of History* and *The Individual in a Revolutionary World.*

LEWIS NICHOLS has served as a drama critic, reporter and book columnist for *The New York Times.* He wrote "In and Out of Books" and now writes the "American Notebook" column for *The New York Times Book Review.*

ALAN PATON has served as president of South Africa's Liberal Party and is a strong foe of apartheid. He lives in Natal. Among his books are *Cry, the Beloved Country, Too Late the Phalarope* and *South African Tragedy.*

ORVILLE PRESCOTT served as daily book reviewer of *The New York Times* from 1942 to 1966. Among his books are *The Undying Past, A Father Reads to His Children* and *The Five-Dollar Gold Piece*.

A. H. RASKIN is assistant editor of *The New York Times* editorial page. Since joining the newspaper in 1931, his labor reporting has earned him the major journalistic awards. He is a frequent contributor to magazines and commentator on educational television.

RICHARD RULAND teaches American literature at Washington University, St. Louis, and has served on the faculty at Yale and the University of Michigan. He is the author of *The Rediscovery of American Literature: Premises of Critical Taste, 1900-1940*.

ARTHUR SCHLESINGER, JR., Schweitzer Professor of Humanities at City University of New York, is author of *A Thousand Days, The Bitter Heritage: Vietnam and American Democracy, The Age of Jackson, The Age of Roosevelt* and *The Coming of the New Deal*.

LEONARDO SCIASCIA is a Sicilian novelist who makes his home in Palermo. His works include *Mafia Vendetta, The Council of Egypt, A Man's Blessing* and *Pirandello and Sicily*.

RICHARD F. SHEPARD is a reporter on the staff of *The New York Times*, a linguist and authority on ethnic New York. He frequently comments as a reporter and critic of the cultural scene.

CHARLES SIMMONS is on the staff of *The New York Times Book Review*. His stories, articles and criticism have appeared in *Esquire, The Noble Savage* and *Saturday Review*. His first novel, *Powdered Eggs*, received a William Faulkner Award.

WILLIAM M. SPACKMAN has taught the classics at New York University and the University of Colorado. He is the author of *On the Decay of Humanism*, which is based on a lifetime of devotion to literature in general and the classics in particular.

JOHN B. STARR is a frequent contributor to American publications and a longtime observer of the literary scene.

SIMEON STRUNSKY became an editorial writer on *The New York Times*, contributed to the "Topics" column, and then was its sole writer from 1932 until his retirement after the Second World War. He died in 1948. His books include *No Mean City* and *The Living Tradition.*

HARVEY SWADOS, professor and novelist, is the author of *On the Line, Nights in the Garden of Brooklyn, A Radical's America, The Will* and *The American Writer and the Great Depression.*

JAMES TUITE is assistant sports editor of *The New York Times* and a longtime observer of the New York scene.

L. V. UPDEGRAFF came to *The New York Times* out of Yale, '08, where he had marked Sinclair Lewis's English papers. He retired in 1958 and died in 1961. As head of the Sunday copydesk, he was famous for his scholarship and knowledge of the classics.

DAVID VIENNA, a free-lance journalist, formerly on *The New York Times* business news staff, often comments on the American scene.

E. B. WHITE, long associated with *The New Yorker* magazine, is an essayist, poet and journalist. Among his books are *Stuart Little, Charlotte's Web, One Man's Meat, Here Is New York* and *The Points of My Compass.*

MITCHELL WILSON is a novelist and physicist who lives in New York. Among his books is *Live With Lightning.*

WILLIAM G. WING is a free-lance writer and consultant on conservation. Among his expeditions has been a trip to the Georges Banks on a Gloucester trawler.

GEORGE A. WOODS is children's book editor of *The New York Times* and a frequent writer on the pleasures and perils of his large family at home in New Jersey.

HERMAN WOUK, novelist, is the author of *City Boy, Aurora Dawn, The Caine Mutiny, Marjorie Morningstar, This Is My God, Youngblood Hawke* and *Don't Stop the Carnival.*